Semiotics of Landscape: Archaeology of *Mind*

Edited by

George Nash

BAR International Series 661
1997

Published in 2016 by
BAR Publishing, Oxford

BAR International Series 661

Semiotics of Landscape: Archaeology of Mind

ISBN 978 0 86054 854 6

COVER IMAGE *Red deer on the Laxe da Rotea de Mende Panel, Campo Lameiro
(after E Anati in* Miscelanea y homenage al Abate Henri Breuil (1877-1961),
1964)

BAR Publishing is the trading name of British Archaeological Reports (Oxford) Ltd.
British Archaeological Reports was first incorporated in 1974 to publish the BAR
Series, International and British. In 1992 Hadrian Books Ltd became part of the BAR
group. This volume was originally published by Archaeopress in conjunction with
British Archaeological Reports (Oxford) Ltd / Hadrian Books Ltd, the Series principal
publisher, in 1997. This present volume is published by BAR Publishing, 2016.

Printed in England

BAR
PUBLISHING

BAR titles are available from:

BAR Publishing
122 Banbury Rd, Oxford, OX2 7BP, UK
EMAIL   info@barpublishing.com
PHONE   +44 (0)1865 310431
FAX   +44 (0)1865 316916
www.barpublishing.com

To Pilky

CONTENTS

PREFACE

I have always regarded the preface as a platform for personal and informal chit–chat and a pat–on–the–back for all those who helped with 'that' book. It could be also a platform for making comment on the mechanisms of producing 'that' book.

This volume is the result, in part, of papers presented to the Theoretical Archaeological Conference held at Bradford University in December 1994. The theme of the session was the social construction of the landscape and it was thought that a specific discourse concerning landscape, cognition and, the relatively new buzz word, phenomenology, were going somewhere.

Chris Tilley's two monumental volumes, one on deconstruction of rock art at Nämforsen, Sweden (*The Ambiguity of Art*) and the other on landscape form and monumentality form (*The Phenomenology of Landscape*) had a profound effect on the way I looked at the past. Since then, few theorists have taken on board the important implications of landscape and text. Indeed, in witnessing the general comments at (Euro) TAG held at Southampton in 1992, it emerged that even theorists were divided. The Renfrew and Binfordian school were still entrenched in the rigidity of post–processual archaeology, which is in itself, a functional approach to theory. Tilley, and the more vocal John Barrett, however, argued the contrary, putting forward a more philosophical approach and relying less on 'isms' and compartmentalisation. The radical views taken were intended to shake even the most reactionary of archaeology departments. But, what of the outcome? Well, TAG still 'acts' as a general 'diving–board' that is controlled and manipulated by middle–class pseudo Marxists–feminists and the occasional Tory peer. Each year new 'isms' and buzz–words are put forward with the hope that theoretical archaeology is going somewhere. Certainly, over the past few years, social–theory has been wandering around in the wilderness with no cohesive or coherent direction. Maybe, this is an ideal 'state' to be in?

However, by wandering, can new approaches stand the test of time? For example, is the cognitive approach to landscape, or whatever, still an adequate discourse for a theoretical critique? Equally, are the radical approaches of Tilley's phenomenology of landscape, Shanks' experiencing the past or Thomas's hermeneutics valid within mainstream archaeology? The answer to this is probably yes (well, I would say that wouldn't I). As long as discussion and, more importantly archaeology in general is forced to either disregard or argue against such approaches, reactionary theory provides an alternative approach. This is certainly prevalent within a climate whereby research grant aid is cut/frozen (depending on one's political persuasion) by central government policy year by year and the quantity of such research is restricted. The role of commercial archaeology, too, requires now only the bare minimum of interpretation (a dig–and–record strategy). This doom and gloom, however, will not diminish my passion for the discipline.

I am grateful to the following people for help in putting this volume together. Firstly, to George Children, long–time friend and writing colleague, for help with the editorial and layout of this volume; his patience is most certainly a virtue. Sincere thanks also to all the contributors for time and energy spent on the papers, in particular Trevor Kirk, who not only shares a similar academic stance on theory discourse but is always there for a good chat and a pint. A big thank you also to Rajka Makjanić (Tempvs Reparatvm) for putting up with the usual excuses concerning delay of the text – she has heard them all before! Finally, I wish to thank Chris Tilley for his energy and influence whilst I was a post-graduate student.

George Nash
Department of Archaeology
St David's University College
Lampeter

December 1996

FOREWORD

Michael Shanks

Department of Archaeology University of Lampeter

Archaeology has been associated with a topographical interest since long before its formalisation in the nineteenth century. David Clarke, in his scientific vision of the 1960s and 70s, listed a geographical paradigm as one of the constitutive features of archaeology, referring particularly to connections with the positivist new geography and to the potentials of a subject at long last finding its disciplinary maturity. Landscape, as the interrelationships of people and environment, has since become, in the 1980s and 1990s, a major focus of theory–building. But not just for theory's sake. As well as offering some fascinating examples of humanistic interpretation, landscape archaeology holds, I believe, the prospect of a set of integrated practices and interpretative strategies, ranging from environmental reconstruction of existential phenomenology, which avoid the familiar partisan fissures of processual and postprocessual, scientific and culture–historical archaeology. This book is a significant contribution to this future.

Attention ranges across Europe through Hungary, Spain, France, Britain, Germany and Denmark. Here is a mixture of approaches, from traditional culture history to interpretative archaeologies at home with some of the current theoretical debate about Heidegger's phenomenology of human being–in–the–world. Many of the papers display a particular intellectual trajectory, developing from the symbolic and structural archaeology of the early 1980s and the emerging programme of a theoretically–aware social archaeology interested in human agency and the active construction of social pasts. More generally there is a strong flavour of cognitive archaeology, a concern with the reconstruction of past symbolic and ideological systems. This breadth is welcome.

New cultural geographies of the last two decades have applied social and cultural theory to interpretation of the landscape. Interest lies in the sociocultural and political processes that shape landscapes and the way lived environments are intimately part of social and political strategy. So too in archaeology, and very well evidenced in this collection. the concept of landscape has received the sort of theoretical development and refining which has been so evident in the social sciences and humanities since the 60s. Let me mention some of the issues before outlining what I see as a rewarding way ahead, towards an archaeology of deep maps.

The old separation of environmental science and cultural perceptions of landscape is untenable as it is clear that the natural environment has been a cultural landscape for millennia, so deeply affected by human activity. The concept of landscape signals making and perceiving as fundamental attributes of the environment – land not as neutral backdrop but product of perception and an active component in the structuring of social identity. This notion of landscape as product of human labour, land as artifact, brings landscape archaeology within that fascinating interdisciplinary field of material culture studies. It is to remember too that there is continuity from land through to the built environment, to architectural forms, and indeed many other components of the lived environment. Hence the prominent interest in site location, not simply as determined by natural or environmental factors, but within a seamless web of active relationships between people and materials, people and artifacts.

Ideology is a fundamental concept in dealing with another element of landscape, that relating to ways of seeing. I recall a colleague pointing out that so often archaeologists have looked at sites from the outside in, literally standing facing a monument or house. So much could be gained by reversing the prospect and considering what might have lain in view from the inside out, looking out from window or door, from rampart or gate. Intervisibility studies are an obvious starting point, but the main message is perhaps one of engaging with the construction of space as place and locale, imbued with the textures of social practice, lived experience. Here there is another continuity: the imaginary is coextensive with 'the real'. States of subjectivity such as perception and belief may be very active in making the lived environment what it is for people. And this is not simply a neutral process ('objective' perception of 'the way things are') but one tied to political strategy and structures of inequality. Our land, not yours. Home territory may be treated analytically as a local environment of resources, but in terms of the lived experience that is social practice it may be as well thought as something like the Welsh concept of *y filltir sgwar* – the square mile of intimate landscape of childhood, the patch we know in detail, a web of favourite places, others to avoid; neighbours and their stories; the beginnings of geography, history and society, difference and similitude.

This semiotic mix has led to approaches which treat landscape as a text to be read. Very much a legacy of the influence of structuralism and poststructuralism upon archaeology, there are problems with this textual analogy which need not be dealt with here, for no one in this volume holds rigidly to it. Instead the wider and vital point is evident and realised, that *interpretation* is endemic to the social world. People are forever immersed in uncertainty and the necessity of trying to make sense of their surroundings and the things that befall them.

This has led some to delve into existentialism and particularly Heidegger as one who has dealt deeply with the human condition of being–in–the–world. Here some phenomenological constants are assumed about how people deal with life, experience and environment – cultural constants or a cultural uniformitarianism, if you like. Appreciation of such constants is, in fact, aided by awareness of the diversity of culture, and the use of ethnographic analogy is apparent in some studies in landscape archaeology. Rather than supplying ready–made explanations, unfortunately a common use of ethnographic analogy such as an interpretive strategy of referring to the experience of other cultures is best treated, I believe, as a more general confrontation with difference – things could be different.

The land is not static, but constantly changing, particularly as people move through it. Paths and lines of association (lines of sight or conceptual connection) may join locales. This travel and movement also brings in event and the 'performance' of landscape, two categories which refer interpretation to time. Here is that breaking down of categories, time and space, that used to be treated as fundamentally separate; as well as abstract backdrops, time and space are to be treated as constitutive of society. The visibility of a monument in the land may reference lines of sight and movement, the actions of a group of people made permanent, the temporality of endurance beyond the mortality of the human frame, picked up perhaps also in monumental scale. Several papers in this volume theorise such basic phenomenological categories, basic experiences.

A blurring of categories that I am very much interested in is that which occurs through application of the idea of life-cycle or biography to both people and artifacts, including landscape. This is part of a more general tendency now to develop specially archaeological theory, applying to the materiality of the human and artifactual world. It is coming to replace the wholesale import of theory from anthropology, sociology and cognate disciplines. Artifacts travel. And monuments in the land are designed to endure for perhaps millennia. There are temporal and architectural continuities running through landscape which so often make it what it is. Appropriately there is a chapter in this volume about such continuity.

The book contains a variety of styles of writing, all closely clustered around the academic paper, as is appropriate. The methodology of survey is attended to, as is the practice of excavation. However it is clear that the humanistic treatment of landscape which is on offer here is requiring alternative modes of expression and address, including visual illustration. There are some hints of close reading accompanying thickly–textured narrative, and I think many of the contributors would agree with my advocacy of a loosening of the structures of academic discourse as it has come to be in the 90s with a revival of more traditional styles of humanistic writing as well as experiment with less familiar genres. These may well be more suited to the practice which is coming to lie at the heart of landscape archaeology – making sense of a complex of meanings lying between past and present, between natural history (in the fullest of sense of that term) and cultural narrative.

For in dealing with landscape as a flowing set of unfixed social experiences, the task is set explicitly in this book of rehumanising archaeology. Attending to as full a range as possible of cultural sources that make land what it is to people today, that succession of living characterised by heterogeneous continuities, the archaeological challenge is to develop 'deep maps', making sense of this notion of landscape so dear to senses of belonging and identity. I write 'senses' deliberately, for a rehumanised archaeology is one which, in its attention to lived social practice or experience, recognises the foundation of society in *sensoria*, which I define as cultural arrays of *all* the human senses. Subjective states are the form through which the objective world is experienced and there is no avoidance for social archaeology, ultimately, of working with the fact so conspicuously evident in notions of landscape, that society is not only a set of formal structures uniting social actors and resources, but it is lived, felt, enjoyed, and suffered.

Establishing a Discourse: The Language of Landscape

George Children and George Nash

St David's University College, Lampeter

Introduction

Like an orally–transmitted story, archaeology changes its rules. Language – discourse – is fluid. In the introduction, and throughout, we emphasise the need to rehumanise the interpretation and language of archaeology. Of course, there is always the problem that, when creating a language, it is made exclusive and elusive – and in some ways this book is guilty. However, lessons are being learned, and ideas being reformulated, which are influenced by pre–1960s archaeology. Although imperialisitic and empiricist in places, the approach to archaeology was such that many individuals were prepared to have a go!

After a good four hours of tramping, that is to say about eleven o'clock, we drew near to the Valltorta Ravine. There is a wide glen whose banks fall steeply down to a stream. Bushes and scrub cover the sides from the top to the bottom but cannot hide the large stones and boulders. If one chanced to step upon or against a stone it went tumbling, rumbling down right into the brook below. The ravine twisted and turned. Sometimes it was a quite narrow canyon and then again the gorge would widen out somewhat. The cliffs contain a number of natural recesses, little rock–shelters, from three to six feet deep. Many of them present no pictures, but then again others are crowded with paintings and drawings. (Kühn 1958:126)

This quote originates from a book which in 1958 went against the grain of the traditional archaeology. Kühn had turned his ideas very much into a book about personal experience. Here, archaeology had become a narrative. Henri Lhote (1959) attempts a similar type of discourse with his expedition in search of the Tassili frescoes in Southern Algeria. Both men are concerned, not with the idea of data and statistics, but with the notion of making the archaeology of landscape coherent. By expressing their experiences, they are establishing a narrative based upon social and historical geography. Shanks and Tilley (1987:19–21) tend to attack this traditional historical narrative. They claim that the narrative should be analytical and retrospective, viewing the past from the present. However, this is somewhat contradictory, in that a landscape and a history must have a beginning, a middle and an end. In the words of Shanks and Tilley, one cannot open a book at the end and understand the meaning. Furthermore, history must have an end at the point where the subjectivity is being analysed; in this case the deconstruction of landscape. It is only after this deconstruction that the narrative can begin. Recently, Shanks (1992:186) has suggested that the narrative (stories) is the basic means of '*making sense of the archaeological past*'. It would appear here that he has re–addressed the ideas of narrative. The story cannot start from the middle or the end. The characters, the plot and the setting need to be placed into context i.e. the start or the beginning. Therefore, landscape, comprising natural features, is a series of stories that are constructed through time and space and formulate a series of histories; not history.

The papers in this volume follow a particular theme – landscape. Each one attempts to construct 'landscape' in a particular way. For example, landscape can represent order, social stratification and control. However, it can also be perceived as chaos, turmoil and social disorder. Over the past five years, the term landscape has received much discussion, albeit based upon the mechanics and form of landscape. What has been omitted is the construction of landscape in terms of knowledge, interpretation and application.

One might ask; what is landscape? We know it's there; the hills, mountains, rivers, streams, trees and so on. These features, although natural, are socially constructed within our minds. Although landscape is there, the imagination and the cognitive construction is controlled by ourselves.

This book is divided into two parts. Although both parts are inextricably linked, one deals with the built environment – landscape constructed around monuments – while the other deals with monuments or buildings within a landscape. Although both represent the same thing, they can be perceived in different ways. Fundamentally, landscape is a series of spaces which become places, thus establishing territory (Children & Nash 1994:21). Chris Weedon (1987:32), discussing the principles of post–structuralism, goes further and states:

'it is language in the form of conflicting discourse which constitutes us as conscious thinking subjects and enables us to give meaning to the world and to act to transform it.'

Recently, Tilley (1994) has adopted the ideas of space, place and landscape as part of an historical/geographical discourse. Linked with this idea are the human emotions of power, time, memory, social interaction and politics. It is important to note that landscape, although natural in its construction, does rely on the mechanics of the mind. For this introduction we want to deconstruct landscape using a number of philosophical arguments related to phenomenology, cognition and semiotics. All three components are fundamental to the construction of landscape. We use the term semiotics in the hope that the reader can draw on the notion that landscapes can be read. Levi–Strauss (1962:56) has stated that language is a social phenomenon, that it acts as a form of linguistic behaviour relying upon the unconscious. We also take landscape for granted. We know it is there. But within our world, this language is unread. We are not advocating that landscape should be deconstructed using a structuralist theory; we merely suggest that features within a landscape act as signs and that these signs control social and political behaviour. During early prehistory, the construction of monuments, the formation of territories is not based merely on political behaviour, but is symbolically and socially constructed with landscape in *mind*. Similar to Bradley's idea that monuments evoke memories (1993:2), landscape, too, creates a sense of time, in that people create a sense of belonging. This is not a notion that can be created overnight, but one that takes generations. Bourdieu (1977:4) suggests further that on a human level, landscape, or the phenomenology of landscape, is created as a lived experience. Furthermore, that the mode of knowledge is inherent in all acts; this is a precondition to the construction of landscape. In the words of Bourdieu, landscape should constitute '*a social world as a system of objective relations independent of individual consciousness and wills*' (ibid.). We would suggest therefore that the construction of landscape becomes a critique; a collection of chapters that are chronologically and geographically ordered. Each moment in time, the individual adds more to these chapters, creating this sense of space and belonging.

Cognitive Perception and the body

Monika Langer's commentary on Merleau–Ponty's phenomenology of perception discusses the idea of space and the body. It is important that, although we perceive ideas and place them cognitively within our own minds, our body too becomes part of the landscape – it interacts with and becomes a component of landscape, forming a sense of space. Langer (1989:87) states that 'the anchoring of the body' as a 'natural self' institutes a physical or 'natural space' and thereby opens up a 'human space' which encompasses the world of emotions, dreams, myth and madness, as well as the world of reflection. The description of this human space overturns our traditional distinctions – such as those between form and content, clarity and ambiguity, reality and appearance – and revolutionises the role of philosophy itself.' Quite clearly, Langer is not content with the ideas of the body as a microcosm. She is creating a series of structural oppositions both outside and inside the body. We would suggest that many more oppositions can be applied, in which the 'self' and the landscape are one. Landscape as a form of research has, over many years, been entrenched in the realms of geography. It is from this base that much empiricist archaeology has sprung.

Landscape has been described geomorphorologically, its mechanics neatly calculated and land use formalised. From these initial ideas there has arisen some interest in the construction of landscape on a social/political basis. Indeed, during the 1960s and 70s, workers such as Chorley and Haggett went one step further to create a whole social-theoretical discourse of landscape, formulating their ideas on territories. Recently, however, research and landscape has been adopted by post–processual archaeology. Initially, researchers such as Darvill (1987) and Bradley (1987, 1993) attacked the middle ground and formulated a general discourse which relates society to its surroundings. It is only recently that workers such as Christopher Tilley, Julian Thomas and John Barratt have gone further and applied a complete philosophical discourse encompassing archaeology – instead of archaeology embracing philosophy.

Qualitative or quantitative analysis

One of the mainstays of traditional archaeology is that the more one wishes to know about a period or site, the more one needs to excavate. Of course, one can dig sites for a lifetime and add very little to the sum of information already at hand. The quantitative approach is problematic in achieving an overall intepretation. It requires the application of a theoretical discourse. Theorists, on the other hand, claim they can achieve an interpretation without data, but can they? Are they building theories without foundations? We would argue that each approach is invalid without the support of the other. Likewise, landscape archaeology relies, not only on a fleeting glance at a map, the odd walk in the landscape. A series of structured rules must be applied. In some ways, a theoretical discourse follows a similar line to that of the processual archaeological and scientific approach still practised today. Similarly, the scientific approach only arrives at the data stage. Previously, the authors have looked at landscape as a series of quantitative data that both interact with, and set apart, certain aspects of the landscape. We have used, for example, intervisibility of monuments, visible topographic features, orientation and the interrelationship of settlements, mortuary buildings and defence structures (Children & Nash 1994 & 1996). One element that cannot be quantified is personal experience. Many will be aware that interpretation varies from experience to experience. At a fundamental level, many field archaeologists look at sites and conveniently categorise them into site type, period and probable use. What is ignored is the cultural and symbolic encoding of that site. For example, the chambered tomb becomes merely a 'long mound' with aligned stones arranged in a particular classified way; the site is nothing more than an estate agent's brochure. Taking the argument further, a similar, more rigorous description is apparent in the majority of Sites and Monuments Records (SMRs). It would appear that, although this scientific approach is necessary in order to create a database, archaeology needs to claw back some of the ideas expressed by the pre–Childean antiquarians, who, in the words of Shanks & Tilley, romanticised the discipline. In other words, the expression and experience of the archaeology of each site is as important as the rigorous data that is applied. Taking this one stage further, we would suggest that, if landscape forms part of the archaeological record, then the landscape too is an archaeological site, which is not only constructed of sites, topographical features and an environmental record, but a landscape of human experience – the phenomenology of landscape. This involves the personal understanding of landscape and, in the words of Chris Tilley (1994:12), it is about the relationship between being and being–in–the–world. Arguably, Tilley could expand on this to suggest that the indivdual, too, is the archaeology.

The built environment

As stated earlier, we have identified two approaches to landscape archaeology within this book. Part 1 deals with the idea that the monument, the site, is part of a landscape. Part 2 with the landscape being part of the site, and emphasis is placed upon the built environment. It is important to understand that, although the approaches are different, there are similarities. This is based mainly on the availabilty of data: the more visible evidence one has, the more one feels one is able to say. Thus, when one is dealing with Roman or, in this case, Mediterranean temple archaeology, there is a wealth of specialisms that can be applied to achieve an overall discourse. In all cases, the authors are trying to put forward the idea that landscape is more than just a collection of sites. Moreover, landscape is a series of places which are dependent on both visuality and a chronological materiality. In the case of Andrew Townsend's paper on the temple-building of Malta and, in some respects, the research carried out in the Black Mountains (Nash 1994), what appears to be achieved is a distinction between organic and inorganic space. Now, arguably, both spaces may be human–induced. However, one is of direct experience, that is, everybody concerned knows that the building exists: whereas, the other is an indirect experience based upon restricted visual access. In the case of the Neolithic monuments of the Black Mountains (Wales), there is emphasis placed upon incognito – the site hidden within the landscape – as oppposed to the direct monumentality connected with temple–building. Again, both examples place a statementing upon landscape. Both Foucault (1977) and Miller and Tilley (1984) have put forward the idea that restricted access is concerned with *power over*, rather than *power to*; that is, the control of landscape, procession and visual access by a hierarchical society; the power of the individual over the masses.

We talk quite freely about grammar and the narrative, and in many ways we arbitrarily attempt to link these words with monumentality, rock art and, in the case of this volume, landscape. Nordbladh (1978) talks of the need for a cohesive, structured syntax in order to create a narrative. It is very easy to write words: it is more difficult to formulate these as a coherent sentence. Likewise, the authors have used the terms 'narrative' and 'grammar' in a very generalised way. It is important within the introduction, and in the papers, that grammar and syntax are placed within narrative: people, artifacts, monuments and landscape become components or chapters within the narrative. Therefore, we may consider landscape to be the dominant component. Indeed, visually, our social construction of landscape, the visuality of landscape, is by far the biggest influence upon our cognitive interpretation within archaeology. Landscape, therefore, can be read as a narrative, albeit from the eyes and experiences of a group of late 20th century archaeologists.

Addressing the problem: landcape as artifact

It has been covnenient within the textbooks to discuss distribution, site type, shape and even orientation; but very little has been said of why sites are placed where they are. For example, the location and distribution of chambered monuments in Britain is, for the most part, restricted to a single north arrow next to the site plan. No references are made to its relationship with landscape. Powell et al (1969), Megaw and Simpson (1979) and Darvill (1987), are all guilty of this. Even Bradley (1984) appears to be obsessed with the materiality of sites; the distribution of pottery, for instance, and the position of grave goods. Within this volume we are guilty, in that we only present half of the narrative. What is omitted is the materiality of landscape. Landsape may be construed as an artifact in its own right. It may well

be a wish of the indivdual/group to locate a monument in a particular place. This act, this desire, is as important as the deposition of certain artifacts within the tomb itself. In the words of Danny Miller (1985:1), this volume could be placed within an area of 'material culture studies'; landscape employs a language of artifact, an object which is created by people and embodies the princples of organisation and categorisation within the human experience.

Bibliography

Bourdieu, P. (1990), *Outline of a Theory of Practice*, Cambridge University Press, Cambridge.

Bradley, R. (1984) *The Sociological Foundations of Prehistoric Britain – Themes and Variations in the Archaeology of Power*, London. Longmans.

Britnell, W. (1979) 'The Gwernvale Long Cairn', *Antiquity*, 53. 132–4.

Britnell, W & Savory, H. (1984) *Gwernvale and Penywyrlod: Two Neolithic Long Cairns in the Black Mountains of Brecknock*, Cambrian Archaeological Monographs No.2 Cardiff.

Children, G. & Nash, G.H. (1996a) *Monuments and the Landscape: The Prehistory of Herefordshire*, Logaston Press, Hereford.

Children, G. & Nash, G.H. (1996b) *Pathways, Stone and Monuments: The Chambered Monuments of South-west Wales*, BAR International Series (in press).

Corcoran, J. X.W.P.(1969) 'The Cotswold–Severn Group' in Powell, T.G.E., Corcoran, J.X.W.P., Lynch, F. and Scott, J.G. *Megalthic Enquiries in the West of Britain*, Liverpool University Press, Liverpool.

Crawford, O.G.S. (1925) *The Long Barrows of the Cotswolds*, Gloucester.

Daniel, G. (1950) *The Prehistoric Chambered Tombs of England, and Wales*, Cambridge. Cambridge University Press.

Frampton, K. (1992) *Modern Architecture: A Critical History*, 57–63, Thames and Hudson, London.

Gavin Robinson, R.S. (1934) 'Flint workers and flint users of the Golden Valley'. *Transactions of the Woolhope Naturalists' Field Club*. 54–63.

Grimes, W. (1936) 'The Long Cairns of Brecknockshire Black Mountains', *Archaeologia Cambrensis*, 259–282.

Grimes, W. (1939) 'The excavation of Ty Isaf Long Cairn, Brecknockshire', *Proceedings of the Prehistoric Society*, V, 119–42.

Hemp, W.J. (1935) 'Arthur's Stone, Dorstone, Herefordshire', *Archaeologia Cambrensis*, XC, 288–92.

Hodder, I (1986) *Reading the Past: Current Approaches to Interpretation in Archaeology*, Cambridge, Cambridge University Press.

Jencks, C. (1969) (ed.) *Meaning and Architecture*, Design Yearbook. London

Kühn, H. (1958) *On the Track of Prehistoric Man*, London. Hutchinson

Langer, M.M. (1989) *Merleau–Ponty's Phenomenology of Perception*, Macmillan Press, London.

Lhote, H. (1959) *The Search for the Tassili Frescoes: The*

Story of the Prehistoric Rock–Paintings of the Sahara, London. Hutchinson

Megaw & Simpson (1979) *Introduction to British Prehistory*, Leicester. Leicester University Press

Miller D. (1985) *Artifacts as Categories: A Study in Ceramic Variability in Central India*, Cambridge. Cambridge University Press

Miller, D. & Tilley, C. (1984) *Ideology, Power and Prehistory*, New Directions in Archaeology, Cambridge. Cambridge University Press

Nordbladh, J. (1987) 'Bird, fish or something in between? The case for the rock–paintings of the Swedish west coast' in G Burenhult, A Carlsson, A Hyenstand and T Sjovold (eds.) *Theoretical Apporaches to Settlement and Society: Studies in Honour of Mat P Malmer*, Oxford. British Archaeological Reports International Series 366, 305–20

Powell, T. G. E., Corcoran, J. X. W. P., Lynch, F. and Scott, J. G. (1969) *Megalithic Enquiries in the West of Britain, a Liverpool Symposium*. Liverpool. Liverpool University Press.

Shanks, M. (1992) *Experiencing the Past: On the Character of Archaeology*, London. Routledge

Shanks, M. & Tilley C. (1987) *Reconstructing Archaeology – Theory and Practice*, Cambridge. Cambridge University Press

Thomas, J.S. (1993) 'The politics of vision and the archaeologies of landscape', in B. Bender (ed.) *Landscape, Politics and Perspectives*. Berg.

Tilley, C. (1993) 'Art, architecture and the landscape in Neolithic Sweden', in B.Bender (ed.) *Landscape, Politics and Perspectives*. Berg.

Tilley, C. (1994) *A Phenomenology of Landscape – Places, Paths and Monuments*, Oxford. Berg

Weedon, C (1994) *Feminist Practice and Poststructuralist Theory*, Oxford. Blackwell.

From Anneville to Zedes: A Ritual Seascape? Megaliths and long-distance contacts in Western Europe

Stéphane Rault

'It is, however, the study of these long–distance relationships and the underlying economic network that will help us to understand all the factors involved in the emergence of funerary gigantism in the Europe of 5000 years ago'

(Bougot and Cassen, 1993:487)

Introduction

Binford was wrong. There are not only three 'big questions' which can be addressed in prehistory (Binford 1983:26–30). Aside from the issues he mentions, (regarding the origin and basis of human socio–economic organisation), the origin and spread of the earliest complex building in stone demands an explanation, the implications of which run deep and fast for such issues as the beginnings of social complexity and sedentary lifestyle in temperate Europe.

Megalithic structures were tombs, first built in the Neolithic period, by farming communities: Since the days of F.C. Lukis (1849), these base–lines for the interpretation of prehistoric structural monuments have hardly been questioned. There has indeed been a certain amount of discussion recently as regards the precise socio–economic context of the earliest 'chamber–tombs', for example Bradley (1993), Scarre (1992), Patton (1993) and most recently Sherratt (1995), but the existence of a fully agricultural settled community (generally believed to be that of the builders, but almost always thought to be contemporary with them) has been thought necessary to explain their existence. Since the publication of *Before Civilization* (Renfrew 1976), the setting for the rise of megalithic monuments along the Atlantic seaboard has been seen as the result of independent and unrelated local responses to the arrival of farming communities from the East – a sort of modern *ex oriente lux*, which precluded the possibility of large–scale, long–range contact.

This paper follows on from ideas presented in the author's *Neolithic Passage–graves reconsidered* article (Rault 1993/4a) and suggests an alternative possibility, which sees repeated long–range contact as forming the setting for the initial growth of the 'passage–tomb' tradition, thus proposing a possible 'Atlantic seaboard' ritual landscape at the turn of the Mesolithic period. This article suggests evidence for contact in the form of the geographical locations and common plans employed for a considerable number of monuments between Iberia and Scandinavia.

There are four main sources of information from which we can attempt to interpret the earliest phase of European passage–dolmens[1]. These are the form, petrology and orientation of the monument itself, its setting (both geographical and in relation to other monuments), parallels between it and other monuments, and the artifactual/ecofactual evidence which can be ascribed with certainty to the initial construction phase, and parallels, both in the European archaeological data–base and from ethnography. The nature and quality of the available evidence, particularly in the form of accurately–planned monuments, will be discussed, resulting in the postulation of a comprehensive and long–range ritual landscape across the Atlantic seaboard at the transition between the Mesolithic and Neolithic periods.

As was discussed at length in Rault 1993/4a, (e.g. pp. 94–107), there is very little material throughout the entire range of passage–dolmens which can be ascribed reliably to the initial construction phase of any monument. Almost all the published dating rests on what can be proved, or, at the very least, strongly argued, to be secondary material, with the result that 'The evidence for passage–dolmens originally having been 'Neolithic' or 'graves' is weak. A stronger case can be made for them originating in the Mesolithic period and having a non–sepulchral function (Rault 1993/4a:117). The conclusion of the paper, based on the recovered evidence which included a large body of Mesolithic–type artifacts (for example 1993/4 figs 8–9) was that: 'They may have been constructed by coastal fishing communities capable of long–distance sea travel and having the capacity to build closely similar monuments hundreds of miles apart. This may prompt a reconstruction of the origins of social complexity and the relationship between Mesolithic and Neolithic communities, reaching far beyond the study of megalithic monuments themselves' (Rault 1993/4a:117).

Surprisingly perhaps, our most useful starting–point, as regards the possibility of inter–regional contacts, is to be found among the plans of passage–dolmens, and the evidence which they provide for inter–regional contacts.

Possible 'blueprints'

In order to decide whether there were any common and rigid architectural rules used in the construction of some passage–dolmens over a wide geographical area, the best available modern plans and sections, such as those by l'Helgouac'h and Lukis in Armorica, or the Leisners for Iberia, were accurately enlarged or reduced, using photocopiers which had first been calibrated for their accuracy throughout the desired range, to a common scale of 1:100. This value was chosen as the smallest at which it is still possible to see the detail of each monument, and was the scale used by the Leisners (for example: 1956; 1959) for what remains, to this day, arguably the best published collection of plans of megalithic monuments. The fact that their work covers the Iberian peninsula allows of easy comparison of plans on the same scale, when searching for possible external contacts. Among others, two other major recent works of synthesis

---

[1] From this point, the term 'passage–dolmen' (Daryll–Ford 1927:6–7) will be used rather than the more usual 'passage–tomb', 'chamber–tomb' or 'passage–grave'. The reasons for this are described in detail in Rault 1993/4a: 84–5, but basically refer to the non–interpretationally–laden terminology, and the fact that its direct translation into the French terms 'dolmen–à–couloir' and 'dolmen–à–galerie' facilitates' standardized international translation.

(l'Helgouac'h 1965 and Twohig 1981), also centre around 1:100 (with slight variations), which confirms this as a standard scale.

The results of analysing all the site plans of acceptable quality suggest that it may just be possible that *some* of the passage–dolmens were built to common, repeated, and accurate plans. What is perhaps even more surprising is that there are two carving–types, found in Armorica at Petit Mont and in Ireland, for example, at Sess Kilgreen and several of the Loughcrew dolmens, which appear to show on a different scale an impression of the chamber–forms of monuments like Nelhouët, and la Ville–Pichard, respectively. Naturally, this does not demonstrate that the carvings *themselves* actually need have been used as templates for monument–construction, but it does suggest that their shared, complex and accurate geometrical designs may indicate contemporaneity and/or a means of visually representing a shared design, not apparently functional in origin, which the depicters/constructors considered sufficiently important to be executed in great detail over a wide geographical area.

With the exception of the menhir next to the Sess Kilgreen dolmen, none of the carvings showing what may be 'Ville–Pichard' and 'Nelhouët' site–plans occur from sites which themselves share that plan. The presence of the 'blueprint' at sites of different morphology does not invalidate its existence, and in view of the alterations which are now ever more clearly shown to have occurred in the plan of some monuments over their period of use, it is also possible that the stones bearing such motifs may have originally come from monuments of different form. La Hougue des Geonnais

(Rault and Forrest 1992), for example, has shown how drastically chamber morphology could alter during the Neolithic period at a single dolmen, and recent work at Petit Mont by Lecornec (*pers comm*) shows how much structural alteration went on in this monument which bears carvings of both the 'blueprint' forms.

The earliest dated passage–dolmen (Kercado in Brittany) is among the sites which appear to possibly share the 'Ville–Pichard' blueprint at the same scale. This in itself emphasises the importance of plan–types in assessing the *origins* of passage–dolmen construction, since, as there are no monuments which are known to be older than Kercado, there can be no empirical evidence that passage–dolmens need have existed prior to the period when this 'blueprint' appears to have been in use. The two plan–types are named after the monuments where they were first identified.

The Ville–Pichard 'blueprint'

This hypothetical 'blueprint' was originally cumulated by the author from superimposing site plans, after having noticed the striking similarity between the chambers at la Ville–Pichard. This was before becoming aware of the similarity with prehistoric carved motifs. During the course of work on the art, the similarity was noted of the Loughcrew T and Sess Kilgreen carvings, resulting in the superimposition of the cumulated 'blueprint' at a scale of 1:100, onto a representation of the Sess Kilgreen carving at 1:10, leading to analysis of other similarities between the 1:12 relationships carving and site–plans (Fig. 1).

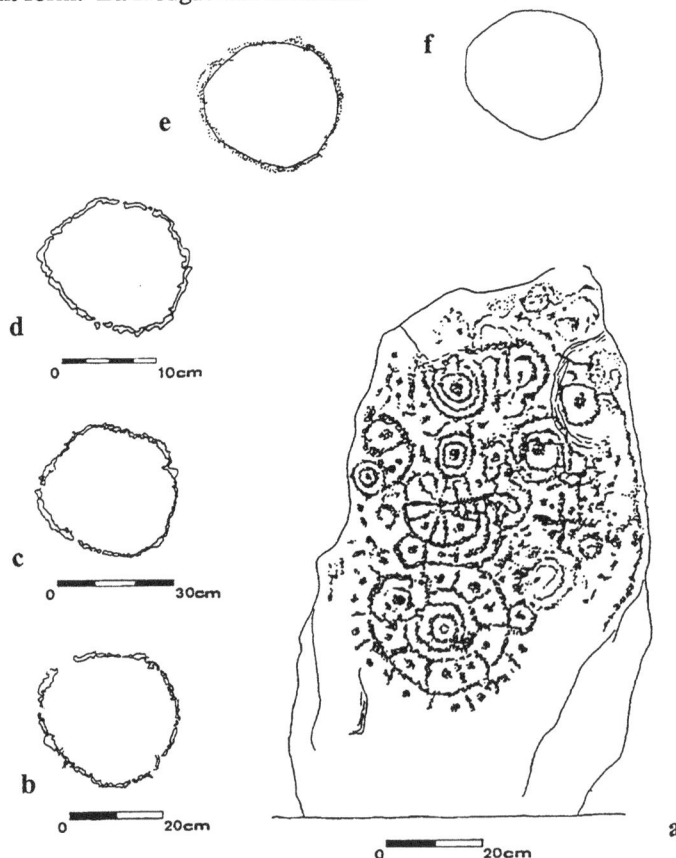

Figure 1. Some 'Ville–Pichard' carvings: a. Stone L1 from Loughcrew, Cairn T, showing carvings; b. 'blueprint' isolated from surrounding carvings; c. 'blueprint' from Sess Kilgreen; d. further 'blueprint' from Loughcrew, Cairn T; e. L1 'blueprint' overlain on cumulative 'best–fit' plan inside faces of sites of 'Ville–Pichard' scale, with mutual relationship of 1:12; f. cumulative 'best–fit' plan for the 'Ville–Pichard' monuments, arrived at independently from comparison with the art.

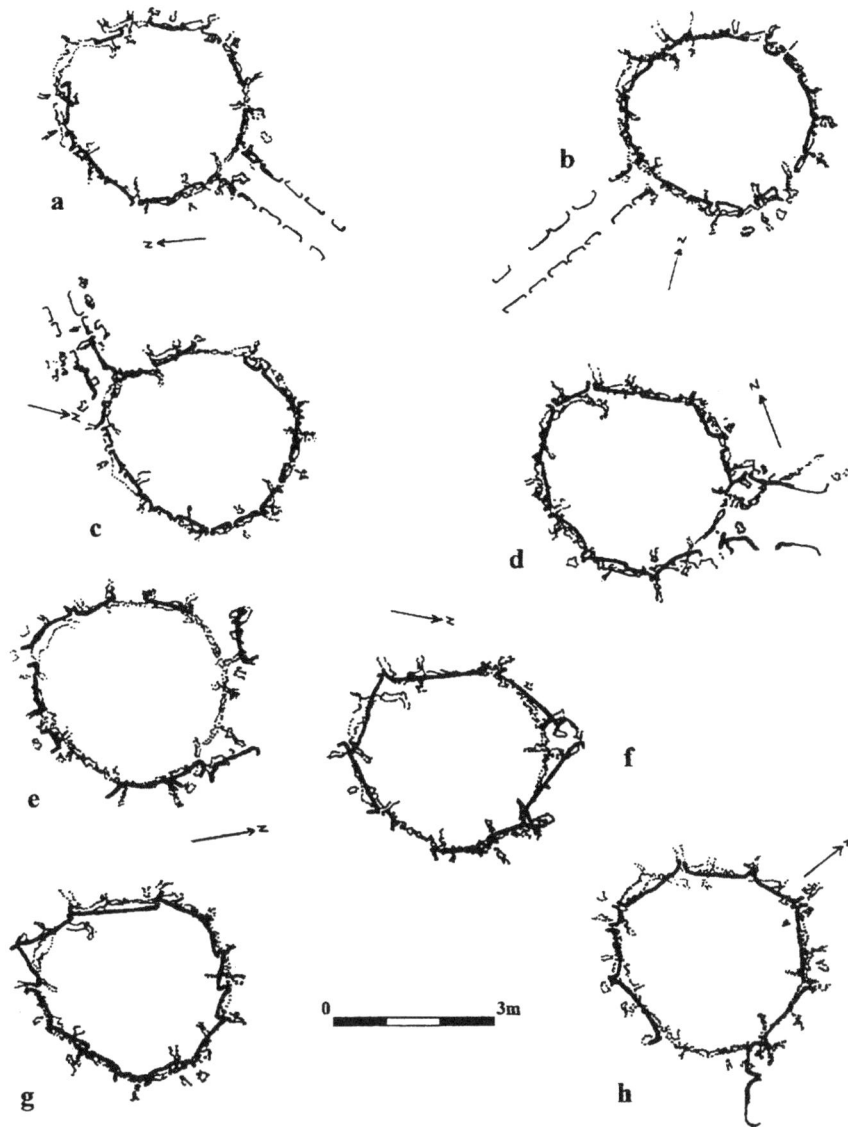

Figure 2. Selection of 'Ville–Pichard' site–plans superimposed on the Loughcrew T, 'L1' 'blueprint' (dotted): a. La Ville–Pichard, South Eastern dolmen, Côtes d'Armor; b. La Ville–Pichard, central dolmen; c. La Ville–Pichard, north–western dolmen; d. Kerdrain, Morbihan; e. Lazaros, Reguengos; f. Matinho 1 (Jardim), Portalegre; g. Cha de Mezio 4, Minho; h. Revellado, Badajoz.

This plan–type is named after the site at la Ville–Pichard, at Pléneuf (Côtes d'Armor in modern Brittany), where three monuments sharing the same chamber–plan (Figs. 2a–2c, after l'Helgouac'h 1965) occur under the same mound (which does not imply any necessary contemporaneity between the mound and the dolmens). As shown in figs. 1–4, this possible 'blueprint' consists of a chamber which is basically of 'egg–shaped' form, but with distinct, and repeated, irregularities. The chamber–plan could be described as a collection of accurately–scribed arcs of different radii, with identifiable points of intersection. The 'Ville–Pichard' scale is always of the same dimensions, approximating to 3.25m x 3m, with the passage inserted at varying locations along the perimeter. One monument – Cha de Mezio 4, Arcos de Valvedez, Minho, in Iberia – does not even have a passage at all (Fig. 2g).

The carvings shown in Fig. 1 are from the Irish monuments of Loughcrew T and Sess Kilgreen, whereas the vast majority of the monuments which employ this 'blueprint', at whichever scale, come from Iberia, Armorica or the Channel Islands.

The choice of illustrated carvings underlines the apparent long–distance links between areas utilising this plan. The carving from the Sess Kilgreen menhir was executed at a scale of 1:10 in relation to monuments of Ville–Pichard dimensions; whereas illustrated motifs from Loughcrew T were at 1:12 and 1:24 respectively, relative to the monuments.

It may be of interest to note, in view of the preponderance of Irish 'blueprint' carvings in areas without comparable sites, that there is a monument which appears to combine a 'Ville Pichard' chamber with an 'Irish–type' cruciform ante-chamber and passage. This is the dolmen at Anneville (also known as Faldouet) in Jersey (Rybot 1932), shown in figure 2a. In fact, if one superimposes and rotates the plan on top of that of Newgrange at exactly the same scale, the similarities are quite striking. Although the excavation records are scanty, material of definitely Chassean date appears to be associated with a secondary phase at Anneville (Rybot 1932; Hawkes 1937). Whether this implies a very early example of a cruciform, or structural alteration is impossible to say without further excavation.

A final possibility, of course, for the presence in Ireland of what *may* be a 'blueprint' for many Armorican megaliths, is that the design was copied from Armorica, and brought subsequently to Ireland. There are certainly striking (although later) similarities between the art at Gavrinis and certain motifs in the Boyne Valley (Eogan 1986). One has only to look at Kerbstone 56 at Newgrange (O'Kelly 1989: fig. 52) to see familiar Gavrinis carving-types, such as both

rounded and square-topped 'boxed-U' motifs and equally distinctive boxed-Us with rounded top leading to converging straight lines. Recesses between carved elements on Kerbstone 56 resemble the familiar Armorican axes, both of classic form, and with splayed out-cutting edges (Mané-er-H'roëk type), both of which types occur at Gavrinis. The central part of this composition looks, at least superficially, as if it is a bas-relief copy of the unique, and very deeply-engraved composition of hollowed basins found on stone $C1^2$ in the chamber at Gavrinis.

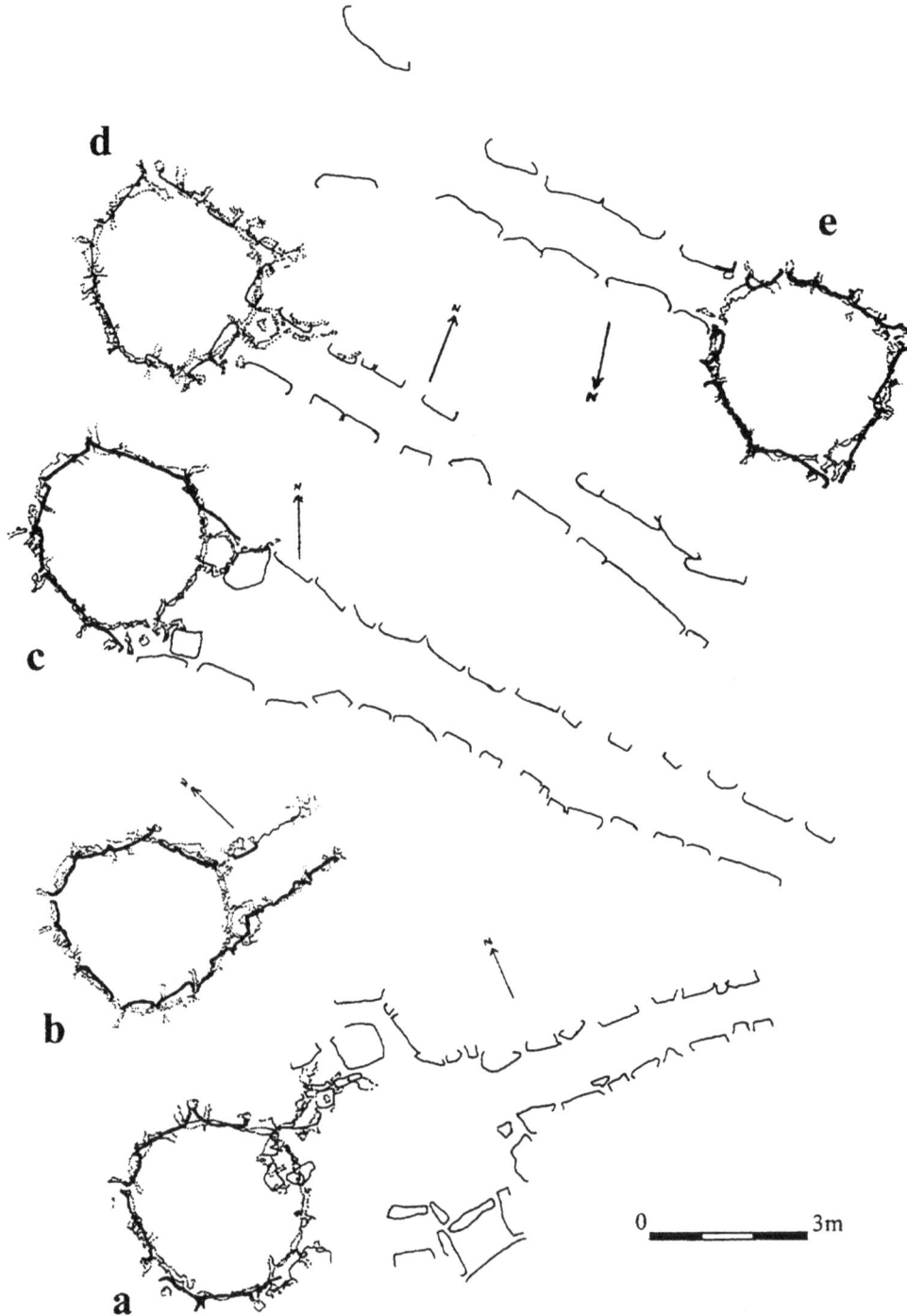

Figure 3. Some Armorican examples of 'Ville-Pichard' monuments: A. Anneville, Jersey; b. Colpo B, Morbihan; c. Mané Ruthual, Morbihan; d. Ile Longue, Morbihan; e. Kercado, Morbihan

---

[2] Typology as per E. Shee Twohig (1981)

The fact that there are other carvings of different form on the same stones as the 'blueprints' need not mean that all carvings on the stone need to be contemporary. There is ample evidence (Eogan 1986, C. O'Kelly 1973) for alteration and superimposition at different periods *on the same stones* in the Meath art, so other motifs should not be assumed to form any context for the function or chronology of the carving-form. The longevity of carved megaliths as a forum for later 'artwork' is amply demonstrated by the 'Deferre' inscription on the carved stone 53 at Stonehenge, or the word 'Gazelle' scribed onto the end-stone of the Table des Marchand at Locmariaquer. In both those latter cases, had the carvings been less obviously modern, they may have been accepted without question as being contemporary with their fellow art, using that dangerously two-edged deterrent to comparative investigation: Occam's Razor[3].

It must be stressed that the carvings need not *necessarily* have represented a 'blueprint' in themselves. Equally, it may be that the complex geometrical form found on the carvings, and in the monuments, represented in different media a similar concept or 'symbol' (used in as unloaded a way as possible), which it was found necessary to portray in great detail, and to rigid size criteria. To establish this for certain would necessitate a far more exhaustive search. It is just put forward as a tentative possibility, but one the possible implications of which would make it dangerous to ignore.

Different scales of the 'Ville–Pichard blueprint' (Fig. 3)

Although the first monuments to be recognized as having this ground-plan are on the Ville-Pichard scale, the majority of monuments so far identified belong to different sub-groups, which all share precisely the same geometry and construction lines, but on different, although internally-consistent, scales. By far the most numerous of these is the *Béhélec* group (Fig. 4), which has the same number of identified sites as the Ville-Pichard scale. It is named after the dolmen at Saint-Marcel (Morbihan), and consists of monuments whose scale is precisely at 10:1 compared to the Loughcrew T ('L1') motif; whereas as Ville-Pichard sites are at a 12:1 relation with this carving. The dolmen at Sess Kilgreen, next to the menhir which includes a carving of the 'blueprint' itself, belongs to the 'Béhélec group'. The great majority of known monuments using this scale come from the Alentejo region of Iberia (33 out of 44 sites), with other sites in Badajoz, Beira, Extramadura, Huelva, the Algarve, and Braganzia.

There is also a number of sites which share the 'Ville-Pichard blueprint', but are of a different size to the two main scales. Fourknocks 1, County Meath, Ireland, is at a scale of 2:1 against Ville-Pichard, or 20:1 against the Sess Kilgreen menhir and 24:1 against the Loughcrew T 'L1' 'blueprints', the construction guidelines for upright-location of which it also shares. The Danish passage-dolmen of Gronhoj, near Horsens also shares the morphology, but at a scale intermediate between the two major groups.

In Iberia, where most of the monuments bearing all scales of the geometry are found[4], nine megaliths – all except two of which are found in the Alentejo region – are larger than the 'Ville–Pichard' group, for example, Anta Grande da Comenda da Igreja, Evora and Saragonheiros 1, Poralegre, Nisa. Ten sites are of intermediate scale between the 'Ville-Pichard' and 'Béhélec' sites, but are between themselves of identical scale (see Fig. 3). These latter are found in the Alentejo (for example, Murteira de Cinna, Evora, Evora), Beira (for example Pedra da Moura, Campo d'Arca, Cambra), and Huelva regions (Mesa de las Huecas 2). Finally, five sites appear to employ a miniature version of the 'blueprint', although still sharing the construction lines. Three of these are in Alentejo (such as Brissos 6, Evora, Evora), one in Extramadura, and the last in the Algarve.

The Nelhouët 'blueprint'

This is an extremely rare form, found only in one dolmen in Armorica and a small number in the Badajoz region in southern Iberia. The eponymous monument for this plan-type is the large, though now sadly neglected, dolmen of le Nelhouët, near Caudan in the Morbihan. The only sites so far discovered with this blueprint are considerably larger than most known monuments bearing the *Ville–Pichard* plans (with the exception of Fourknocks 1), and all known monuments which employ it have been built to a single scale, measuring a little below 5m x 4.5m. As in the case of monuments built according to the first 'blueprint', the junction with the passage may be at any point along the perimeter of the chamber. No site using this plan has yet been identified without a passage.

Unlike the *Ville–Pichard* geometry, there is only one carving which appears to show the Nelhouét 'blueprint'. However, it makes up in accuracy what it lacks in number, as can be seen in Fig. 5a (after Twohig 1980). This extremely accurate facsimile of the blueprint (at a scale of 1:10 in relation to the monuments) is engraved on the WSW (chamber) face of the stone marking the junction between the left-hand face of the passage (viewed from its mouth) and the chamber. The motif appears to show the construction lines used to set out the chamber-plan, radiating from a point a little above the centre.

Orientation of the Iberian Ville–Pichard and Béhélec chambers: a test for the 'blueprint' hypothesis

It is generally accepted that, if passage dolmens were ever meant to be orientated, it was along the axis of the passage (one only has to read the numerous accounts of Newgrange being orientated to the midwinter sunrise). If the chambers were each unique in conception, or, at most, designed to be roughly of the same size or vaguely circular, then it follows that there should be no distinctive patterning of their orientation. One can go further – at first sight, it would seem almost impossible to discern any meaningful axis from examining the plans in isolation.

---

[3] See Rault 1993/4b for a detailed discussion of this form of problem, and the misinterpretations it may have caused in the past, applied to the carvings and other features at Stonehenge.

[4] 94 monuments out of a total of 114 so-far identified

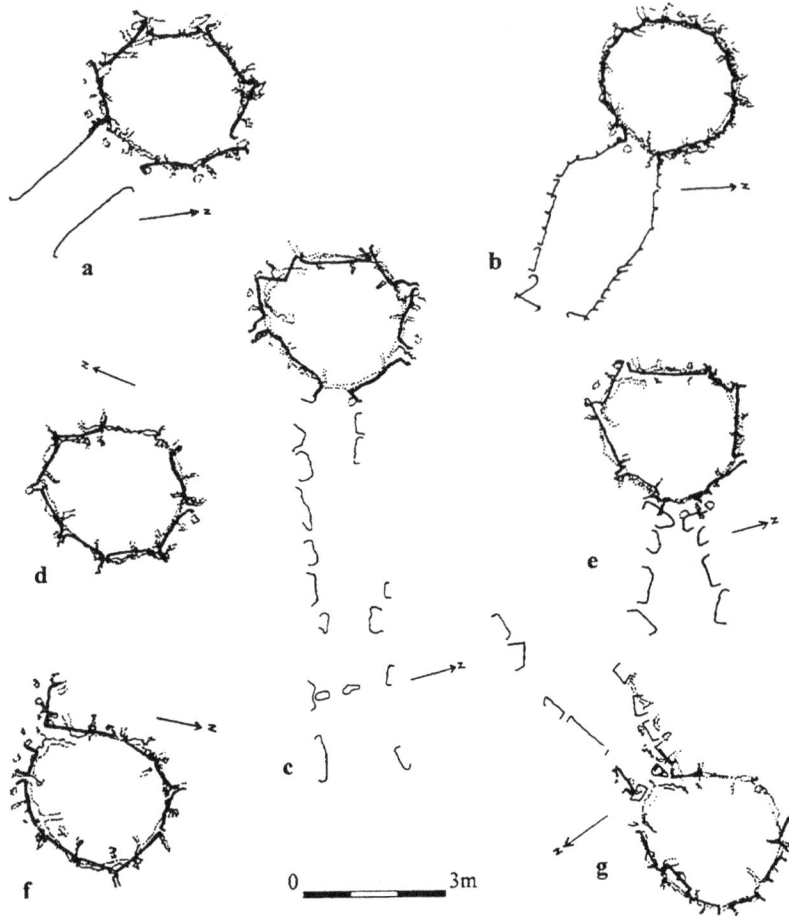

Figure 4. Selection of 'Béhélec' scale plans (stones in bold where they overlap with the Loughcrew T'L1' 'blueprint' shown dotted): a. Regato de Cajiron, Caceres; b. Tholos de Monte Velho, Ourique; c. Anta 2 dos Arneirinhos, Alentejo; d. Dehesa de la Lapita, Badajoz; e. Olivera 1, Alentejo; f. Sess Kilgreen, Tyrone; g. Béhélec, Morbihan

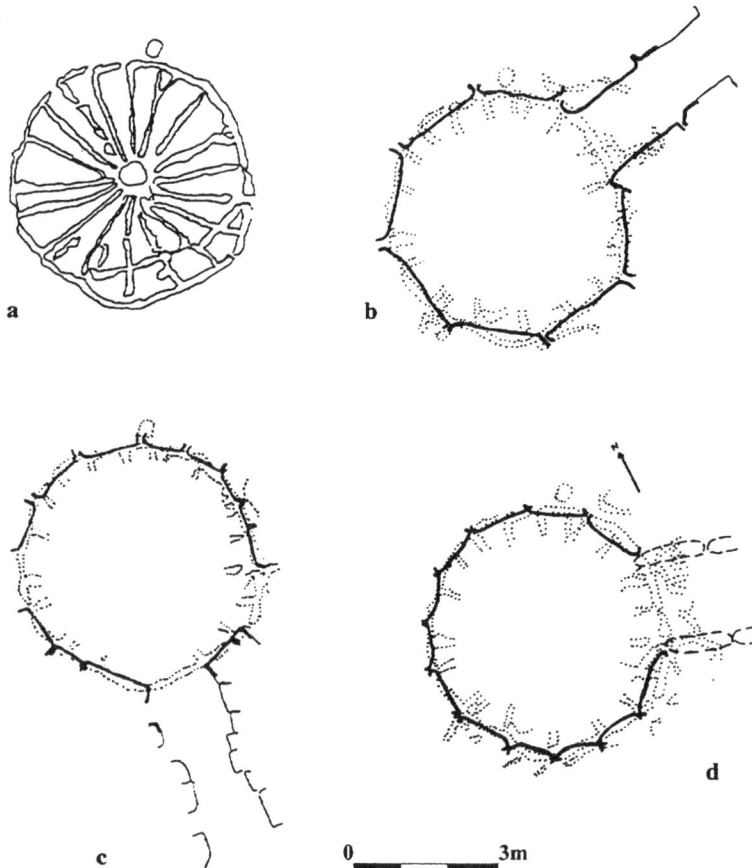

Figure 5. Selection of sites employing the Nelhouët 'blueprint: a. The 'blueprint' carving, isolated from stone 'C1' at Petit Mont, Morbihan; b. Dehesa de Majorga, Badajoz; c. Nelhouët, Morbihan; d. Cerca del Marzo, Badajoz

If we accept the blueprint hypothesis, however, a ready means of testing comes to hand. We can overlie the blueprint on the site's ground–plan, and choose an imaginary line bisecting any two points of the carving. If the carving cannot be used as a template, the results will be meaningless; and there should be no observed exclusivity between clusters of different 'orientation' since there was no common design in the first place. If, however, such mutual exclusivity is observed, then the case becomes very strong for a causal link between the passage–dolmen and the 'blueprint'.

In order to test this hypothesis, an imaginary line was drawn between the midpoints of the two sets of concentric circles at the top–left and centre of the Loughcrew Cairn T 'blueprint', filling the bottom third of the art on stone L1 (Fig. 1a). This seemed an obvious bisecting–point for the motif, and one that cut the two *foci* of the carving. With the chamber–plan superimposed upon a drawing of the blueprint at the appropriate scale, and using the north–point supplied by the Leisners, it was a simple matter to plot the resulting distributions.

The first two maps (Figs.6a,b) show the distributions of the Ville–Pichard and Béhélec monuments, whose exact positions are securely located. Southern Iberia has been singled out, because there are too few sites located to sufficient accuracy in the north for any valid comparisons to be made. There follow Figs 6c through 7d, which show a selection of the site distributions for monuments whose chamber faces in the directions quoted, using the methodology described above.

In all the sorted maps, 'Ville–Pichard'–scale sites are shown as circles, and 'Béhélec' scale dolmens as triangles. Open circles denote monuments for which the attribution is less than certain, but still highly probable.

Only those sites whose geographical location can be pinpointed accurately have been included. The smaller number of sites in areas to the north of Iberia prevents their information from having the same value for this purpose, hence their not being treated in a similar way. A plus or minus sign on the symbol signifies that the orientation is a few degrees to either side of that designated, but less than half the amount towards the next designation.

It is hoped that this evidence will show that, although the numbers are small, the distribution pattern is not random. The contrast between the north–facing chambers, concentrated towards the centre of the area under consideration (Fig.7a), and the east–facing chambers forming a great–arc over a much wider geographical area to the north (Fig. 7b), is quite remarkable.

Most of the monuments lie close to long rivers, many concentrated along the Tagus, where enormous shell–middens of an almost industrial scale flank the estuary from around the mid–eighth millennium BP (Scarre 1992:150). The south, and south–south–western (Fig. 7c) –facing chambered sites follow the river on its south–westerly flow towards the sea, whereas the south–westerly–orientated

chambers (Fig. 7d) cut across river lines in a south–south–easterly line. It must be stressed, however, that more surveying needs to be done to increase the number of accurately located sites, as other sites which cannot be precisely pin–pointed nonetheless seem to confirm the general picture.

It is worth mentioning that when both Ville–Pichard and Béhélec versions of the site–plan share chamber–orientations (as defined from the Ville–Pichard 'blueprint'), their distribution is always mutually exclusive (except for the two examples facing north–east). In the case of the east–facing chambers, this is resolved into a SE–NW line for Ville–Pichard, and NW–SE line for the Béhélec dolmens, with the lines intersecting to the north.

As an example to show that this is not all the patterning which is discernible from the plans, the distribution–plots for the sites in the same groups with *passage* orientations in the east–to–south–east sector in Iberia were also included in the study.

The patterning is very distinct in these cases also, with the large number of east–facing sites (Fig. 6c) formed into an NW–SE core, and the outlying 'arc' reminiscent of the corresponding chamber orientation. The south–south–east–facing sites form an almost exact N–S line, flanked by Ville–Pichard monuments, and with its body formed of Béhélec dolmens. The mutual exclusivity between like-facing dolmen types seen for the chamber seems not to have been important when it came to passage–orientation.

The south–eastern facing dolmens, only three in number, are situated either side of a river–bend, with the Ville–Pichard dolmen to the outer, western arc, and the two Béhélec sites to the east–south–east.

In conclusion, the evidence from the site–plans tends to confirm that some aspects of the design motivation were indeed related to orientation, and that, in certain cases, this incorporated or engendered mutual exclusivity. Further evidence is also thereby produced for the existence of a link between the Ville–Pichard type carvings and certain groups of monuments. Unfortunately, there are too few sites of the Nelhouët type to undertake a similar analysis.

Geographical scope of the 'blueprints'

Although the original research which led to this paper concentrated mainly on Armorica, the Channel Islands, and the borders of the Irish Sea, it soon became apparent that the great majority of passage–dolmens possessing all three 'blueprints' actually occurred on the Iberian peninsula. This is probably partly due to the fact that no other area rich in megaliths has benefited from the wealth of published plans provided by the Leisners (exemplified by Leisner & Leisner 1956; Leisner & Leisner 1959).

The list of passage–dolmens employing the blueprints must, of course, remain very tentative, as only sites whose correlation reach a high degree of probability should be

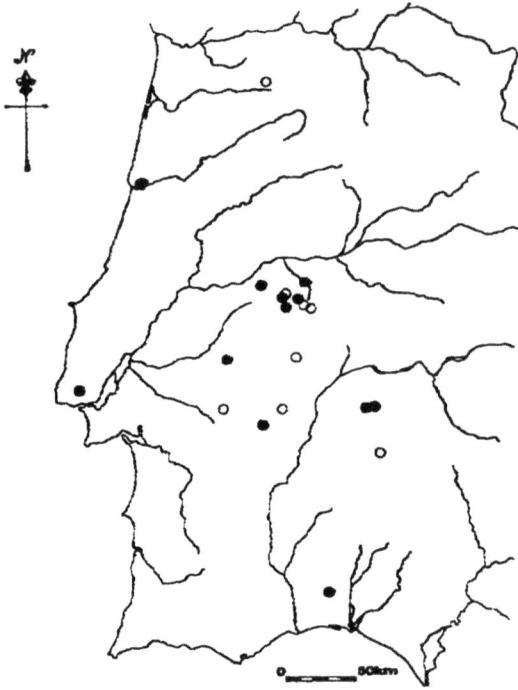

Figure 6a. 'Ville–Pichard'–scale dolmens in S Iberia

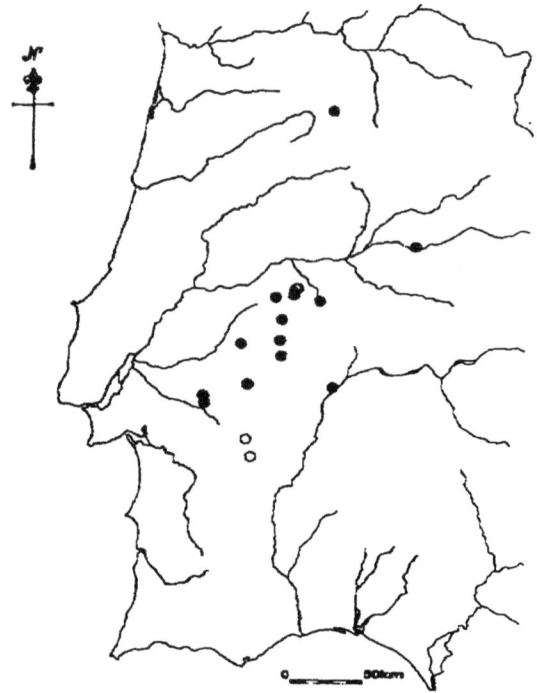

Figure 6b. 'Béhélec'–scale dolmens in S Iberia

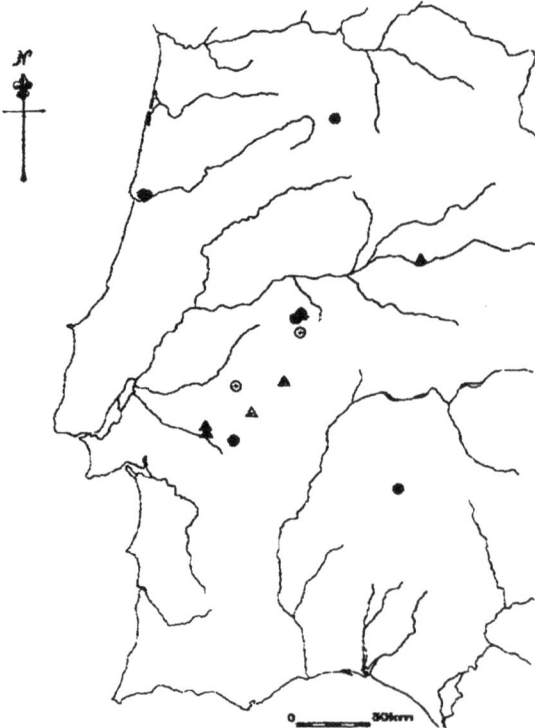

Figure 6c. 'V–P+B' dolmens with E facing passages in S Iberia

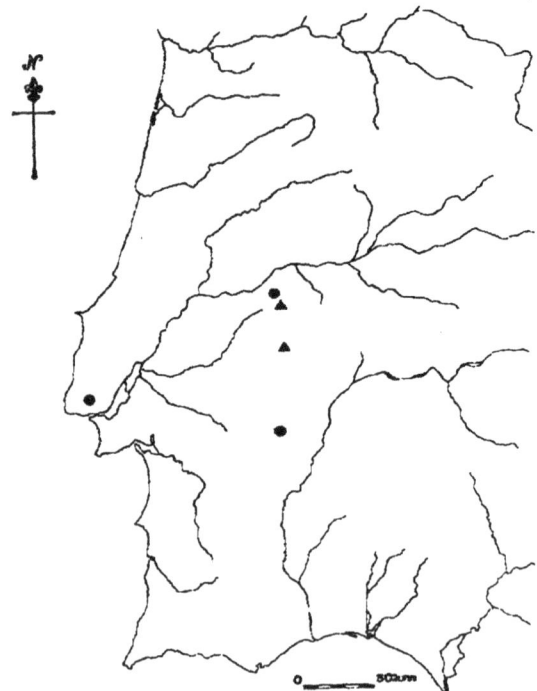

Figure 6d. 'V–P+B' dolmens with ESE facing passages in S Iberia

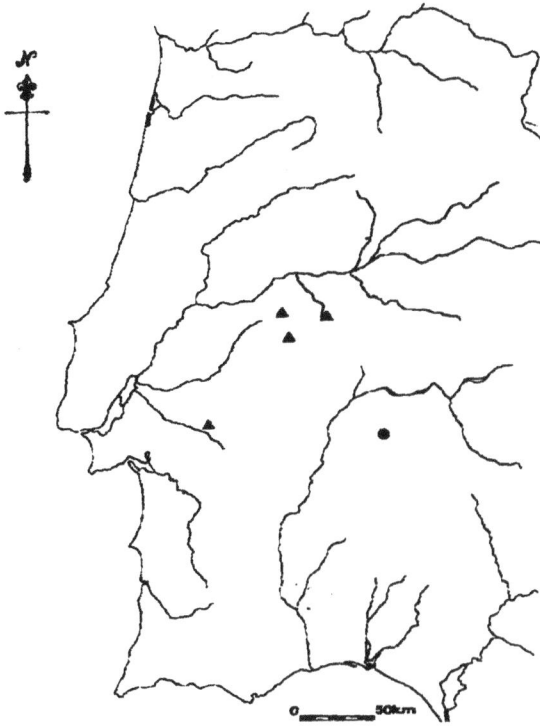

Figure 7a. 'V–P+B' dolmens with N facing chambers in S Iberia

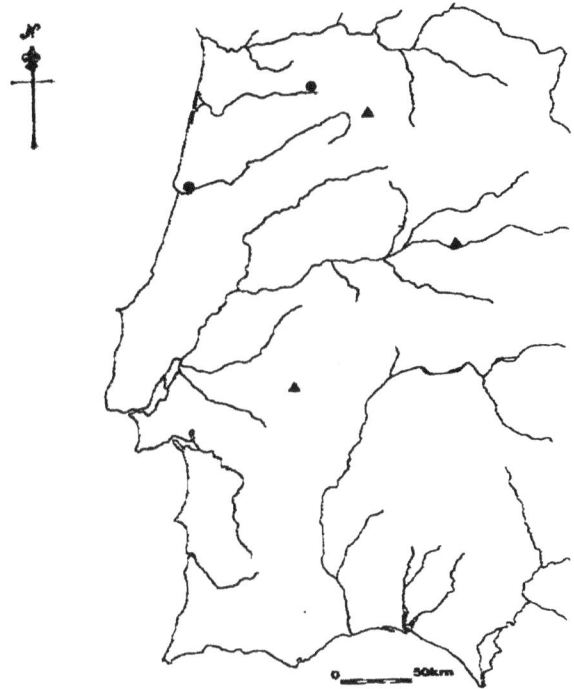

Figure 7b. 'V–P+B' dolmens with E facing chambers in S Iberia

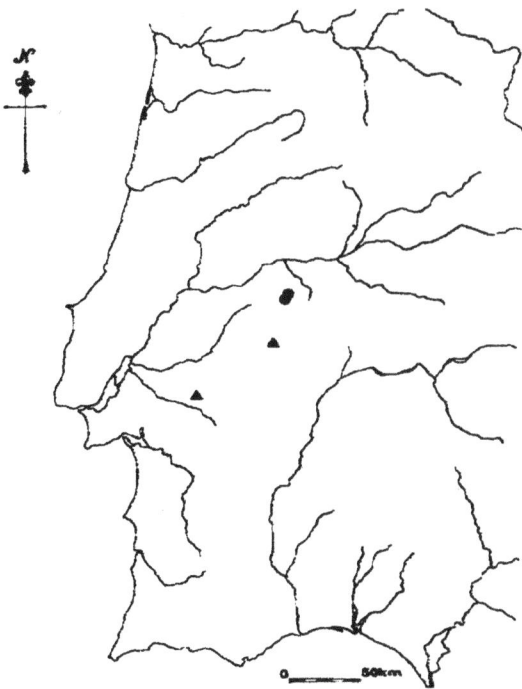

Figure 7c. 'V–P+B' dolmens with SSW–facing chambers in S Iberia

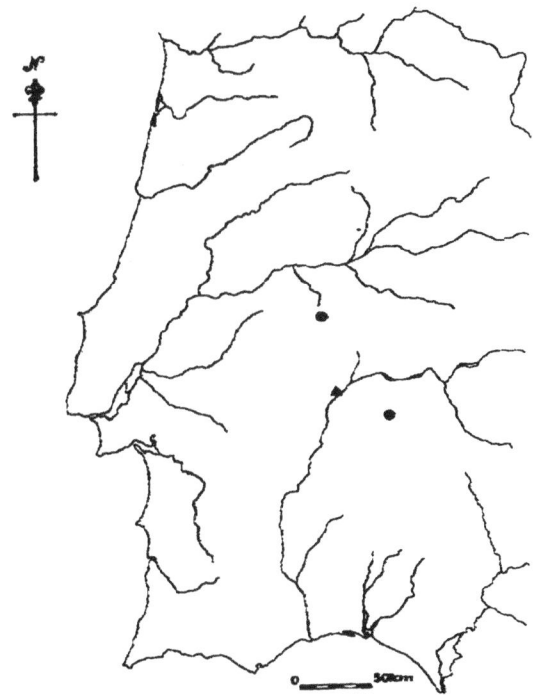

Figure 7d. 'V–P+B' dolmens with SW facing chambers in S Iberia

included. The numbers should, therefore, be only seen as the minimum for each class. Also, with new plans being published every year, and more sites being discovered, the final quantities will change, allowing the relative proportions between areas to be refined.

There are other monuments of 'Ville–Pichard' type and scale from Armorica and the Channel Islands (for instance, the central dolmen at the Ile Carn [l'Helgouac'h 1965: fig. 12.1], Tossen–ar–Run, at Yvias [l'Helgouac'h 1965: fig. 12.2], Ile Bono, in Perros–Guirrec [l'Helgouac'h 1965: fig. 15.3] and Parc er Guren in Crac'h [Twohig 1981: fig. 95] and Anneville in Jersey [Rybot 1932: Plan B]). However, no other certain examples of the Béhélec or Nelhouët types can be isolated from the areas north of Iberia. There is one example, however, of a site which conforms to the same 'blueprint', but at a scale intermediate between the 'Ville Pichard', and Béhélec sizes, from the eastern coast of Denmark. This is the site of Gronhoj, near Horsens (Thorwildsen 1946: fig. 1). Again, there are at least ten passage–dolmens from Iberia using the 'blueprint' at this scale.

There is, at present, only one Ville–Pichard 'blueprint' site which has been recognized in France, not counting Armorica. This is the dolmen of la Grosse Pérotte, at Fontenille in the Charante (Twohig 1981: 199, fig. 201). The match is not as good as most of the other examples, however, it does share the construction lines for stone location of the other monuments.

Proportions of different monument–types/scales

There are 114 monuments which so far have been identified as certainly, or probably, possessing the Ville–Pichard 'blueprint', of which 94 come from the Iberian peninsula, 15 from the Armorican province (including 3 from Jersey), and one from the Charante. Of the two major magnitudes, 44 are of the Ville–Pichard scale and 44 of the Béhélec. As mentioned earlier, 10 monuments are larger than Ville–Pichard, 11 are between Ville–Pichard and Béhélec in size, and five are smaller than Béhélec.

There is a marked difference, however, in the proportions between different scales in different provinces where the 'blueprint' is used. Whereas the numbers of Ville–Pichard and Béhélec monuments are the same, the larger dolmens form 30.1% of the total for Iberian monuments, against 88.2% in Armorica (including the Channel Islands). The greatest number of 'Ville–Pichard–scale' dolmens do, however, occur in Iberia (63.6%), where at least 28 megaliths employ the Ville–Pichard 'blueprint', in the districts of Beira, Galicia, Badajoz, Minho, Huelva, Caceres, Braganzia, and, particularly, Alentejo, along the Tagus river.

The 'Béhélec scale' monuments, however, are almost entirely found in Iberia (95.5%), as are the largest monuments bearing the 'blueprint' (80%), monuments between Ville–Pichard and Béhélec in magnitude (90.9%), and the few very small sites (100%). As regards the second 'blueprint', the 'Nelhouët' monuments form such a small group that

meaningful conclusions from the surviving distribution (one monument in Armorica and four in Iberia) appear impossible.

Discussion

In order to be certain whether this phenomenon of repeated, long–range replication of plan–morphology, side–by–side with carvings of identical geometry, represented one simultaneous burst of activity, or else a slow and perhaps discontinuous process, it would be necessary to ascertain as far as practical the chronology of the monuments involved. Regrettably, the majority of the excavation reports which we possess for passage–dolmens which may belong to an early stage in the construction of megaliths date from the nineteenth or earlier twentieth centuries.

The work at Knowth and Newgrange, for example, refers to monuments which, in their present state at least, can be demonstrated to be over a millennium later than the earliest megaliths dated in Armorica or Iberia. Giot's work at Barnenez (Giot 1987) is a notable exception, in that it contains a number of radiocarbon determinations placing use at the monuments well into the fifth millennium Cal BC. There is also considerable evidence from the latter group of monuments that these dates may be much later than at least some of the dolmens concerned in their original form, which appear, as at Geonnais (Rault and Forrest 1992) to have been in a ruinous condition when the final structure and mound were erected.

In Rault (1993/4a: 94), the possible stratigraphic locations from which data recovered from any passage–dolmen must belong were classified as follows:

a. Sealed below a layer cut by primary sockets
b. Sealed below structural alterations
c. Sealed below cairn or mound
d. Sealed below kerb
e. In area inside sockets of primary structure
f. On floor level sealed at initial phase
g. Inside sockets relating to structural alterations
h. Inside sockets relating to kerb
i. On lowest floor level, but not sealed at initial phase
j. On interface with structural alterations
k. On interface with cairn or mound
l. On interface with kerb
m. From any context stratigraphically later than the above

Before any dated material from a dolmen can be used as chronological evidence for its initial construction phase, it is obviously necessary to ascertain from which of these categories it proceeds. Data from an **a** location would provide a *terminus post quem* for the first phase of the monument, whereas **c**, **g**, **j**, **k**, and **m** locations supply terminus *ante quem* material. Only material from **e** and **f** can be regarded as contemporary with the initial monument phase, with any evidence from the remaining categories (**b**, **d**, **h**, **i**, **l**) requiring further stratigraphical relationship to the first phase of the dolmen before it can be used for dating the latter.

At the time of writing, there is no secure *terminus post quem* material, as defined above, for the monuments employing the 'blueprint', nor any skeletal evidence that need be primary and suggest a necessarily funerary purpose for the structures (see also Rault 1993/4a *passim*). That some at least of the Ville–Pichard monuments must be early in the sequence of passage–dolmen construction is certain.

The fact that Kercado shares the 'Ville–Pichard' blueprint is not alone in confirming this. Early dates from cairn material at La Hougue Bie in Jersey, which must be secondary to the enveloped megalith, and much of the material from the Iberian monuments appears to be Mesolithic in date (see the detailed discussion in Rault 1993/4a: 109–117). The fact that many monuments possess what appears to be an industry far earlier than generally realized suggests that some monuments, and the exact context of the finds within them needs to be looked at more on their own merits, but that would require another article outside the remit of this paper.

Conclusion

In conclusion, we have seen that there is strong evidence for the use of two 'blueprints' from a large group of sites separated by vast stretches of water. This makes it probable that the areas involved were in contact during the initial period of construction, and that at least some megalithic art is contemporary with the stone structures. The fact that the art pertaining to site–plans does not generally occur on sites bearing that shape, suggests that those responsible for the motifs may have been aware of at least some of the constructional complexities of the architecture of distant monuments.

The fact that one of the earliest monuments 'dated' so far, Kercado in Brittany, itself conforms to the 'Ville–Pichard' site–plan; follows the construction lines for upright–location from a carving at Loughcrew in Ireland; and is of a type most heavily represented in Iberia has implications which run deep and fast for the origins of passage–dolmen construction, as do the large number of very early finds from many of these passage–dolmens.

The possibility that some of the earliest monuments had been built according to replicated and accurate plans at set dimensions questions the foundation of some of the rarely challenged interpretative background for the beginnings of monumental architecture. It suggests that rather than being a local reaction to an overwhelming agricultural 'light from the East' by disparate, moribund, epi–Mesolithic communities, or pre–deciding that they were built by a fully agricultural society centring on ancestor–worship, the origins of our earliest stone buildings may be seen rather as the culmination of a long–standing and vibrant economy based on long–distance contact, almost certainly based on fishing. This follows the model suggested by Clark (1977), but suggests that it may be extended backwards in time and complexity. If we are to use ethnography in the study of European passage–dolmens, it is important to look at work such as that on the patterns of social complexity linked to economy & subsistence level (for example, Keeley 1988 *passim*),

artefact–ecofact distribution linked to precise use–determination (for example, Binford 1983 *passim*), and techniques of long–distance navigation (Goodenough & Thomas 1987 *passim*) or moving heavy weights on land (for example, Garfitt 1979 *passim*).

One final quote is also of importance, as regards the possibility of a Mesolithic origin for certain passage–dolmens, and the form of social complexity which may already have existed, notwithstanding the low–level complexity which was, until recently, assumed for non–agricultural societies. I. Saksida emphasises (Saksida 1991: 27) that he 'would also be very cautious of using that ethnographic material deriving from living or recent hunter–gatherer groups, which serves as a classic comparative clue in constructing ... mesolithic 'sociological' models. Most of these groups may be regarded as a secondary response to inter–group relations in some chosen region: most of them were once forced to choose this kind of social mode of survival. This was usually done in a less than promising (or even completely unpromising), extreme environment, and usually, in some ways, these groups were dependent on neighbouring, settled, and highly structured groups ... we might see that Mesolithic human agglomerates were, therefore, highly structured complex societies, producing their own 'social' worlds in as effective and sophisticated a way as we do'.

It is perhaps in this context that we should view the architects (in more senses than one) of what was possibly among the earliest and most geographically–widespread 'ritual landscapes'. Perhaps we see in these inter–related monuments an attempt at emphasising social identity over the breadth of the 'Atlantic seaboard' at a date when the coastal population would have comprised a scattering of small–scale fishing communities along the seaboard. The building of these imposing monuments would have necessitated co–operation between many such groups, perhaps separated by tens or even hundreds of miles, which could have only been achieved through a recognized and reliable means of long–range contact, and sufficient unity of purpose between the groups to embark upon such non–obviously practical projects. The result of these, in turn, sited as they would have been on the high lands overlooking both the coastal and river fishing–grounds, would have served to re–emphasise the unity between the disparate communities whose group effort was so visibly and lastingly enshrined.

Note on the figures: orientations (where supplied on the original plans) are true, not magnetic.

Bibliography

Binford, L. (1983) *In Pursuit of the Past*, London.
Boujot, C. & Cassen, S. (1993) A pattern of evolution for the Neolithic Funerary Structures of the West of France, *Antiquity*, 67, 477–491.
Bradley, R. (1993) *Altering the Earth*, Edinburgh.
Eogan, G. (1986) *Knowth and the Passage–Tombs of Ireland*, London.

Daniel, G. (1963) *The Megalith Builders of Western Europe*, 2nd edn, London.

Hawkes, J. (1937) *The Archaeology of the Channel Islands, Volume II*, Jersey, Jersey.

Giot, P. (1987) *Barnenez, un grand cairn mégalithique*, Châteaulin.

Hodder, I. (1990) *The Domestication of Europe*, Oxford.

Clark, G. (1977) The economic context of dolmens and passage–graves in Sweden, 35–50, in Markotic, V. (ed) *Ancient Europe and the Mediterranean: studies presented in honour of Hugh Hencken*, Warminster.

Daryll Forde, C. (1927) The Megalithic Monuments of Southern Finistère, *The Antiquaries Journal*, 4–37.

Goodenough, W. & Thomas, S. (1987) Traditional Navigation in the Western Pacific: a Search for Pattern, *Expedition*, 29, 3–14.

Keeley, L. (1988) Hunter–gatherer Economic Complexity and "Population Pressure": A Cross–Cultural Analysis, *Journal of Anthropological Archaeology*, 7, 373–411.

Leisner, G. & Leisner, V. (1956) *Die Megalithgräber der iberischen Halbinsel: der Westen*. Band I, Berlin.

Leisner, G. & Leisner, V. (1959) *Die Megalithgräber der iberischen Halbinsel: der Westen*. Band II, Berlin.

L'Helgouac'h, J. (1965) *Les sépultures mégalithiques en Armorique, dolmens à couloir et allées couvertes*, Rennes.

Lukis, F. (1849) On the Sepulchral Character of Cromlechs in the Channel Islands, *Journal of the British Archaeological Association*, 4, 323–336.

O'Kelly, C. (1973) Passage Grave Art in the Boyne Valley, Ireland, *Proceedings of the Prehistoric Society*, 39, 354–382.

O'Kelly, M (1989) *Early Ireland*, Cambridge.

Patton, M. (1993) *Statements in Stone Monuments and Society in Neolithic Brittany*, London.

Renfrew, C. (1978) *Before Civilization*, 2nd edn, London.

Rault, S. & Forrest, T. (1992) La Hougue des Geonnais, (Jersey, Channel Islands): Interim Report on the 1985 – 1989 Seasons of Excavation, *Annual Bulletin, la Société Jersiaise*, 25, 691–710.

Rault, S. (1993/4a) Neolithic Passage–Graves Reconsidered, *Journal of Theoretical Archaeology*, 3/4, 83–121.

Rault, S. (1993/4b) Rings and Recesses: Problems in Archaeological Visibility at Stonehenge, *Journal of Theoretical Archaeology*, 3/4, 167–178.

Rybot, N. (1932) The Dolmen of Faldouet, *Bulletin Annuel, La Société Jersiaise*, 12, 73–85.

Saksida, I. (1991) On the Historical and Structural Meaning of the term 'Mesolithic', *Journal of Theoretical Archaeology*, 2, 25–28.

Scarre, C. (1992) The Early Neolithic of Western France and Megalithic Origins in Atlantic Europe, *Oxford Journal of Archaeology*, 11, 121 – 154.

Sherratt, A. (1995) Instruments of Conversion? The Role of Megaliths in the Mesolithic/Neolithic Transition in North–West Europe, *Oxford Journal of Archaeology*, 14, 245–260.

Thorvildsen, K. (1946) Gronhoj ved Horsens, en Jaettestue med Offerplads, *Årboger for Nordisk Oldkyndighed og Historie*, 73–94.

Twohig, E. (1981) *The Megalithic Art of Western Europe*, Oxford.

Monumentality and the Landscape: The Possible Symbolic and Political Distribution of Long Chambered Tombs around the Black Mountains, Central Wales.

George Nash
St David's University College, Lampeter

Posing the question

If one looks at Luttra (Plate 1), a few kilometres south of Falköping (central Sweden), or La Hougue Bie, Jersey (Plate 2) in south-west Wales, or at Arthur's Stone (Plate 3), on the Welsh borders, one sees a series of monuments that are truly megalithic – monumentality at its most dramatic. For example, from Alleberg Mountain, Luttra dominates and controls the surrounding landscape; it forms a cognito within the landscape. But would the same visual impact exist if Luttra was covered by an earthen mound? I would say not. In fact, I would argue that this megalithic tomb would then become part of the landscape, rather than opposing it, as it does now. The only visual opposition comes from within. Likewise, if one looks at Spreckelsen's Grande Arche de La Defense[1] (Plate 4) in Paris, one sees a building that is blatantly monumental. If this design was to be incorporated into say, a small townscape, the visual impact would obviously be greater than in its present position. However, when placed within a familiar space, i.e. the Defence Park (Plate 5), the building becomes organic, merging with other similarly-designed buildings, while nevertheless, retaining its visual identity.

Introduction

In this paper, I wish to explore the relationship between the landscape and the siting of megalithic (Chambered) monuments. In particular, I am interested in tomb orientation, passage view and chamber alignment with prominent features in the landscape, for example rivers, streams, U-shaped valleys, upland escarpments and spurs. For this, I will use the Black Mountains Long Chambered Tomb Group of Central Wales as a basis for my arguments. In addition, I am interested in applying an architectural approach to the perception of both inside and outside, paying particular attention to the 'sense of occasion', the cognitive values to tomb space and design. I will argue that internal space replicates the landscape. In other words, the outside is drawn within, creating a cultural and symbolic map. So, rather than a tomb 'statementing' the landscape, it becomes part of an homogeneous whole – it is the landscape itself, a microcosm replicating the outside.

The problems

Throughout the Neolithic core areas of Britain, indeed, of Europe, there has been a problem of ignoring the landscape.

Plate 1. Luttra, Falköping, Central Sweden, Megalithic Monumentality

---

[1] I am indebted to Steve Moore (architect) for discussion concerning this building.

Plate 2. La Hougue Bie Passage Grave, Jersey

Plate 3. Arthur's Stone, Black Mountains Group

Plate 4. Spreckelsen's Grande Arche de La Defense, Paris – Organic or Inorganic?
(Photo: S.J. Moore)

Plate 5. Ty Isaf, Black Mountains Group. Facade Area looking South–East

However, endless attention has been paid to the monuments themselves. Each tomb has been excavated, drawn, measured and in some instances, weighed. In the case of the Black Mountains Group, there has been very little emphasis upon landscape perception. Only Grimes (1936a, 1936b), Darvill (1982), Daniel (1950), Britnell and Savory (1984) and Kinnes (1992) have paid limited attention to the landscape. Moreover, this research is largely empiricist and the text rather tedious. The tomb has become a static object, devoid of human association, an object with no landscape, no history and no relationship with the social.

Recently, Julian Thomas (1994) has stated that the earlier tombs played an important part in 'presencing the ancestors' into the surrounding landscape. In other words, the dead were being returned whence they came. I think, however, this is only part of a more complex story in that the tombs themselves, rather than the socio–political–symbolic nature of the body, are of paramount importance to design and location. Christopher Tilley and Julian Thomas (1994) have suggested a relationship between design and the body. Again, this is a plausible idea. However, I feel there is a problem with this argument in that tomb design could well be in direct conflict with the body. I would argue that tomb space is organised so as to oppose body symbolism. Hence, the necessity to disarticulate human skeletons within the inner space of the tomb. Such disarticulation blatantly dehumanises space. Therefore, the inner and outer tomb space may be divided into a series of structural oppositions:

Life v Death
Public v Private
Nature v Mechanical
Social v Ritual
Open v Closed
Familiar v Unfamiliar
Seen v Unseen

Many have argued that the siting of tombs is fundamentally a form of 'statementing' the landscape – turning a space into a place (Bradley 1993, Patton 1993). Both ritual and political knowledge make this place special. In part, this is fair comment; but I would stress that each monument is hidden away, organic and incognito with its surroundings. When one looks at tomb architecture, one is faced with only part of the monument, usually a few uprights and a fragmented capstone. One may refer to this as the 'frame' or 'skeleton' of the monument. Thomas and Tilley (1994) have also applied the term 'rib cage' to the design plan of the Brittany monuments. Gone is the drystone walling, cairn decoration, the mound, the facade and small internal and external features such as doorways, kerbing, roofing slabs etc. The frame, becomes structurally and visually opposed to the landscape. The frame, angular and mechanical, clashes instantly with the irregular, disorganised organic landscape. The structure suggests order, control and design. However, during the Neolithic the frame (or skeleton) would have possessed flesh. Each capstone, each upright would have been hidden by either an earthen mound or cairn, thus merging the form and design into an homogeneous whole. In this way, the monument becomes part of the landscape,

rather than opposing it. However, inside the tomb space, nature is, in part, rejected. Here, social and symbolic order dominates. The space becomes legitimated, humanised and clinical. Although the raw materials (i.e. stone and earth) are organic, the construction is not. Can we, therefore, describe the tomb as organic?

Monument location

The Black Mountains Group consists of at least eighteen monuments (Map 1). Earlier literature suggests that as many as twenty–three tombs were sited in and around the fertile valleys of the Dore, Usk and Wye (Daniel 1950, Powell et al. 1969). The group extends in an arc around the northern and western peripheries of the mountains. The tombs within this group are all locally–orientated, either to the valley or to prominent features within the landscape. Another distinction is that many are located on high upland ridges and plateaus, close to, and in full view of, the Black Mountains. Only two tombs, Gwernvale and Carn Goch, are sited on low ridges above the flood plains of the lower Usk valley. These two tombs may constitute meanings that are different from those of other monuments within the group farther north and east, although both are locally orientated – Carn Goch to Table Mountain, and Gwernvale to the directional flow of the River Usk.

Territoriality

In addition to local orientation, the Black Mountains Group also possesses a possible territorial relationship. Tombs are organised into distinct groupings. Usually, each group will consist of one valley–orientated monument and one tomb aligned with a particular topographic feature. Dividing the tombs in each group are major rivers and streams. For example, Pipton Long Cairn, orientated to the valley (or river), is allied with Little Lodge Barrow, which is aligned towards Y Das, a prominent west–facing spur of the Black Mountains. The River Llynfi separates the monuments, which are only 1.5km apart. Arguably, each river acts as a boundary between territories. However, I would suggest rivers play a ritual, rather than a political role in the siting of monuments. Tombs appear to be arranged in pairs, each fulfilling a separate symbolic function.

Creating an organic architecture

To discuss this further, one must look at the concept of modern organic architecture. One of the main protagonists of this concept was Frank Lloyd Wright. Many of his ideas on the use of materials in an organic form may be applied to some of my own ideas on mechanical and natural forms in the landscape (Hanks 1979, Frampton 1992). The Winslow House, River Forest, Illinois (Fig. 1) presents a dichotomy; a metaphor of private and public space. Here, Wright's design projects two meanings (or aspects): a rural facade, with its irregular distortions, the relationship between garden space and the random, almost organic fascia; that of the urban facade, regimented, symmetrical and mechanical. Another example is the Falling Water (Fig. 2) concept at Bear Run (1936). This design typifies the organic principles whereby concrete and glass are applied to an organic design, where "the place of the living is fused into nature" (Frampton 1992). The building incorporates the structural and spatial principles of falling water. In both instances, Wright considered that the materials used, did not necessarily have to be organic in the true sense of the word. Many buildings designed by Wright were, in fact, made from concrete

blocking. It is the way in which the materials are used that creates an organic architecture. Therefore, one cannot contemplate the stone frame of any tomb as being organic. These structures are truly mechanical in form. It is the mound material, the outer space, that is organic. However, this form is contrived so as to organise the visual impact of landscape and, in particular, prominent topographic features.

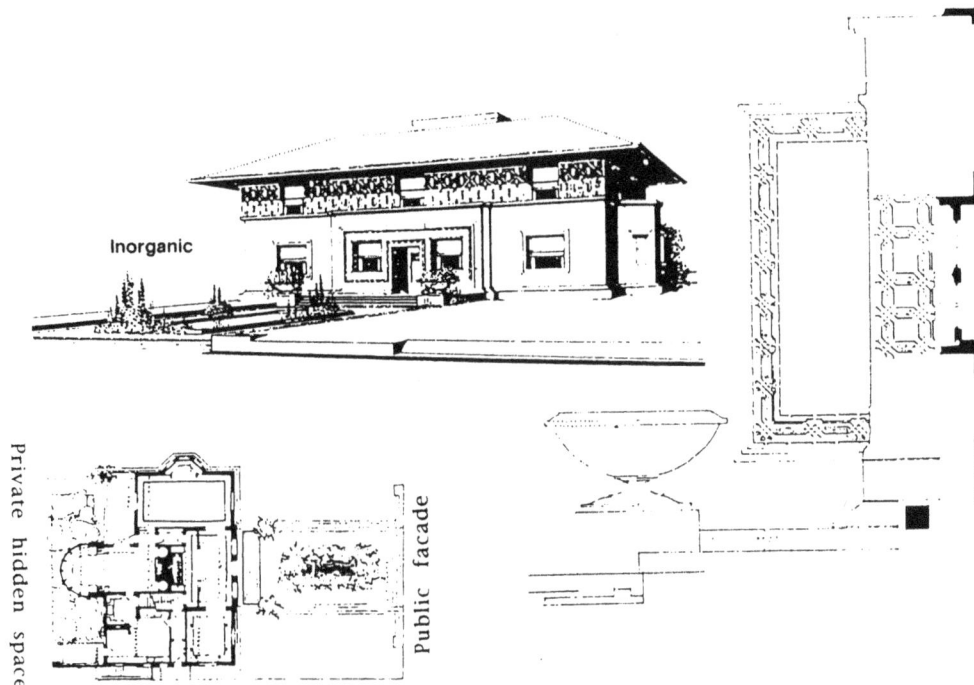

Figure 1. Winslow House, River Forest, Ill., 1893. View and site plan.

Figure 2. Wright's Falling Water Building, Bear Run, Pa., 1936. Here, Wright embodied a place for the living and fused it into nature.

Replicating the landscape

I have suggested that many of the features within the inner and outer space of the tomb are orientated towards various features within the landscape. I will now argue that the tomb plan and layout replicates that landscape – it draws the outside, within. The mechanical form metamorphoses the inner space into a stylized ritual map, in that certain topographic features are symbolically mapped and incorporated within the tomb plan. So, although the inner space opposes the outer, the outer space, when replicated within, becomes manipulated and controlled – it is subdued.

Regarding the actual replication, each monument has developed its own unique morphology. It appears to be responsive either to valley orientation or a particular topographic feature. With eight tombs (Gwernvale, Mynydd Troed, Ty Isaf, Penywyrlod, Ffostyll North and South, Pipton and Arthur's Stone) both tasks are initiated. Certain features such as rivers, valley spurs and scarp edges are being symbolically incorporated within the tomb plan. Horns, the facade, passages and chambers are utilised. Of the tombs with clear horns and facade, all appear to be aligned on a north/south axis – sharing direction with the Rivers Dore, Rhiangoll, Usk and Wye. In all cases, the orientation of the horns and facade is the same as that of the directional flow of the rivers. One might suggest, therefore, that the elongated shape of the tomb replicates river direction.

The most complex (inner) architecture belongs to the Ty Isaf monument (Fig. 3). Here, passages and chambers are organised in the direction of steep mountain slopes to the west, and mountain spurs to the south and east. The tomb acts as a 'compass', a central point within the landscape. Moreover, the tomb plan is orientated to the flow of the River Rhiangoll. The chambers are aligned in an east–west direction so as to 'catch' the rising and setting sun (also representing a life–and–death cycle). In addition to the

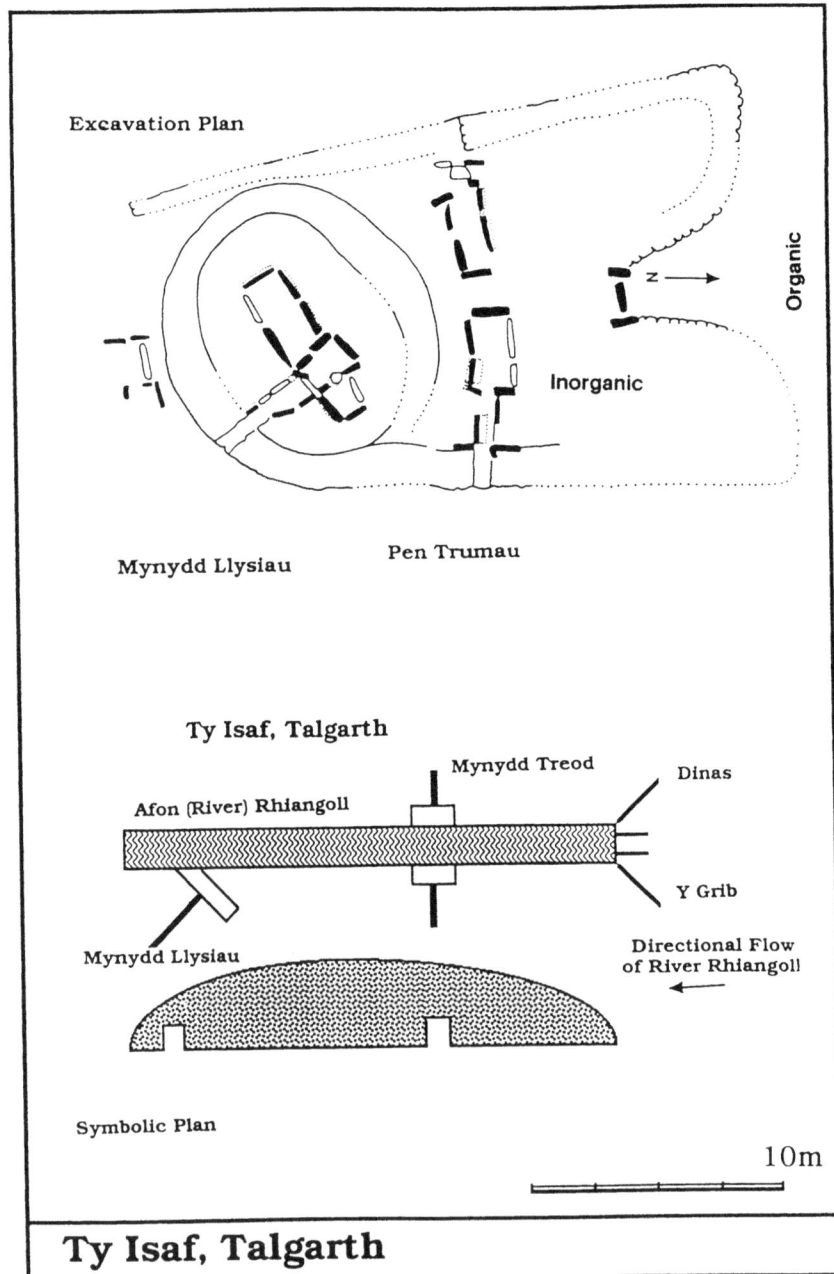

Figure 3. Ty Isaf, Talgarth

ground plan, the original shape of the mound would have been similar to the surrounding mountain peaks. At Ffostyll South, a clear similarity exists between the cairn shape and Mynydd Troed, looking towards the south–west. So, one can suggest that a three–dimensional replication is in operation. Ty Isaf, Ffostyll South and other monuments in the group are not therfore dominating the landscape, so much as merely forming part of it.

A similar pattern occurs at Penywyrlod. The orientation of this tomb is the same as the directional flow of the River Llynfi. The two chambers point towards Y Das and Hay Bluff, the northern extent of the Black Mountains. No passages or chambers occur on the west side of tomb, where the Brecon Beacons are in full view. It would appear that the inner space of this monument is only interested in the draw of the Black Mountains. Looking to the south, the mound shape appears to replicate the northern extent of Mynydd Troed.

A more pronounced attempt to encapsulate landscape can be seen with the unorthodox redirection of the passage at the Arthur's Stone "chambered structure", Dorstone (Herefordshire). At the entrance, one cannot see into the chamber. Likewise, one is unable to see outside from within the chamber. The transition point between what is human space and what is nature appears to be located where the passage changes direction. This point is equidistant between the chamber and the entrance. From both the chamber and the entrance, the doorway can be seen, and it is at this juncture that the human meets the natural, order meets disorder and the tame meets the untamed. But, I think that this is only forms part of the meaning behind monument construction and the socio–political nature of territoriality.

Arguably, there may well be an alternative explanation for the redirection, in that the entrance to the passage points towards Hay Bluff, an impressive spur at the northern extent of the Black Mountains. The capstone is orientated NE–SW with the south–western end pointing towards the southern section of the valley and Black Mountains. One can therefore suggest that the outer passage and the capstone deliberately encompass the whole aspect of the Black Mountains. But why? I would suggest that, in addition to the ambiguity (or opposition) between human and nature, the Black Mountains has been incorporated into the social and, more importantly, the symbolic identity of the settlers during the middle Neolithic. In other words, their landscape created a sense of belonging. Many other tombs sited in the upper Wye and Usk valleys appear to 'act' in the same way.

Monumentality of perception

Socio–ritual knowledge and the consciousness and manner in which people perceive objects within their own surroundings is fundamental to the formulation of a sense of belonging. However, is the building of a mortuary structure enough to statement the landscape? Perhaps, it is not the place that is important but the space. By focusing upon one small point in the landscape (i.e. the monument), one does not construct a cognitive and visual perception of a complete landscape. Many other components are required, such as valley spurs,

rivers, scarp edges and slopes, to bring about a visual totality. By initiating the outer tomb space the tomb becomes an integral part of a greater outer space (the landscape) – the monument becomes part of that visual impact. Therefore, the tomb is not visually monumental – it does not exist – but the consciousness and meaning of monumentality does. This is controlled and manipulated by knowledge – ritual knowledge. Organic architecture or not, the French architect, Le Corbusier (1923), one of the main exponents of functionalism in architecture, has established the idea that architecture is not a physical medium but a conscious awareness of concept, design and ideology. He states,

"By the use of inert materials and starting from conditions more or less utilitarian, you have established certain relationships which have aroused my emotions. This is Architecture".

One can suggest that these emotions form part of what is both a sense of belonging and the familiarity and association with landscape. Objectivity, although constituting meaning within language, can be interpreted differently by different individuals. In other words meaning is shared but the concept of meaning is multivalent (Jenks 1969:13). This basic component adds complexity to the visuallity of monuments within the landscape. Applying a semiotic approach (triangle), the concept or thought (the signified) to the symbol (the form or signfier creates or establishes the referent or thing. The way in which we make judgment on things is dependent upon a large number of sociological, economic and political determinants. The individual creates his or her own story; the way of the person being–within–the–world. Thus, the monument becomes a thing for all those who percieve it. To the archaeologist, it becomes the site. To our Neolithic ancestors it conveyed a multitude of meanings; symbols of individuality and restricted meaning.

Acknowledgements

I wish to express sincere thanks to the following people. Firstly, to George Children and initially, Chris Tilley, who spent many hours visiting the monuments within the Black Mountains. Thanks also to Trevor Kirk, who put forward ideas on the Ffostyll tombs. Finally, to the organisers of the Megalithic Conference in Falkoping, Vestegötland (Sweden) at which this paper was first presented.

Bibliography

Bourdieu, P. (1990), *Outline of a Theory of Practice*, Cambridge University Press, Cambridge.
Britnell, W. (1979) 'The Gwernvale Long Cairn', *Antiquity*, 53. 132–4.
Britnell, W & Savory, H. (1984) *Gwernvale and Penywyrlod: Two Neolithic Long Cairns in the Black Mountains of Brecknock*, Cambrian Archaeological Monographs No.2 Cardiff.
Children, G. & Nash, G.H. (1994) *Monuments and the Landscape: The Prehistory of Herefordshire*, Logaston Press, Hereford.
Children, G. & Nash, G.H. (1996) *Pathways, Stone and*

Monuments: The Chambered Monuments of South-west Wales, (in press).

Corcoran, J. X.W.P.(1969) 'The Cotswold–Severn Group' in Powell, T.G.E., Corcoran, J.X.W.P., Lynch, F. and Scott, J.G. *Megalthic Enquiries in the West of Britain*, Liverpool, Liverpool University Press.

Crawford, O.G.S. (1925) *The Long Barrows of the Cotswolds. Gloucester.*

Daniel, G.E. (1950) *The Prehistoric Chambered Tombs of England and Wales*, Cambridge University Press.

Frampton, K. (1992) *Modern Architecture: A Critical History*, 57–63, Thames and Hudson, London.

Gavin Robinson, R.S. (1934) 'Flint workers and flint users of the Golden Valley'. *Transactions of the Woolhope Naturalists' Field Club.* 54–63.

Grimes, W.F. (1936) 'The long cairns of the Brecknockshire Black Mountains' *Arch. Camb.* xci (1936), 259–82.

Grimes, W.F. (1939) 'Bedd yr Afanc', *Proceedings of the Prehistoric Society* 5, 258.

Hemp, W.J. (1935) 'Arthur's Stone, Dorstone, Herefordshire', *Archaeologia Cambrensis*, xc, 288–92.

Langer, M.M. (1989) *Merleau–Ponty's Phenomenology of Perception*, Macmillan Press, London.

Patton, M. (1992) *Statements in Stone*, Routledge.

Thomas, J.S. (1988) 'The Social Significance of Cotswold–Severn burial practices' *Man* 23, 540–559.

Thomas, J.S. (1993) 'The politics of vision and the archaeologies of landscape', in B.Bender (ed.) *Landscape, Politics and Perspectives*. Berg.

Tilley, C. (1993) 'Art, architecture and the landscape in Neolithic Sweden', in B.Bender (ed.) *Landscape, Politics and Perspectives*. Berg.

Vulliamy, C.E., (1921) 'The Excavation of a Megalithic Tomb in Breconshire', *Arch. Camb.* 7th ser. i (lxxvi), 1921, 300–5.

Vulliamy, C.E., (1923) 'Further excavations in the Long Barrows at Ffostill', *Arch. Camb.* 7th ser. iii (lxxviii) (1923), 320–4.

Vulliamy, C.E., (1929) 'Excavation of an Unrecorded Long Barrow in Wales', *Man*, xxix (1929) no.29, 34–36.

Gazetteer (a *Body* of Evidence)

As stated earlier it is important to recognise empiricist data. In some ways this paper creates a dichotomy; that of the monument and the theory of the monument. It is important to stress that no social–theoretical discourse can function without data. Archaeology still requires 'flesh', as well as the 'bones', in order to create a body (of evidence). In order to discuss and theorise, I have outlined a 'database' of evidence for each of the eighteen monuments within the Black Mountains Group.

1. Parkwood

SO 3565 3347

The precise location of this monument is unknown although Crawford (1925) suggests otherwise. At present, the whereabouts is still a mystery, although on a recent visit to the immediate area, there was a large limestone slab still visible. Whether or not this represents the Parkwood capstone remains debatable.

It is has been argued that Parkwood represents the south-eastern limit of the Black Mountains Group (Children & Nash 1994). However, a possible long mound is present on Garway Hill, to the south–east. Crawford (1925) describes the monument as a single capstone.

2. Long Barrow, Dunseal

SO 39133382

This monument along with the now destroyed Park Wood (SO 356 334) chambered tomb, marks the most southerly extent of Neolithic influence in the Golden Valley. Possibly, Dunseal long barrow and Park Wood represent territorial (boundary) 'markers'. Beyond these monuments, southwards, there are no other monuments and very little in the way of artifacts. These monuments, and others sited around the valley peripheries, could well be delineating a defined territory using tomb distribution and location. This delineation creates control and, above all, identity for the valley's inhabitants.

The origins of the site remain a mystery. The few surface finds (from ploughing) suggest a Neolithic or Early Bronze Age date. The mound itself is oval, approximately 27m x 14m in diameter and 2m high. The mound may once have been circular, hinting at a Bronze Age date. However, I would argue that, due to its location (high on a west facing ridge and occupying dominant views, especially to the south and west) the monument can be none other than a Neolithic long barrow. It's location, similar to that of other burial monuments in the valley, reinforces this idea. Furthermore, evidence for the Bronze Age is negligible along this part of the Welsh borders.

3. Cross Lodge Barrow, Dorstone

SO 33254168

This monument is located about 2km south–east of Arthur's Stone. Possibly much larger during the Neolithic, the mound is an elongated oval, approximately 18m x 10m and 2.5m high. Locally orientated (NW–SE) to the Golden Valley, Cross Lodge Long Barrow (as well as Arthur's Stone) embraces a commanding view of the Black Mountains. During the recent past, this monument has suffered plough damage to the northern section of the mound. Indeed, a large number of stones now litter the corner of the field, some of which may belong to the original tomb structure.

During the Neolithic, Cross Lodge Long Barrow would have been visible from the valley floor and also form the large Neolithic settlement (SO 3260 4230) approximately one kilometre north. Discovered between the two tombs in the early 1960s', the settlement is located on a prominent spur overlooking the Black Mountains. It is central to both tombs, yet there is no intervisibilty with them. The positioning of both the settlement and the tombs appears to be deliberate. The settlement, moreover, represents a link between the socio–economic and the ritual/symbolic.

Arthur's Stone and Cross Lodge long barrow are constructed in different ways, suggesting that the monuments were either constructed at different times and/or that they represent two different meanings. Cross Lodge barrow is aligned with the the valley, whereas Arthur's Stone may represent a valley-end territorial marker. It is probable that Arthur's Stone considerably predates Cross Lodge long barrow. A number of Mesolithic flints were found underneath Arthur's Stone, suggesting that the site was in use prior to the monument's construction .

The size and weight of the uprights and the capstone suggest that the construction time was indeed long and the number of people involved must have been considerable. Bill Startin (1981) has argued that a tomb such as Arthur's Stone might take between 7,000 and 16,000 labour hours (between three and seven months to build)! Judging by the size and construction of Cross Lodge long barrow, the investment of time and labour would have been much less. Obviously, construction time depends on the availability of local materials (sandstone) and the labour needed to transport blocks across the landscape. This being the case, the spare time available to the first farmers must have been considerable. Time for tomb building may have possibly been taken during the winter months, when the growing season was limited. Alternatively, tomb building may have been the first 'task' undertaken by valley settlers in order to establish control and social–political identity within the locality.

4. Arthur's Stone, Dorstone

SO 31804313

Arthur's Stone dates from around 3500 BC and is one of the most northerly chambered tombs of the Cotswold–Severn Group. It is one of five tombs dominating the Neolithic landscape of the northern reaches of the Golden Valley. Set in an oval mound (originally 26m x 17m), the tomb has nine upright stones (forming a polygonal chamber), an unorthodox right–angled passage and an enormous capstone, estimated to weigh more than 25 tonnes.

The capstone (5.8m x 3m) is split in two and is orientated NE–SW, with the south–western portion pointing towards the southern section of the Golden Valley. The chamber has, at its western end, a false portal stone (partly blocking the doorway to the main chamber) and a passage orientated north. However, the passage changes direction to the north-west, pointing towards the impressive Hay Bluff (the northern extent of the Black Mountains). This unorthodox redirection of the passage and the orientation of the capstone suggests Arthur's Stone was positioned deliberately so as to completely encompass the whole aspect of the Black Mountains. The tomb also incorporates views of both the

southern and northern extents of the Golden Valley. Indeed, many other tombs sited in the upper Wye and Usk (in Powys) appear to be positioned in a similar way.

In addition to landscape familiarisation, Arthur's Stone along with other tombs in the area represents a continuous human presence since at least the Late Mesolithic (6,000–3,500 BC). Mesolithic flint has been found underneath and around Arthur's Stone and also at Gwernvale (near Crickhowell). The latter also has flint and chert material from the Late Upper Palaeolithic (Britnell & Savory 1984). So, even during the Neolithic, Arthur's Stone would have possessed a 'history' and, more importantly, an affinity with the ancestors.

5. Bach Long Barrow, Bach

SO 2773 4294

Bach long barrow, a possibly Neolithic, is badly damaged at the northern end. Drystone walling can be clearly seen on the woodland side of the mound, which is oval–shaped, approximately 13m x 10m, and 2m high. This tomb is the most north–westerly of the Golden Valley Group. Interestingly, it is sited on a north–facing slope, overlooking the upper Wye Valley. Its position suggests, therefore, that it may not be associated with any of the Golden Valley tombs. The location and localised orientation (E–W) suggests an association with nearby Clyro Court Farm long barrow (SO 212 315) and the now damaged Clyro long barrow (SO 215 437), both just over the border in Powys. All three would have had dominant views over the upper Wye Valley and all would have been intervisible. Unfortunately, to the north of Bach long barrow is dense woodland, making visibility of other monuments difficult to ascertain.

6. Clyro Court Farm Long Barrow, Clyro

SO 21234313

The visible remains are restricted to a low mound and a few uprights. The uprights delineate the remains of a small chamber and passage. However, the tomb has outstanding views right across the upper Wye valley and incorporates the north–western extent of the Black Mountains. In addition, Mynydd Troed, an isolated peak, can also be seen, approximately 15 km SSW.

This monument is valley orientated, that is, the mound shape follows the direction of the valley (SW–NE). Close by and now destroyed, was Clyro long barrow (SO 2159 5377). It is possible that this tomb may have functioned quite differently to the Court Farm monument; similar to Arthur's Stone and Cross Lodge barrow at Dorstone. In neither case, is there any intervisibility – the Clyro Court Farm monument is positioned so that Pen yr Wyrlod (3.5km,) and Little Lodge barrow (4.6km) are completely hidden, but at the same time having outstanding views right across the south–western flanks of the upper Wye valley.

7. Little Lodge Barrow, Glasbury

SO 18222944

Excavated in 1929 by C.E. Vulliamy, Little Lodge barrow revealed a wealth of artifacts, including human remains. The mound, now much disturbed, is orientated north–south and has two, perhaps three chambers: a simple terminal chamber, the remains of a lateral chamber opening out from the west and possibly, a third chamber, now marked by a single upright at the northern end.

Although the mound is orientated north/south, the impressive Hay Bluff (spur) is in full view. In addition, there is intervisibility with Pipton Long Cairn, 2.3km due west of Little Lodge barrow. It would appear that this tomb is topograpically aligned, rather than valley orientated, although a small stream does flow close by.

8. Pen yr Wyrlod, Llanigon

SO 22483986

All that survives of this tomb is a series of four uprights and traces of an elongated (pear–shaped) mound approximately 18.5m in length. The uprights form a small rectangular terminal chamber. At the north–eastern end of the mound are traces of a small chambered structure. Corcorcan (1969) suggests that the tomb, is in fact, a multi–phase structure. If this is so, Pen yr Wyrlod would have been in use over a long period of time. Its position within the landscape also suggests a symbolic strategic importance in that the orientation (SW–NE) of the mound is the same as that of the upper Wye valley. In addition, the tomb is located on a high truncated spur and therefore commands views right across the Wye and Llynfi valleys; but it does not have any direct intervisibility with the Clyro Court Farm monument (3.5km), Little Lodge barrow (4.7km) or Pipton long barrow (7 km).

The monument was originally excavated between 1920 and 1921 by Rev W.E.T. Morgan and George Marshall (and members of the Woolhope Field Club). Very little in the way of artifacts were found, except for a few fragments of "rough pottery and a few flint flakes". The excavation methodology came under much criticism. The spoil heaps were investigated by C.E.Vulliamy and later by Gwynne. Both found flint, traces of Beaker pottery, a Roman coin (dated AD 317–26) and what was believed to be a large quantity of blue glass beads from an early (possibly 6th century) Anglo-Saxon burial.

9. Pipton Long Cairn, Glasbury

SO 16033728

Pipton long cairn, one of four 'hybrid' Severn–Cotswold monuments within this group, is located on an east–facing slope overlooking the north–western extent of the Black Mountains. Pipton's mound, 32m in length is constructed of a drystone revetment wall (excavated by Herbert Savory in 1956). The mound is oriented north–south and overlooks the upper reaches of the River Wye. Many similarities exist between this tomb and other monuments within the Black Mountains Group. For example, Pipton's northern chamber and passage arrangement is identical to that of Arthur's Stone, Herefordshire (Houlder 1978, Castleden 1992). The west–facing passage is angled in two places, thus making any visibility between the outside and the chamber impossible. The outer cairn shape and architecture include a trapezoidal mound with extended rounded horns and a false portal (constructed of two uprights). These features are also present at Penwyrlod, Ty Isaf and Gwernvale. A second chamber, south–west facing does not have a passage. However, Castleden (1992) recognised an earlier 'cultural' phase of construction for which a passage would not be required. The plan suggests a similarity with the multi–phase construction at Ty Isaf. Present within the chamber, was an assemblage of disarticulated human bone. Houlder (1978) suggests that the bone had probably come from elsewhere. Whatever, Pipton was either the final resting place for the dead (the bones) or else it may have 'acted' merely as an interim resting place.

The topography surrounding Pipton is similar to that of other nearby tombs. Ffostyll North and South, Little Lodge barrow as well as Pipton, appear to point to corresponding features within the landscape – the spurs of Y Das and Hay Bluff. This small cluster of monuments within the group also shares a common intervisibility. From Pipton, Penwyrlod, Ffostyll North and South, and Little Lodge barrow can be clearly seen. Arguably, this cluster constitutes a territory.

10/11. Ffostyll North & South, Llaneliew

SO 178348

Both monuments were only partially excavated between 1921–23 by C.E.Vulliamy. The Ffostyll North mound is orientated east–west, while the Ffostyll South runs north–south, creating a directional opposition. Ffostyll South, the smallest and best preserved of the two, has a single 3m gallery–type chamber located at the north eastern end. Two dislodged capstones are supported by ten uprights.

The larger northern mound is considered to be multi–phase monument and possibly trapezoidal in plan (Corcoran 1969). The mound incorporates three chambers: a destroyed eastern chamber plus two others located centrally and at the south-western end. Unfortunately, there is no evidence of passages leading from any of the three chambers.

Both Ffostyll North and South have commanding views towards the south–west and may be intervisible with Penrwyrlod. Directly to the south and east, Ffostyll North appears to be aligned to the dominant spurs of Y Das and Rhia y Fan, whereas Ffostyll South is aligned to the valley and the nearby Afon Ennig (2.5km). Two small tributaries close to both tombs run westwards into the Ennig. The northern mound is sited slightly higher up slope than Ffostyll South and may be considered the more dominant and possibly earlier of the two mounds.

Both monuments are well over 310 metres above sea level and the highest within the Black Mountains Group. The orientation of the northern mound suggests a symbolism linked to the life/death (east/west) cycle.

12. Cwmfforest, Talgarth

SO 18332944

This monument, once considered to be partially destroyed, is sited approximately 300m north of Ty Isaf, close to the Afon Rhiangoll. The only visible remains today are drystone walling and a large capstone (possibly in situ). Crawford (1925, 54–55) claims that the chamber is constructed from drystone walling with the capstone set over. Both are centrally placed within a small SE–NW mound, at the south–eastern end of which is a possible passage (Corcoran 1969).

Cwmfforest shares its landscape with nearby Ty Isaf: that of a dramatic valley/pass locate. It has also been suggested that the two share a similar architecture (Castleden 1992). This being case, both tombs could well have been in use at the same time, but like Ffostyll North and South, each having different social and symbolic obligations to their communities.

13. Ty Isaf, Talgarth

SO 1819290

Ty Isaf was excavated in 1938 and is regarded as a 'hybrid' form of the Severn–Cotswold classification. Typically, it has a complex series of chambers and passages, as well as a trapezoidal plan (orientated N–S), false doorway and extended horns and facade. Although complex in plan, all that remains visually of this monument today are a few protruding orthostats and the remnants of the elongated mound (30m x 18m). However, the landscape setting can be regarded as an element of equal importance to the overall 'meaning' as its location and structure (plan).

The plan reveals that Ty Isaf is a multi–phase monument, possibly with at least three phases of construction and use. Phase I shows a small oval cairn structure located at the southern end of the mound and measuring about 12m in diameter. Within the oval cairn is a south–east facing passage and a SW–NE orientated chamber. It is argued that this structure was an addition to the larger mound plan (Corcoran 1969). However, more probably it is the earliest structure, the larger trapezoidal mound being a later addition (Castlden 1992). Phase II, the main mound structure, has two chambers (with passages), and a curious false doorway. The mound itself is constructed of a double drystone revetment wall. The doorway is located at the northern end, between two horns. The plan and orientation are very similar to another 'hybrid' tomb in this group: Pipton long barrow. Both the west and east lateral passages look out towards dominant topographic features: Mynydd Troed (west) and Waun Fach to the east. Approximately 100m to the west is the southward flowing Afon Rhiangoll. These landscape features

may be regarded as vital and necessary symbolic components of the overall plan and shape of Ty Isaf (see text).

When excavated, Ty Isaf revealed a wealth of information about interring the dead. It would appear that all chambers and passages were utilised, but in different ways. In total, the remains of no fewer than 33 individuals were recovered. In the west chamber, crushed bones from 17 individuals, along with leaf–shaped arrowheads, a polished stone axe and undecorated Neolithic pottery were found. In the east chamber, one complete(?) skeleton was found along with six or more Western (Neolithic) bowls. Within the passage area, the remains of two articulated skeletons were recovered. Outside, within the entrance area, a sandstone pendant and more pottery was found. Incidentally, pottery was also recovered from the old land surface against a section of the eastern wall (Daniel 1950). From the chamber and passage of the southern circular cairn more human remains were recovered; two articulated skeletons from the passage and broken bones from the chamber, plus a small quantity of undecorated Neolithic pottery. Phase III, a small isolated chamber at the southern end, contained a middle Bronze Age cremation urn and a series of burnt boxes.

The phases of construction plus the different ways in which the dead were interred suggests Ty Isaf was in use over many hundreds of years, and certainly throughout the latter part of the Neolithic and early Bronze Age.

14. Mynydd Troed, Talgarth

SO 16142843

Mynydd Troed, one of the Black Mountain Group's less impressive mounds, is located at the foot of the mountain of the same name. Very little has been discussed about this monument, due in part to its poor state of preservation. Potentially though, Mynydd Troed has one of the more impressive landscape settings of all the Black Mountains Group. It is located between Mynydd Troed and Mynydd Llangorse and faces south–east towards Cwm (valley) Sorgwm and Pen Allt–mawr. The tomb also commands views westwards over Llangorse lake. Mynydd Troed and Ty Illtyd are equally distant from Llangorse Lake (approximately 3.5km) and therefore may be linked territorially. Grimes (1936) suggests that area around the mound marks the boundary between open scrub and woodland. This being the case, very little would be intervisible with Mynydd Troed despite the fact that it is 254 metres above sea level. This tomb is sited in order to be seen. A large area of bracken–scrub and woodland would have been cleared in order to expose the mound to the surrounding landscape.

The mound, oval in shape, is orientated NE/SW and encloses a probable simple terminal chamber with at least one other chamber present. The recent historical disturbance of this monument makes any reconstruction impossible.

15. Penwyrlod, Talgarth

SO 15053156

Penwyrlod long cairn (not to be confused with Penywrlod, Llanigon) has only recently been discovered. It was subsequently excavated by Herbert Savory in 1972. For many years, the cairn material from Penwyrlod was quarried for hard core. Much of the chamber and passage plan at the southern end of the mound remains intact. The mound shape is that of the 'hybrid' type similar to that of the later designs of the Severn–Cotswold Group. Originally, Penwyrlod would have possessed two extended horns and a false portal at the southern end. However, these are not visible. Clearly present though are three chambers with disturbed capstones and the remains of two passages. Both chambers and passages look out towards the Black Mountains, even though, to the west, the Brecon Beacons are also in full view. It would appear that the internal architecture is concerned only with the Black Mountains. This monument is clearly valley–aligned, even though the orientation points towards Mynydd Troed. Also worth considering is the intervisibility with three other nearby tombs – Ffostyll North and South, and Pipton (Map 1). All appear to have similar architectural forms as well as close affinities with various aspects of landscape topography and valley alignment.

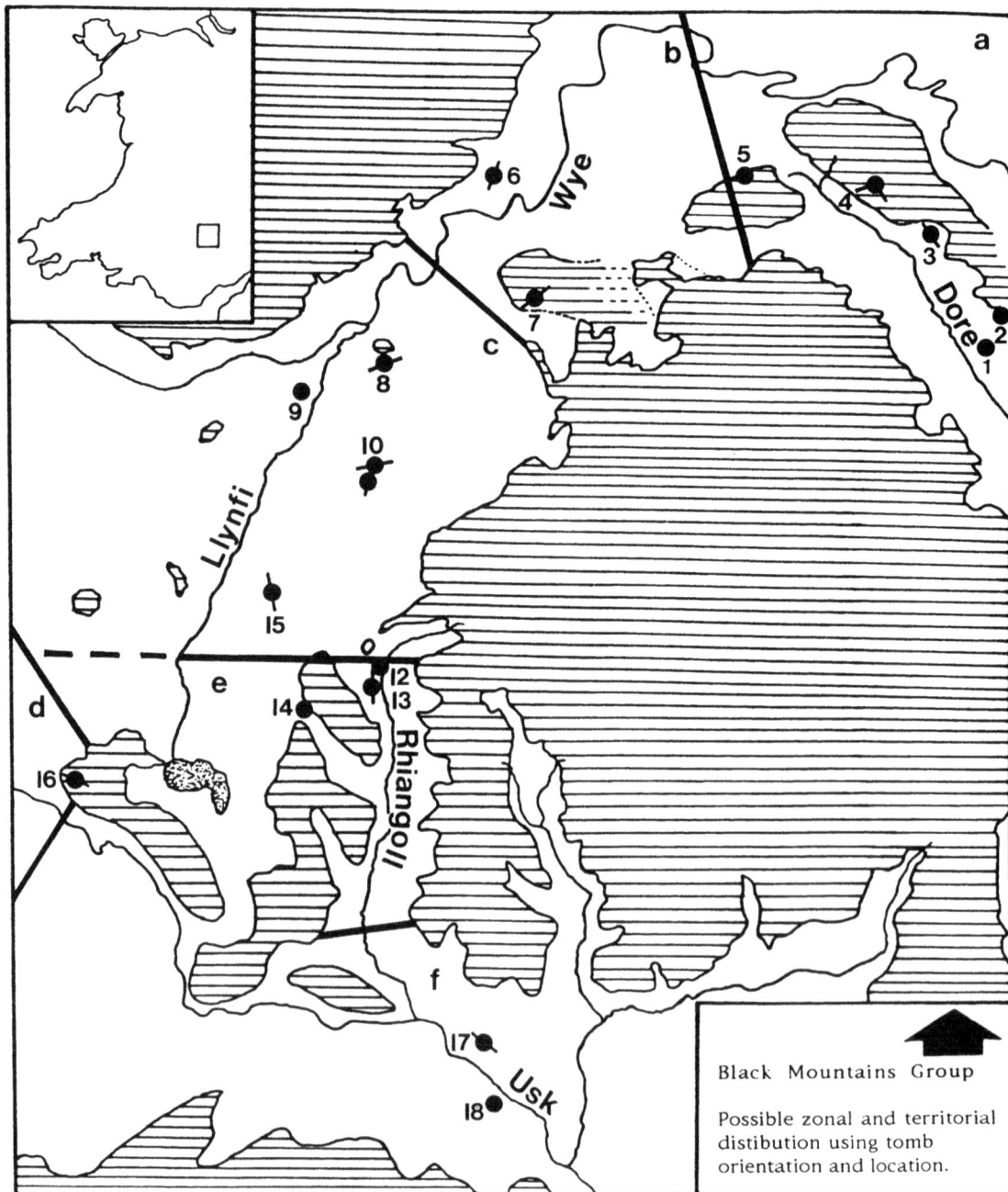

Map 1. Black Mountains Group

16. Ty Illtyd, Llanhamlach

SO 09842038

This tomb, although classified within the Black Mountains Group, is the only tomb that has a landscape affinity with the Brecon Beacons. Situated on a west facing ridge, and approximately 6.6km due west of Mynydd Troed, Ty Illtyd incorporates the whole of the eastern extent of the Brecon Beacons. Both the chamber and the capstone are aligned towards Pen y Fan, the highest point within the Brecon Beacons.

The monument itself is constructed of a single capstone overlying a rectangular chamber, delineated by eight uprights and set into a raised oval earthen mound. The mound and chamber is orientated north–south with a small rectangular forecourt or antechamber at the northern end. Corcoran (1969) suggests that the forecourt area may in fact be a second chamber.

On a number of uprights, a series of probable medieval–type inscriptions (graffiti) exist. The faded rock art includes a harp and two dates of 1312 and 1510. Other inscriptions include crosses (some set in lozenges) and circles. Longueville Jones (1867) considered them to be the work of "shepherd boys".

17. Gwernvale, Crickhowell

SO 21111920

Excavated many times, the last in 1978, Gwernvale is sited on a Neolithic settlement. Evidence also suggests that flint from the Upper Palaeolithic is also present. The elongated mound (45m in length), constructed of a double revetment wall, is orientated east–west with the Usk valley. Britnell (1979) has noted that traces of a possible (ancient) cement was found between the uprights and the drystone walling during the 1977–78 excavation.

Forty–five metres in length, the mound was once thought to be circular (Fenton 1804, Crawford 1925). At the eastern end are two horns and a false portal. Two lateral chambers are located at the southern end of the mound. The largest chamber, polygonal in shape, comprises six large uprights and has a passage that opens out towards dominant topographic features – the Afon Wysg (River Usk) and Mynydd Llangatwg in the south–west. A third chamber also exists, but has been badly damaged, along with a small single chamber on the northern side. Very little in the way of human remains were found in the 1978 excavation. However, it is believed that remains were removed during the 1804 excavation. Furthermore, Gwernvale suffered much damage during recent widening of the A40. The 1978 excavation did reveal, however, six large post holes in the forecourt area, suggesting that a possible mortuary structure existed.

18. Garn Goch, Llangattock

SO 21231771

Garn Goch is located on a small rise overlooking the River Usk and surrounding mountains to the north and south. The form of this monument is very difficult to decipher. The mound is oval shaped with its northern end orientated towards Table Mountain, a prominent truncated spur on the southern extent of the Black Mountains. Both Crawford (1925) and Grimes (1936) suggest that Garn Goch is indeed a long cairn, possibly similar in form to nearby Gwernvale. Daniel (1950), however, argues that it is no more than a cist or round mound. The mound is oval thus typical of other megalithic structures in the region. There is also a number of large stones 'placed' on top of the mound and delineate a simple rectangular chambered structure. Finally, many of the landscape 'traits' attributed to the monuments in this region such as topographic orientation also apply to Garn Goch.

Table 1: Monument Location

No.	Tomb	Lowland	Inter	Upland	Metres O.D.
1	Park Wood		X		200
2	Dunseal Long Barrow			X	175
3	Cross Lodge Barrow		X		180
4	Arthur's Stone			X	280
5	Bach Long Barrow			X	304
6	Court Farm, Clyro		X		90
7	Penyrwyrlod			X	250
8	Little Lodge Barrow		X		137
9	Pipton Long Cairn		X		145
10	Ffostyll North			X	312
11	Ffostyll South			X	312
12	Cwm Forest		X		280
13	Ty Isaf		X		310
14	Mynydd Troed			X	358
15	Penywyrlod			X	260
16	Ty Illtyd			X	215
17	Gwernvale	X			79
18	Garn Goch	X			84

Table 2: Quantitive Analysis

Site No.	Name	Parish	Grid Ref	Metres O.D.	Landscape Position	Nearest Tomb (No.)	Distance (km)	Second Tomb (No.)	Orientation Cap.St./Pass.	Nearest/Prominant Topographic Feature	Intervisibility (Tomb No.)
1	Park Wood	St Margarets	35653347	200	Dore Valley	16	3.5.	15 (8.5)	-	Black Mts., Dore Valley	?
2	Dunseal	Dorstone	39133382	175	Dore Valley	15	9.7*	14 (11.8)	Mound NW-SE	South Black Mts.	-
3	Cross Lodge Barrow	Dorstone	33254168	180	Dore Vally	14	2.0*	16 (9.7)	Mound NW-SE	Black Mts., Dore Valley	-
4	Arthur's Stone	Dorstone	31804313	280	Dore Valley	15	2.0*	1 (9.8)	Cap (SE) Pass (SW)	Hay Bluff, Dore Valley	-
5	Bach Long Barrow	Dorstone	27654287	304	Upper Wye Valley	14	4.4.	15 (5.7)	Mound E-W?	Black Mts., Upper Wye Valley	-
6	Clyro Court Farm	Clyro	21234313	90	Upper Wye Valley	1	3.5	10 (6.0)	Mound SW-NE	Wye Valley	-
7	Pen yr Wyrlod	Llanigon	22483986	251	Upper wye Valley	13	3.5	10 (4.6)	Mound SW-NE	Hay Bluff, Gosop Hill	-
8	Little Lodge	Glasbury	18223806	137	Llynfi Valley	8	2.3	4 (3.1)	Mound E-W	Hay Bluff,	8,
9	Pipton	Glasbury	16033728	145	Llynfi Valley	10	2.3	3 (3.0)	Mound N-S	Afon Llynfi, Y Das	2,10
10	Ffostyll North	Llaneliew	17883487	312	Llynfi Valley	4	0.1	10,8 (3.0)	Mound N-S	Y Das, Afon Llynfi	2,4
11	Ffostyll South	Llaneliew	17883487	312	Llynfi Valley	3	0.1	10,8 (3.0)	Mound E-W	Y Das, Afon Llynfi	2,3
12	Cwm Fforest	Talgarth	18332944	274	Rhiangoll Valley	5	0.4	9 (2.1)	Mound SE-NW	Mynydd Troed, Rhiangoll	5,
13	Ty Isaf	Talgarth	18192905	211	Rhiangoll Valley	12	0.4	9 (2.1)	Mound N-S	Mynydd Troed, Rhiangoll	12,
14	Mynydd Troed	Talgarth	16142843	258	Llynfi Valley	5	2.1	12 (2.2)	Mound NE-SE	Mynydd Troed, Llangorse	2?
15	Penwyrlod	Talgarth	15053156	253	Llynfi Valley	9	3.3	12 (3.7)	Mound N-S	Mynydd Troed	3,4,8
16	Ty Illtyd	Llanhamlach	9842038	215	Usk Valey	9	6.6	9 (2.1)	Mound NW-SE	Brecon Beacons	-
17	Gwernvale	Crickhowell	21111920	69	Usk Valley	11	1.6	9 (10)	Mound NW-SE	Usk, Cerrig-calch	11,
18	Garn Goch	Llangattock	21231771	84	Usk Valley	7	1.6	9 (11.9)	Mound N-S?	Usk, Table Mountain	7,

Places as Timemarks – the Social Construction of Prehistoric Landscapes in Eastern Hungary

John Chapman

Introduction

I begin this paper with the account of an incident which I witnessed in eastern Hungary in September 1991. Police officers from the town of Tiszavasvári were called to prevent three employees of a local construction company from digging away a prehistoric barrow called 'Deak halom'. After several attempts to protect the monument had failed, a ditch was dug across the only track to the barrow to prevent the workers from gaining further access to the damaged site. When museum archaeologists approached the workers to ask why they had wished to remove earth from the barrow when there was a (practically) limitless supply of similar blackearth available from anywhere in the neighbourhood, no satisfactory answer was given. Later, an archaeologist born and brought on the Alfold plain suggested to me that many plainsfolk so loved the view of an unbroken flatness that any deviation from horizontality was offensive to their eyes and they would do their utmost to erase it. In this 'reading', the attempt to destroy the barrow was a deliberate act of landscape 'restoration', a retrieval of the lost perfection of timeless horizontality.

This anecdote raises many questions, including the ownership of the past, priorities of symbolic versus economic rationale, the significance of vertical versus horizontal perspectives, and the symbolism of the earth. Questions are also raised by the conflicting values inherent in the attitudes of the 'restorers' and the 'preservers'. What is it that has led to the creation amongst plainsfolk of a set of visual values that emphasized the horizontal to the (illusory) exclusion of the vertical, the total landscape rather than specific places, while denying a sense of time that led to the fixing of value on those places by another interest group – the museum community? Here is an example from a modern struggle for landscape values of scarcely-articulated ideological preferences: on the one hand, 'educated' professionals with a defined and therefore freshly constructed sense of the past using the traditional legal framework to safeguard a genuinely ancient monument; on the other, working-class plainsfolk using modern technology to defend their traditional, rooted attachment to (the illusion of) a timeless landscape dominated by the immense skies of the Alfold.

This plains tale directs us towards the territory of this paper. Its aim is the exploration of the varied ways in which communities perceive and thus create their own landscapes using the natural materials and socially-defined constructs at hand, among them social time. The special dialectic between places and the landscape is also examined by a consideration of the significance of cyclical time in the lives of the plains communities. Finally, some places considered special in Hungarian prehistory are evaluated to identify the significance of social time in their use, disuse and re-use.

Landscapes and time

The conceptual framework of time–space 'dimensions' in which prehistoric cultures perform systemic tasks in their natural environment has long ago been displaced in favour of a more socially active perspective on time, space and place. The existence of a wide variety of concepts of time is a *sine qua non* in recent archaeology, as it has been in the other social sciences for much longer (Eliade 1955; Fabian 1983; Fortes 1949; Goody 1968; Moore 1963; Young & Ziman 1971). As Sorokin & Merton put it in their classic (1937) paper, in contrast to the uniform, divisible, continuous and objective time of Newtonian physics, social time expresses the changes of social phenomena in terms of other social phenomena, which are taken as the key points of chronological reference. Hence, the starting point of a time-system must be social, for each time-system has profound social implications. Indeed, while the quality of time depends on both duration and sequence and their interactions, the speed of time passing is often closely related to the number and importance of concrete events experienced by members of the social group. In this sense, it can be seen that, instead of time creating social action, social action creates time (cf. Gosden 1994). The life of social frameworks, objects and structures unfolds in their own time; what is true for the social is also apt for the landscape.

One of the most challenging facets of the term 'landscape' is its capacity for extreme variety of meaning. Forman and Goodman (1986) list ten ways of treating landscape: as nature, habitat, artifact, system, problem, wealth, ideology, history, place and aesthetic, to which one may add others, such as as text and stage (Chapman, in press a). Here, attention will be focussed on the landscape as the stage for time–ly social action. The inter-relationship between time and landscape is both complex and recursive. While Shackle (1978) treats time as a landscape, in which we can move about at will in our memories, revisiting known places from our pasts, Tuan (1977) conversely sees landscapes as time made visible, in the sense of the products and experiences of past social action creating the places which define and re-define the landscape. In like vein, the Romanian social scientist Mircea Eliade (1955) has proposed that landscapes represent humans taking upon themselves the role of time, both as viewers at a particular time and place and as creators of a past that carries its own seeds into the future, ripe for re-discovery. What links these views is the notion of narrative, which is central to the relationship between time and places, since it is through insertion into a narrative that a place assumes active meaning and it is through the linking of places in a sequence that a narrative is itself constructed (Parkes & Thrift 1980). Tilley (1994) has compared the construction of narrative to the process of walking through a landscape. The acquisition of significance in a narrative is heightened by the inclusion of local landscape detail, so that the identity of the listeners is reinforced by the place-value of those parts of the landscape which are already well-known. Such thoughts give rise to metaphors of the landscape as a text, a family tree or an archive (Tuan 1978). These metaphors cause us to recast the problem of the social construction of the landscape in terms of how its narrative is

31

constituted and how it is read. Such an approach leads us to the significance of human experience as a vital constituent of the creation of place.

The emergence of place

In a parallel movement to the positivistic geographies of the last 20 years, there has been a group of humanistic geographers who have included in their conceptions of space and place the essential component of human experience (Buttimer & Seamon 1980; Cosgrove 1984; Gregory & Walford 1989; Parkes & Thrift 1980; Tuan 1977). Owing to the paucity of theoretical discussions of landscapes in the anthropological literature until recently (e.g., Bender 1993), these works have provided a major source of ideas about the emergence of place in archaeological discussions (for a summary, see Chapman 1988). In this survey, three different positions are characterised: the humanistic position of Tuan, the early structuration theories of Parkes and Thrift, in which time is a crucial new element, and the integration of structuration and Hagerstrandian time–space geography by Pred, in which social power is introduced as a catalyst in the discussion.

For Tuan (1973: 1977: 1977a: 1978), the notion of 'place' is arbitrary, elusive and protean. In general terms, spaces are transformed into places through the acquisition of definition and meaning, so that places are created by repetitive experience, comparable to a 'field of habit' (1977; cf. Bourdieu's 'habitus': Bourdieu 1977). Tuan sees the identity of place as having two distinct forms. Places are locations in which people have long memories for the bygone generations. But places are also the centre of power as well as meaning relative to their environs, the node at which activities converge. These two qualities of place are defined as fields of care – whereby places are known from the inside through the operation of human emotions – and public symbols, which provide significance in a wider, public milieu (Tuan 1977). Importantly, Tuan argues that the power of symbols in places is dependent upon the depth of the human emotions experienced in the fields of care.

In his other works, Tuan examines three ways in which place is related to time (Tuan 1977a: 1978): place as pause in movement; place as time made visible; and attachment to place as a function of time. If social action is conceived of as flux, movement in time, a transition from state to state – then, place may be viewed as a temporary pause in the flow of human action, which may assume positive qualities distinguishing the place from other mobilities. Tuan also sees places as time made visible through the sedimentation of past memories, activities and changes onto defined places with specific place–value; an example is his notion of the city as history incarnate. Finally, Tuan's third idea relates the attachment to place in terms of a function of time, with intensity of experience related to a longer time–perspective in which a deeply felt sense of place is, in turn, related to a sense of time.

In a coeval work, Parkes & Thrift (1978: 1980) attempt to integrate concepts of time and place within the perspectives of Giddensian structuration theory. For Parkes and Thrift, the realization of place as a day–to–day dynamic lies in the structuring of space. If the essence of place is timed space, the timing component gives structure to space and thus evokes the notion of place. Parkes and Thrift discuss four different, hierarchical levels of spatial and temporal information which act as filters in the social system, enabling individuals to realize place: the highest level of the totality of the political economy, the physical (including the built) environment, the activity system, and the lowest level of individual attitudes and perceptions. Individuals within such an information environment receive two kinds of information – hard (prompting immediate response) and soft (prompting posssible response). Hard information leads to the creation of an appropriate timed space for response, while soft information may never lead to a timed space. Through the learning process, each individual builds up a mental prism of optimal activity pathways for the future; the result of these activities is a sequence of realized places.

The problem of introducing people and their social power into place was faced by Allan Pred in his conceptualisation of place in space–time geography (Pred 1986). Places cannot emerge out of nothing, stop or grow rigid; place is synonymous with the structural processes whereby time–space activities and power relations become each other. For Pred, place involves an appropriation and transformation of space and nature which is inseparable from the reproduction of society itself in time and space. The becoming of place is historically contingent and an empirical content must be found for the theory. Three empirical foci are defined: individual biographies, dominant institutional projects and a sense of place. The biographies of individuals, which intersect and influence one another at particular places, form part of Hagerstrand's influential time–space geographical approach. Wider social decisions to initiate dominant institutional projects indicate the basis of power relations and have a place–specific impact on individuals as well as an imprint on the landscape. Thirdly, and following Tuan and other humanistic geographers, a sense of place is formed through the sedimentation of symbolic and emotional meanings, memories and the attachments to people and things which arise out of past practices and their underlying power relations. Three roles are defined for historically–specific power relations: the selection or rejection of dominant institutional projects, the use and modification of scarce resources, and the extent to which places are allowed to flourish, merely survive or fall into disrepair. While power relations are intrinsic to the social formation, Pred emphasizes the importance of the extent to which social interactions depend on non–local control of resources or transactions. The essential fluidity of social interaction is captured by the notion that place is characterised by an uninterrupted flux of human practice in time and space.

A final insight into the development of landscapes helps to integrate these concepts of place with a wider view of landscape and derives from J. B. Jackson (1984)'s discussion of two inter–dependent forms of landscape – the political landscape and the vernacular landscape. In contrasting these two landscapes, which are always found together, Jackson stresses that the essential function of landscape is to combine the monumental, the landmark, with the transitory. Jackson's classification is based on a distinction between humans as political animals, where the landscape is a human creation belonging to humans, a well–defined domain which gives humans a different status from other species; and humans as inhabitants, with the landscape as a habitat which is essentially pre–human, where humans belong to the landscape in the sense that they are its product and where they take responsibility for nature and other species.

The landscape of the inhabitants – the vernacular landscape – achieves its identity over the course of time, its coherence forming only after generations of unrest, confusion and conflict; when it stops evolving, we can say what it is. In an inhabited landscape, the land implicates its inhabitants as members of a working community on that land. The mobility of people, places and boundaries is typical of the inhabited landscape. If an element in the vernacular landscape is visible, it is because that element is permanent. Yet each place sees itself as the centre of the world, an oasis of order in a sea of surrounding chaos, inhabited by 'The People'. Spaces between dwellings in a vernacular landscape indicate personal relations, the involved and often contradictory traditions of the community.

This incessant re–making of the inhabited landscape is ignored or resisted by the political landscape, whose essential characteristic is a belief in the achievement of identity through the sanctity of place. In the political landscape, the function of place is to make people visible and let them put down their roots: their centrality is altogether more obviously based on social power. The political landscape is an altogether larger arena, more permanent and visible, often with a coherent and imposed design and boundaries which help to create a political or sacred identity. In the political landscape, the 'natural' environment – the land – has no inherent identity of its own but is rather a means to an essentially economic end. It is the permanence of place, in a social as much as a topographic sense, that gives people their lasting identity.

While Jackson can be criticised for the delineation of two idealised landscapes which are related hierarchically, whether diachronically within a social evolutionary scheme or synchronically in the manner of 'high' and 'low' culture, Jackson's own insistence on the inter–dependence of his landscapes should alleviate this problem, even though there is little doubt which of the pair Jackson holds in higher esteem. It is also important to recall that the political struggle continues in all arenas of life, incuding the 'vernacular' landscape (cf. Thompson 1991).

In recent papers, I have attempted to synthesize a schema for the creation of peopled landscapes through a movement from space to place to arenas of social power (Chapman 1988: 1991: 1994: 1994a). The context of cultural change is the time–space framework of social action set within the contemporary social structure. The differentiation of a neutral physical space, not yet colonized by human communities, into a series of places associated with specific functions leads to the emergence of place value and a narrative of peoples' pasts inscribed onto that landscape. As place values accrue, places become arenas of social power in which important and quotidian cultural activities are carried out by individuals and groups in pursuit of their own cultural and social goals (Chapman 1988: 1993: in press b and c). The definition and explanation of time–space sequences of arenas of social power (or ASPs) therefore constitute an important goal in prehistory.The appearance of new ASPs in a given region is always an important change and requires explanation. It has been proposed that one way to resolve otherwise unmanagable contradictions within the existing social structure is a spatial displacement which allows different forms of social action, of a nature otherwise inappropriate or impossible in traditional time–space contexts (Chapman 1993). Three common contradictions have been defined out of many possibilities: (a) new potential for the accumulation of personal wealth in social groups with strongly collective traditions; (b) the expansion of social networks, whether by colonization or exchange network linkage; and (c) changes in gendered power relations.

Our proposition is that significant places – sites and monuments – contain within them a core of what is most important for the social reproduction of the group, the mechanism through which they define their community's place in time and space, especially in relation to their past. Given that the strategies of social reproduction will be reflexively related to the form of the site or monument, it follows that changes in the form of sites and monuments should be related to changes in the underlying ideological strategy of the group. In circumstances where social change is possible, or desirable for part of the group, but in conflict with traditional group ideology, the question of how to renegotiate social reproduction is of particular significance. A familiar pattern of social reproduction concerns the use of opposition to a traditional mode in order to formulate and clarify new principles of social reproduction. In this way, a cycle of ideological strategies may be set up, based on the establishment of difference from the past, which constitutes itself through spatial strategies in relation to re–use of previous monuments, abandonment or continuity of occupation. As an example of some of these processes at work, the sequence of sites and monuments in eastern Hungary will be discussed within the framework of recent research conducted by the Upper Tisza Project.

The cyclical timescapes of eastern Hungary

The Upper Tisza Project is an Anglo–Hungarian inter-disciplinary study concerned to define and explain changes in the landscape, settlement pattern and social structure of a wider area of North East Hungary over the last 12,000 years[1]. The Upper Tisza Project grew out of a concern to

[1] The Upper Tisza Project is an inter–disciplinary Anglo–Hungarian research project, in which a collaboration between the University of Newcastle upon Tyne and Eotvos Lorand University, Budapest aims to define and explain changes in the landscape, settlement and social structure over the last 10,000 years in North–East Hungary (Chapman & Laszlovszky 1992: 1993: 1994). The Project is funded by the British Academy, National Geographic Society, the Society of Antiquaries of Newcastle, the Prehistoric Society and the two universities.

place the northernmost tells in Eurasia in their regional physical and social context. While the Migration and the Medieval Periods are an integral part of UTP research, the focus of this article is on tells, flat sites and mortuary barrows. While the range of problems guiding the research of each project is necessarily diverse, our common aim of the explanation of changes in social action, production and reproduction in a very specific type of landscape provides a unifying theoretical structure to the enquiry.

Eastern Hungary forms part of the middle Danube basin, one of the largest lowland basins in Eastern Europe (Fig. 1). However, within an apparently uniform topography, there is marked diversity in soils, vegetation and subsistence potential, only partly related to the annual or seasonal inundation of much of the plain. Prior to 19th and 20th century drainage works, the Great Hungarian Plain (or Alfold plain) was one of the most water-rich environments in Europe. The three great rivers of the plain – the Tisza, the Maros and the Körös – consistently flooded their banks annually, with biennial floods 2–3 times per decade and with catastrophic flood events on a secular time-scale. On the basis of 19th century hydrological maps and geomorphological fieldwork, several archaeologists have published reconstructions of palaeohydrological conditions

(Bognar–Kutzian 1972: endmap; Kosse 1979: Fig. 2; Sherratt 1983a: Fig. 2–4, 8; Jankovich et al. 1989: Neolithic endmap). Although differing in detail, all the reconstructions agree on the likelihood of 30 – 50% of plains land being seasonally if not perennially flooded. While the potential for subsistence exploitation of seasonal fowl and fish in contrast to the constraints upon cereal cultivation and stockbreeding is well remarked (Bökönyi 1974; Kosse 1979), the implications for prehistoric communities and their creation of social time and space has been less fully explored.

A variety of time cycles can be identified in the community life of the plains dwellers (Fig. 2). Each cycle can be compared with the human life-cycle, provided that the metaphorical nature of the analogy is not forgotten. A preliminary partition is possible between natural cycles, the cycles of individuals and social groups and the cycles of material remains. The interconnections between the three kinds of evidence necessarily raise the most interesting questions, for it is these cycles that intersect and cross-cut, frame and bracket the quotidian, Bourdieu's (1977) *habitus* – the everyday basis for social reproduction.

The cycles of the natural environment are marked by visual changes in vegetation and habitat, in such a way that people

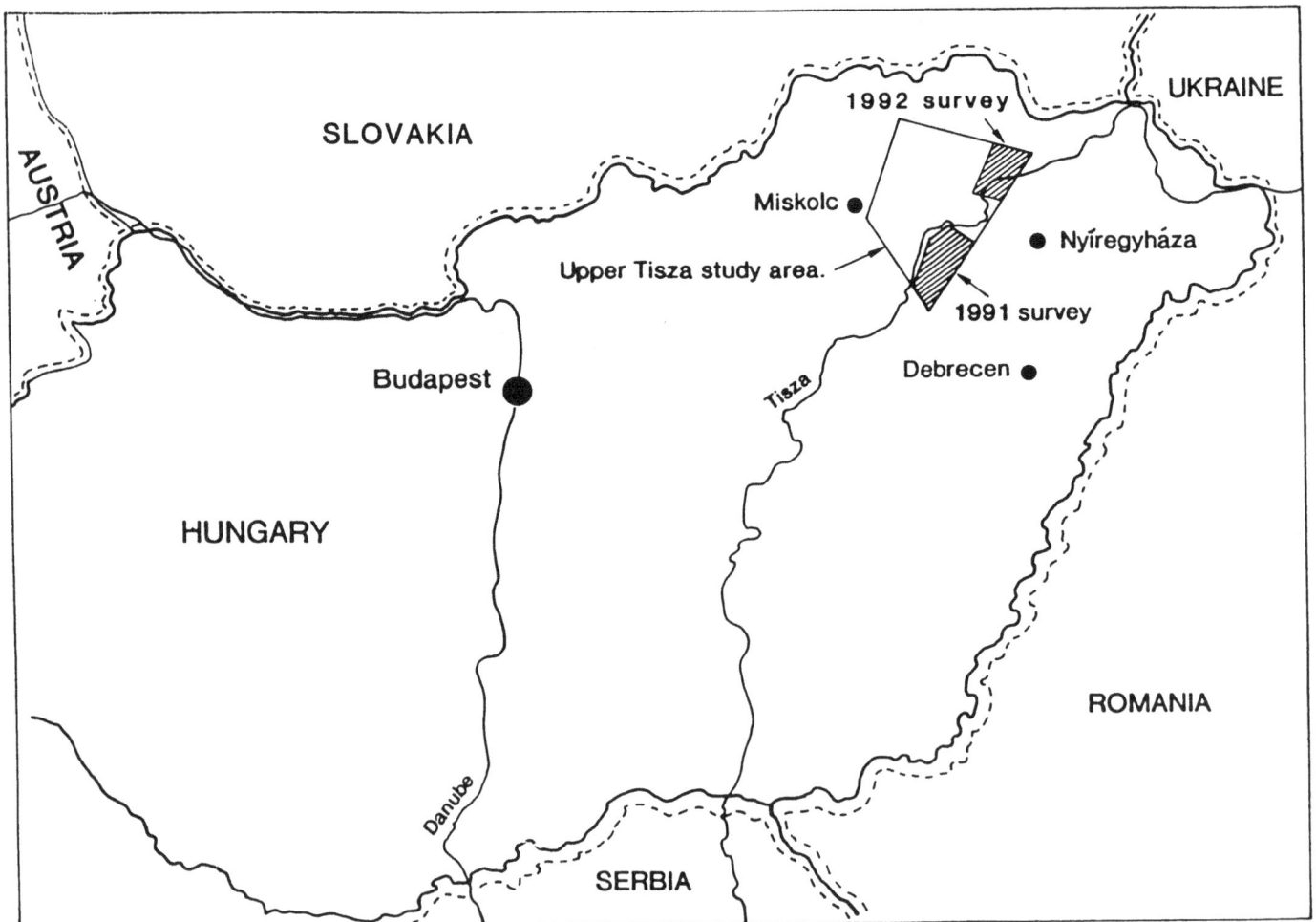

Figure 1. Location Map of Eastern Hungary and Upper Tisza Project.

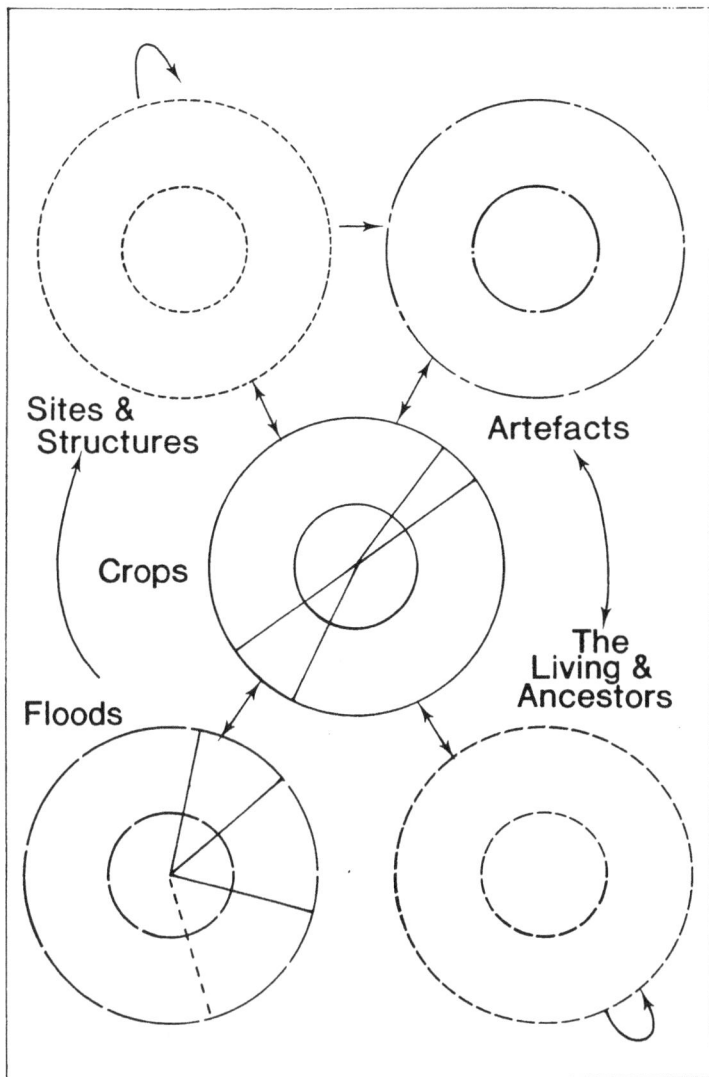

Figure 2. Cyclical patterning in humans, crops, rivers and objects.

can use the environment as their own personal clock to answer Lynch's provocative question – 'what time is this place ?' (Lynch 1972). Evident in all plant species, both wild and domesticated, these changes provide obvious and subtle clues as to the variations in the pace of annual change in climate and weather. Other major timemarks concern the seasonal movement of herbivores from lowlands to uplands, the arrival and departure of the Plain's many species of migratory birds, the cycles of palatability of shellfish and the movement up– and down–stream of anadromous fish, also a rich plains resource.

The other main natural cycle in the Plain concerns the flooding of the main rivers, which covers three different time–scales – the annual, the decennial and the secular. In addition to that part of the plain that was under constant water in the middle Holocene (at least ten and perhaps 20%), snowmelt and spring rainwater from the Carpathians were brought onto the plain each year in spring, flooding a further 20 – 30 % of the plain and subsiding by late spring. Every few years, a second, more serious flood (the 'green flood') hit the plain in early summer, covering perhaps 30 – 40 % more of the plain. Finally, perhaps once or twice a century, a

catastrophic flood would befall the plain, with devastating effects on most villages. The more serious the flood, the less predictable its arrival would be for local inhabitants. Because of the slight gradients on the plain, the onset and ebbing of annual and perhaps decennial floods would be gradual, with the water level rising slowly over weeks rather than days. This leads to a fourfold classification of the surface of the plain: (1) permanently flooded; (2) seasonally flooded (wet enough to cross by boat); (3) boggy land (too wet to walk across, too dry to cross by boat); and (4) permanently dry except for saecular floods (Fig. 3)(Gillings, in press). The mosaic of 'land classes' would structure the movement between, and location of, settlement and all subsistence resources, both wild and domestic. In particular, sites located at the dry/boggy interface, later to become the dry/flooded boundary and later still the dry/boggy interface again, would be important intercept locations for the hunting of wild animals moving from almost flooded to dry and back onto boggy, just–previously flooded 'land'. Such sites would also give access to a wide variety of freshwater molluscs and wild plants in specific seasons. The choice of planting cereal crops on permanently dry or seasonally flooded land or in both areas indicates different kinds of subsistence strategies: high–risk, high–yield floodplain environments versus lower–risk, lower–yield dry farming environments (Fairbairn, in press). But choice of fields also structures social mobility and pathways through the landscape, contributing to the creation of habitus near a settlement. Similarly, the selection of certain pathways for the movement of domestic stock to and from a home base channels human movement along well–known sequences of places, each with a range of different place–values (Tilley 1994).

The symbolic aspects of such a seasonally diverse 'land'–scape are as important as factors of economic choice over activity foci. One topic of interest is liminality, the concept of transitions between different states of being. Boggy land is an illustration of this notion, with its emergent properties of drying out in the late summer and flooding again in the spring and sometimes once more in the early summer. A variety of concepts of fertility, whether based on water or on earth, could find metaphoric referents in the seasonal cycle of flooding and drying out, as could voyages of the living and the dead, moving through liminal areas at times of rites of passage. In this seasonally diversified landscape, the timing of places assumes particular significance.

In terms of the life–cycle of an individual, the basic notions of birth, maturity, ageing and death point to a process of biological 'expansion' and 'contraction' of faculties and capacities. However, many anthropological case–studies underline the continuity in presence of the newly–dead until their transformation into ancestors, from which point they are ever–present in the ritual life of their communities. In some cases, birth implicates the ancestors as much as biological parents, closing the cycle of the living, the dead and the ancestors.

A social parallel to the personal life–cycle is that of the household cycle, a notion theorised by Chayanov (1966) and Meyer Fortes (1949), refined by Sahlins (1972) and

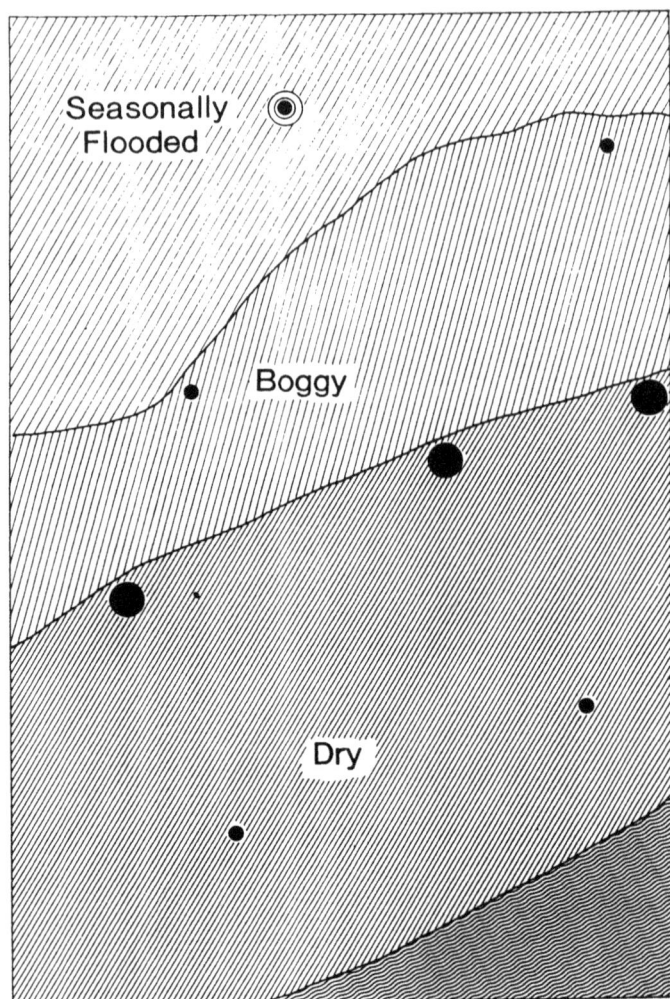

Figure 3. Partitioning of Tisza lowlands. Large circles –
tells; small circles – flat sites; triple circle – seasonal
occupation.

developed by some archaeologists in the 1980s and 1990s
(Wilk & Rathje 1982; Samson 1990; Tringham & Krstic
1991). Fortes identified the household as the nodal
mechanism for social reproduction in many agrarian
communities, arguing that reproduction of the public domain
was critically dependent on the developmental cycle of
domestic groups (Fortes 1949). Mosko (1989) has criticised
Fortes for ignoring the equal significance of contraction,
dispersion and dissolution in households to that of expansion
and extension in group reproduction (for other criticisms of
Fortes, see Bohannan (1958) and Worsley (1956)). Mosko
also theorises the existence of developmental cycles among
public groups which run parallel to, and interact with,
domestic groups. For the public groups, the nodal mechanism
of social reproduction is mortuary ritual and exchange. This
operates in two ways: (1) although involving a small segment
of the social whole, mortuary ritual and exchange stimulate
the configuration of the entire sphere of public relations and
(2) despite representing a small portion of the individuals in
a community, they activate the whole group (Mosko 1989).
In this context, it is important to underline Mauss' (1974)
insight that the person, the group and time itself emerge in
part as the products of a system of exchange (cf. also
Lambek 1990). Exchange relations cannot be ignored in the

exploration of the constitution of the social self through time.

Hence alongside the individual life–cycle we can set two
social cycles – the household and the public, whose various
expansions and contractions are directly related to social
reproduction through the media of exchange and mortuary
ritual. It is an empirical task to discover whether it is the
household or the public groups which play a more significant
role in the social reproduction of specific communities.

Just as we can define biographies of people and households,
it is possible to characterise artifacts, sites and monuments in
terms of their respective biographies. Not only do artifacts
have their own material cycle of manufacture, use and disuse but they also bear qualities of their past history and
associations with previous owners. It is their biography
which allows some objects to be inalienable and some to be
commoditized (Kopytoff 1986). Howell (1989) reminds us
of another of Mauss' neglected suggestions, viz. that in total
prestations between clan and clan, things are related in some
degree as persons and persons in some degree as things. Thus
not only can the value of artifacts be characterised in terms
of raw material, workmanship and rarity but also in terms of
their past biography. The meanings of past contexts can be
brought into the present (Ray's (1987) term 'presencing').
Both Bradley (1990) and Rowlands (1993) have noted how
things have lives and essences and can be 'killed' as easily as
humans, or instead of them, through special deposition. The
deposition of grave goods is, of course, an act of death for
the artifact as much as for the deceased.

The life–cycle of structures which archaeologists interpret as
'houses' may be divided into a daily and a whole–life cycle.
The house as home implies an ontological grounding; for
Eliade (1960), the home is a place from which the world was
founded, the centre of the world, the untold story of a life
being lived. In his discussion of the living house, Bailey
(1990) takes up the theme of the multi–dimensionality of
houses, stressing the varied perceptions of residents, kin and
strangers to the wide range of meanings contained in the
house. As a centre for production, reproduction and
consumption, whether social or physical, the house is an
active component in the construction of social reality. Like
the artifact, the house has its own biography – construction,
use and dis–use in the long–term, waking up, working there
or going out to work, and returning to eat and sleep on a
diurnal scale (Bailey 1990); the residents each provide their
particular associations to the house, whether in the form of
internal fittings and decorations or in the manner of the
spatial ordering of the household. The frequent comparison
between houses and tombs as houses for the dead reinforces
the biographical symbolism of the living house; the
architecture here mediates between the living and the dead as
liminal zone.

Finally, sites and monuments may be compared in terms of
their respective biographies. While sites and monuments
share a basic cyclical biography of creation, use and dis–use,
the prominence of monuments in the landscape provides a
stronger link to the ancestral world than do the often
insignificant remains of previously occupied flat sites.

Nevertheless, the frequency of re–occupation of some flat sites in areas such as eastern Hungary may be related as much to cultural memory and accumulated place–value as to maximisation of local ecological potential. The longer a site or monument is occupied, the stronger the place–values which attach to that place. However, the re–occupation of sites and monuments can bridge the gap since its last occupation or use by a process analagous to presencing; there is much ideological potential in assuming the role of descendants to an unrelated group's ancestors, thereby legitimating the 'new' foundation. Thus old sites can return to life, rather like the ancestral spirits of the deceased, to restart the cycle of occupation, dis–use and re–occupation, in a way that should be related to the larger pattern of social reproduction at group level.

We have seen how the metaphor of the life–cycle can, without excessive distortion, be applied to natural cycles, social groups, artifacts, sites and monuments. But before attempting to paint life–cycles onto too broad an archaeological canvas, we should heed Barrett's (1990:187) words of caution:

> *'these cycles are not explanations of the past but unintended outcomes of routine practices of people who could have acted otherwise'.*

Nonetheless, the cycles which have been discussed contribute to the structuring of timed places and cannot readily be dismissed. Now that a scheme for the variety of cycles has been discussed, it is time to turn to the places in eastern Hungary which emerged as timemarks in the Plains landscape.

Timemarks on the plain

The sequence of ASPs in eastern Hungary in the period 5800 – 2500 CAL BC may be summarized as an overall

preponderance of generally short–term, open, flat settlement sites, punctuated with the sporadic use of tells – settlement mounds consisting of occupational debris of vertically built–up settlement layers. Burial was predominantly intra–mural throughout the Neolithic, while extra–mural mortuary sites in the Copper Age varied between large, flat cemeteries and mortuary barrows, often termed 'kurgans'. This sequence of ASPs (Fig. 4) represents a series of contrasting site types, in which the appearance of new ASPs often contrasts with pre–existing site types (Chapman 1994: in press).

In the Neolithic, Copper Age and Bronze Age of eastern Hungary, there are four basic patterns of ASPs – two based on domestic arenas and two in the mortuary domain. The first pattern concerns flat sites, whose relation with the ancestors is defined by extra–mural or intra–mural burial, as well as an increasing tendency to multiple re–occupation of earlier flat domestic sites. This pattern is seen in the Szatmar group, the Middle Neolithic, most of the Copper Age and the Late Bronze Age.

The second pattern is based on the ancestral home of the tells, where links to the past are based on the domestic domain, on living where the ancestors once lived. This pattern is found in the Late Neolithic and the Early–Middle Bronze Age tells. A basic difference between these two patterns is that the first includes the principle of individual or household accumulation, whereas in the second the principle of communal accumulation and ownership is more strongly rooted in ancestral values (Chapman 1991). However, the existence of settlements larger than single farmsteads in the 'individualising' periods, as much as single farms in the 'communal' periods, signifies the continual need for negotiation and re–negotiation of these social values.

In the third pattern, the dominant places in the landscape were large, flat cemeteries where members of several, perhaps many, different homesteads were buried in

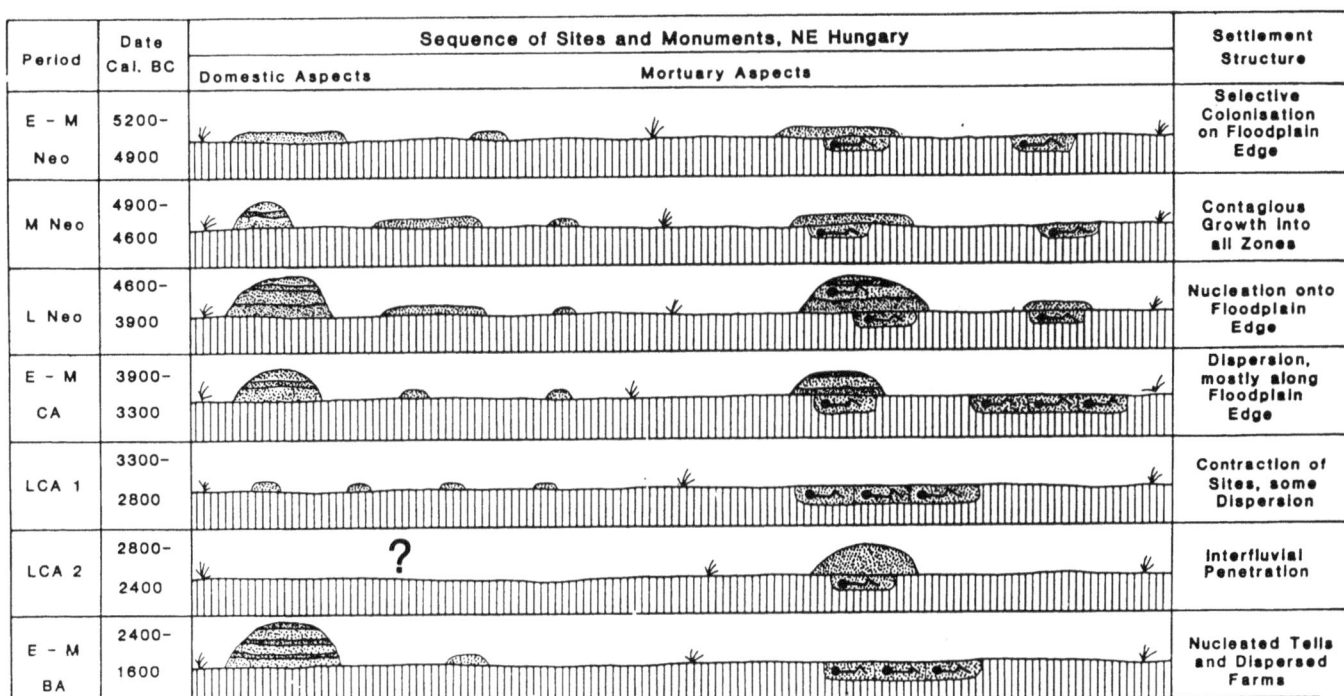

Figure 4. Sequence of sites and monuments, Neolithic–Bronze Age. North–East Hungary.

individual inhumations, often in clusters. This development first occurs in the Early Copper Age and continues throughout the Middle Copper Age and into the first half of the Late Copper Age.

In the final pattern, the combination of the mortuary domain and the domestic domain is symbolised by the mortuary barrow, or kurgan. Kurgans bear a strong visual resemblance to tells and it is postulated that they represent the imitation of the tell monument in the landscape (Chapman 1994: in press b and c). The construction of a burial mound which contains all the ancestral place values of the tell, yet which focuses on the single burial of an individual adult male represents a strong ideological statement about social reproduction, simply because it combines the two oppositional forms of previous social life.

Each pattern is represented by different forms of site or monument, giving the places where they were constructed contrasting values in relation to past, present and future. I now turn to some characteristics of each of these four idealised classes of timed place, using some of the concepts of humanistic and time–space geography.

Flat sites

Flat settlement sites in eastern Hungary are characteristically irregular in shape, varied in size and lacking any central focus. No sites have yet produced evidence for any form of boundaries, whether between individual garden plots or delineating the settlement area; neither is there any evidence for coeval field boundaries. The implication is that such sites may be considered less as public symbols generating their own distinctive status to outsiders and more as 'fields of care' *sensu* Tuan (1977), to be viewed from the inside by inhabitants with their own intimate experience of the paths, open spaces, communal places and surrounding cereal plots and grazing land.

While the practice of superposition of houses on earlier settlements is not strongly developed in such settlements, this is not to deny any sense of time–order in the flat sites. Where regularity has been identified, there is a linear trend in settlement displacement, generally along the beds of palaeo–channels (e.g., Dévaványa-Katonafoldek: Ecsedy 1971), both within sites and in strictly circumscribed microregions. In the Ko. Bekes II survey, 80 % of the prehistoric sites were located in 20% of the area, mostly in clusters of sites in valley segments (Chapman 1983). Wherever such progressive settlement displacements occur, a process in social time is unfolding, in which the foundation of the group's first site can be identified as a 'timemark' – a notion comparable to a 'landmark', a distinctive time in the past when an important event took place. The generation of site shifts to new locations either within the same site or in the same microregion forms a sequence in episodic time which structures other shorter–term activities. The delineation of sites within bounded clusters may be explained by the importance of being able to relate the emergence of new settlements to past shifts from an ancestral timemark, which may be intervisible with other sites in the microregion or

possess other topographical singularities. Nonetheless, after abandonment, the flat sites and the decaying remains of their immediate environs were, by definition, of low visibility, a trait linked to their impermanence.

The re–occupation of flat sites is a characteristic of Plains settlement. In the UTP survey of the Polgar Block, a mean of over five re–occupations per site was found, while the figure was over six for the Bodrogkoz Block. While the subsistence potential of certain areas was doubtless of long–term significance, another factor in re–occupation is the symbolic attachment to the place–value built up on important sites in particular microregions. In the absence of visible monuments on which to bestow significance through legend and myth, the mechanism used to 'presence' the past is not clear; one possibility was the use of surface artifactual remains of past occupations.

While the majority of flat settlements from NE Hungary occur on permanently dry land, a significant minority of Middle Neolithic sites are located at lower altitudes, e.g. on small islands in the floodplain, which would certainly have been covered by water in decennial floods, if not annually (Fig. 5). These sites would have been surrounded by boggy 'land' for several months in the spring and summer, if not flooded during part of those seasons. Thus, seasonal mobility was built into some flat sites, with notions of return, renewal and new life just as significant as in long–term, seasonally re–occupied hunter–gatherer sites (e.g., Lepenski Vir: Chapman 1994). For the more permanent sites on dry land, their interface location would have provided opportunities for interception of wild animal herds twice, if not four times, a year. These activities would have been timed so as not to clash with the departure of small groups for the seasonally –occupied island sites and their return. Together with the seasonal round of cereal cultivation, wild plant and shellfish collecting, these timemarks in the annual calendar provided opportunities for regular meetings and ceremonials, forming the basic elements in a sequence of recurrent time on which the *habitus* of the flat settlements depended.

The range of artifacts found on flat sites varies with the society in question. In general, neither the variety and wealth of material culture nor the range of contexts for artifact disposal is as great on flat sites as on tells or within Copper and Bronze Age cemeteries. This limits the possible range of variations of meanings expressed by the artifacts on flat sites, offering less scope in the narratives in which the artifacts have been included. Nonetheless, both ritual artifacts and exotic finds betokening exchange relations are regular components of the *habitus* of flat sites.

In summary, the landscape comprising flat sites embodied more of the vernacular than the political, with slow but non–cumulative changes in settlement location over generations and an absence of long–term visible monuments. Rather, long–term continuity was vested in a network of settlements, located within a bounded microregion, all of which shared common ancestors who once occupied a timemark that soon became scarcely visible but maintained its special place–value.

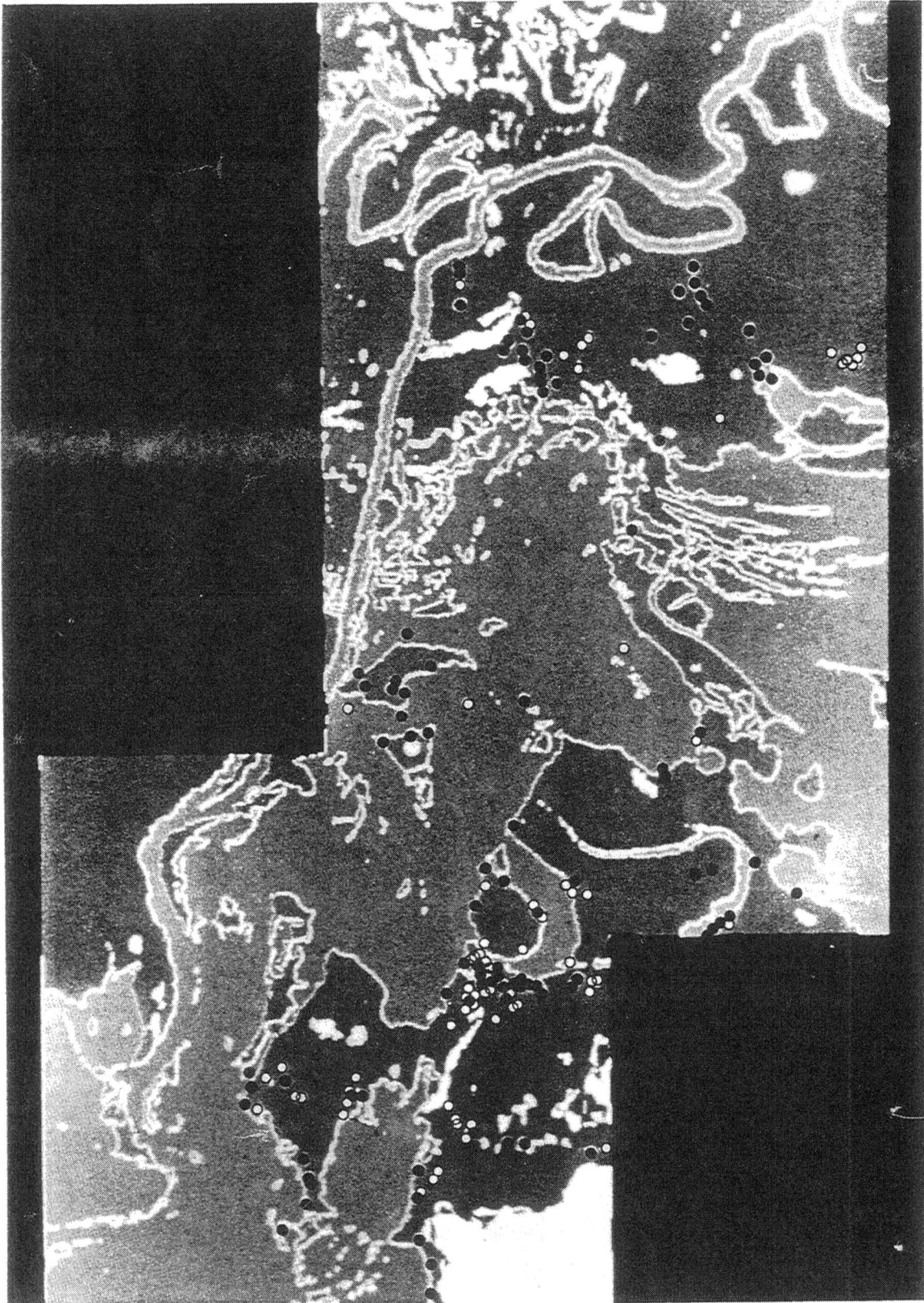

Figure 5. Distribution of Middle Neolithic (Tiszadob) sites in the Polgar Block. Full circles – scatters. Open circles – single finds. Square – tell. Dark grey – flooded up to 92m. Light grey – permanently dry areas. White – potentially flooded areas.

Tells

Tells in the landscape mark a strong contrast, in many ways, to the larger number of coeval flat settlements. While the flat sites continue to exhibit many of those characteristics defined above, tells are an example of a dominant institutional project in the making, in which a relatively small number of settlements were settled longer than the others, gradually building up a physical difference from a flat site through the superimposition of the remains of previous structures. The site type known in the Hungarian literature as the 'pseudo–tell' or the 'tell–like settlement' (e.g., Raczky 1987) refers to sites where fewer generations of inhabitants settled with less intensive deposition of occupation debris.

This kind of site emphasizes that a tell project was not planned from the start as an operation which unfolded over hundreds of years but rather evolved as a multi-generational monument in ways which cannot be inferred from the initial design configuration. The Hungarian tells tend to be defined by lower built-to-unbuilt space ratios (BUB ratios) than those in Bulgaria (Chapman 1989), providing a wider variety of possible structural outcomes in any single building level.

Although the details of the future development of a tell institutional project are necessarily indeterminate, the commitment to the project itself implies certain cultural values. The tell is a particular kind of timemark, in which it marks the time and place of its own foundation for now and the future. If it is possible to define dominant cycles within a timeworld comprising many different types of cyclical activity, then the foundation of a tell can be used to define the start of a dominant cycle of settlement in a particular microregion by later residents of the tell. Any part of the tell occupation sequence, but especially the start, can be used to define a timescale into which the beginning or end of occupation on a flat site can be inserted to produce a local genealogy of place.

As the tell mound grows in height, the dimension of verticality which so distressed the plains workers in the opening anecdote assumed greater significance in terms of the increased visibility which marked the permanence of the site. Even in the open woodland of the mid-Holocene plains (Stevenson 1991), tells with houses built on the top would have been visible from several kilometres around, especially those tells with two-storey houses such as those identified at Herpaly (Kalicz & Raczky 1984). These ancestral places, where inhabitants built structures directly above the levels where their ancestors had lived, emphasized the visibility of not only the ancestors but also the current inhabitants. Unlike the vast majority of flat sites, tells have an overriding geometrical plan, often circular or oval, with a well-defined central place. This central focus may be related to a special building, such as at Polgar-Csoszhalom (Raczky, in press) or it may be related to the centre of a circular ditch (e.g., Gorzsa: Horvath 1987; Polgar-Bosnyak domb: p.c., P. Raczky) or system of ditches and palisades (e.g., Polgar-Csoszhalom: Raczky, in press). While the existence of circular planning may not necessarily imply a central person, whoever has the social power to embody the group identity through significant actions at these central locations may well claim power in other spheres of social life as well. The double centrality of the tell – its own geometrical centre and the tell at the core of a network of flat sites – reinforces the likelihood that central people would be made visible on the vertically-differentiated surface of this special site.

With increasing occupation, the significance of a tell grows in respect of its public symbolism. Its biography – the sum total of the biographies of its occupants over the generations – becomes diversified, with ramifying relationships to most of the flat sites in the neighbourhood. Current kinship leaders have much to draw on in creating a narrative about their tell, with the result that the place-value of the tell is increased.

The longevity of the tell, combined with its visibility and its place-value, contribute to a sanctity of place which flat sites cannot match. This sanctity in turn increases the social power of those in place to lead ritual and ceremony, whether relating to ancestors, to inhabitants of flat sites in the neighbourhood or to the cyclical rites of the agricultural calendar. Since most east Hungarian tells are located at the terrace-floodplain interface above the confluence of major rivers, their occupants are well timed and placed to dominate pathways into a range of ecological zones, to intercept wild animals on their seasonal movements and control activities relating to the liminal position of the tell and its environment.

The disuse and re-use of tells are processes replete with cultural significance. The breaking of a meaningful narrative of long-term occupation in favour of another settlement site marks a major decision, implying at the very least questions of resistance to domination by traditional values. However, the physical presence of the tell enables even those who have moved to a new site the possibility of re-visiting the tell to maintain links with the tell's narrative. This strategy may explain the deposition of small quantities of Copper Age material on tells after the abandonment of occupation in the Late Neolithic (e.g., at Gorzsa: Horvath 1987). But the nature of the tell as monument means that any group, whether possessing ancestral links or not, can use the tell for its own purposes of establishing an identity through links with the past, whether by ceremonial on the tell or permanent re-occupation. The start of another dominant cycle of social identity on the tell can be invested with as much significance as the original site occupation.

While cultural variations do exist, the material remains found on Neolithic and Bronze Age tells tend to be of a richness and variety not found on coeval flat sites. The recent prestigious Hungarian publications on Neolithic (Raczky 1987) and Bronze Age (Meier-Arendt 1992) tells provides a picture of the wealth of material culture deposited in a variety of structured contexts on these sites. The wealth of ritual artifacts, in particular, differentiates the tells from neighbouring flat sites (e.g., the shrines at Veszto-magori halom (Hegedus & Makkay 1987) and Parta (Lazarovici 1989). At the Csoszhalom tell, the percentage of painted pottery rises to c. 40 % in some levels, with fine wares dominated by non-local styles (Tisza, Herpaly and Lengyel: Raczky, in press). The enlargement of the Late Neolithic social network has implications for the timing of social activities, timing presumably dominated by those living on or near the tell. The calendar of deposition of so much decorated pottery, in addition to a wide range of other fine artifacts, would have formed a primary framework for much other activity on and off the tell.

In summary, the establishment and growth of tells contrasts with the flux of more numerous, shorter-term and less impressive flat sites across the Alfold plain. Insofar as the tells and tell communities dominated the flat sites, we can identify an example of the political landscape dominating the vernacular landscape, through the structuring of social action at a regional and local level. Visibility, permanence and sanctity form the holy trinity of the tell timemark, with strong consequences for the balance of social power between the communities of tells and flat sites.

Cemeteries

The initial decision to create cemeteries as bounded, distinct places for the deposition of some of a community's newly-dead can be dated to the Copper Age in eastern Hungary. As in the case of one of the largest examples – Tiszapolgar–Basatanya (Bognar–Kutzian 1963) – the cemeteries often re–occupied former occupation sites but there is no evidence of coeval settlement near the graves. With the exception of a few tell occupations, contemporary settlements were small-scale hamlets, if not farms comprising an extended family, represented in the landscape by small, flat sites.

If Gosden is correct in his claim that social action creates time rather than the converse, the cemetery played a crucial role in establishing a timed framework for social life. The cemetery combines in a special way both essential elements of time – sequence and duration. The sequence of burials embodies episodic time through irregular use; the procession with the corpse of the deceased from the settlement to the cemetery denotes a linear progression, as does the location of the grave within an established pattern of linear groups of graves, perhaps kin groups. The subjectivity of episodic time relates to the absence of mesurement of an interval between occurrences (Young & Ziman 1971); each burial defines a significant social event – a timemark – to which can be related other key ceremonials and other cycles of activity. However, the other aspect of the cemetery is its role as guardian of long–term memory for the social group, in which duration rather than episodic events is stressed. Here, the key narrative to develop is the long–term relation of the living to the ancestors, through their identity with the cemetery and the proliferation of relationships within a narrative which expands with every new funeral.

The spatial contrast between the nucleation of the dead in large cemeteries and the dispersion of the living in farms and hamlets has been noted before (Bognar–Kutzian 1972; Sherratt 1980), without an exploration of the time relations of the two site types. Division of a regional population into extended families means that any major social action requires careful co–ordination of timing and placing between many settlement units related through a spatially larger social network covering longer travel times – a contrast to the nucleated tell population, where major supra–household action can be more readily timed. While tell inhabitants were likely to develop new time frameworks for the integration of their social networks, there was no obvious domestic focus for such timing in a series of potentially equal households – perhaps between ten and twenty per cemetery. However, the grave goods deposited in Copper Age cemeteries such as Tibava and Basatanya suggests a considerable degree of social differentiation, with the implication that certain kin groups or individuals had developed more social power than others through preferential control of exotic prestige goods of copper and gold. While some groups increased social power by success in exchange, others may have done so through

proximity to the cemetery or control of mortuary ritual.

The apparent paradox of the flat Copper Age cemeteries is that they maintained sanctity of place and a strong element of public symbolism despite their seeming invisibility in the landscape. Three factors help to resolve the contradiction. There is a possibility of a distinctive natural marker, such as a sacred grove, denoting the site of the cemetery (with minimal chances of recognition from pollen evidence). Secondly, so few graves in these cemeteries are cut by later graves that the existence of grave markers may be inferred. Thirdly, very few Copper Age cemeteries were re–used as burial places, although later settlement debris can be found near some cemeteries (e.g., the Hunyadi Halom settlement near the Bodrogkeresztur cemetery of Tiszavalk-Kenderfold: Patay 1978). This pattern perhaps supports the notion of cemeteries as sacred, inviolable places. A final point is that, irrespective of the physical evidence, the symbolism of the cemetery may of itself preclude cultural intrusion. In any case, abandonment of cemeteries marked a major break in tradition, the replacement of one ancestral narrative by another, a rupture which denied the opportunity for future expression of that special place–value.

In summary, the flat bounded cemetery played an important role in framing the social action which created a context of time for local Copper Age communities. Time as duration in the maintenance of long–term cultural narratives was as important as time as sequence, in which the order of the newly–dead and their subsequent transformation into ancestors was the basis of kinship calibration. For the first time in Hungarian prehistory, the tension between the political and the vernacular landscape was represented through the opposition between the mortuary domain and the domestic domain.

Kurgans

The appearance of barrow burials in eastern Hungary is dated to the second half of the Late Copper Age. A total of some 3000 barrows is known from the plain (Ecsedy 1979), most of which are believed to be Late Copper Age in date. The extraordinary lack of any form of settlement evidence for the period of barrow building is one of the greatest problems in Hungarian prehistory; it is only logical to assume short–term, small–scale settlement at no more than farmstead level.

In many ways, the time–place characteristics of the mortuary barrow resemble those of the tell, to which it bears a close similarity both as physical monument and as public symbol. All the traits of verticality, visibility, permanence and sanctity based on place–value are present, despite the absence of continuous re–creation though ongoing settlement. The kurgans are generally round and their primary burial is usually central, though at considerable depth. There are a few instances of multiple burials above the primary pit, in which the height of the kurgan has been increased with each subsequent burial (e.g., Ketegyhaza 3: Ecsedy 1979: Fig. 14). Hence, the central focus is on the mound itself, rather than the invisible deceased, whose remains are so deeply buried as to constitute a negation of the newly–dead within the field of a generalised ancestral monument. The barrow gives as much prominence to the living who constructed it as to the ancestors who are stored there. The initial burial is a timemark recording the start of a dominant cycle of social action, an example of a dominant institutional project involving co–operation between several extended families who destroyed the fertility of much topsoil to pile up the fertile blackearth with which mounds tend to be built (Stockdale 1991).

One difference between kurgans and tells is that, while the latter tend to be widely spaced across the landscape, kurgans are often grouped into clusters of two or three, which may form larger barrow cemeteries with clusters separated by up to several hundred metres (Ecsedy 1979). However, large barrow cemeteries exist, such as at Ketegyhaza, with 33 barrows, 11 of which have been excavated (Ecşedy 1979:20–33). The formation of barrow cemeteries provides an opportunity for the overt definition of kinship classification through the location of the latest barrow in relation to previous mounds (Barrett 1990). If burial formed the final stage of a linear patterning in mortuary ritual, the barrows themselves formed the initial point of ancestral ritual.

Kurgans would appear, in essence, to signify the domination of the political over the vernacular landscape, given the strong contrast between the invisibility of the domestic domain and the monumentality of the mortuary domain. However, this interpretation underestimates the significance of the visual similarities between tells and mortuary barrows. The transfer of the domestic narratives associated with tell settlements into the mortuary sphere of monumental barrows enables the combination of the two principal forms of social power into a single context, control of which would have been fundamental for social reproduction. Domestic narratives as represented by local flat sites can also be absorbed into the symbolic world of barrow cemeteries; the best example is Ketegyhaza, where several barrows are constructed above, and incorporate into their mounds, Middle Copper Age and Late Copper Age Period I settlement remains (Ecsedy 1979:20–33).

In summary, the barrow building period of the Late Copper Age widens the gap between the political landscape of the mortuary domain and the vernacular landscape of the domestic arena to a gulf. The principal timemarks are monumental barrows, around which the timed structures of extensive social networks are developed. The minimal visibility of the domestic in Period II of the Late Copper Age is perhaps related to the combination of its main narrative with that of the mortuary sphere.

Summary and conclusions

The social times and places of later Hungarian prehistoric sites have been explored in an attempt to characterize long–term changes in the cultural landscape. This preliminary characterization is based upon four ideal site types – the flat site, the tell, the flat cemetery and the barrow cemetery. It is clearly desirable in future analyses to take account of

specific sequences of ASPs in particular regions and take inter–regional differences more fully into account. Nevertheless, some striking conclusions emerge from an investigation of why and how new ASPs emerge in the Alfold Plain.

The initial settlement of the Plain is defined by the selection of microregions generally close to major rivers and tributaries and the location of flat sites mostly within these microregions. Settlement sequences developed through lateral site re–location along river courses, with few multi–phase occupations. In such communities, there was a dominance of the vernacular landscape over the political, with 'fields of care' radiating out from spatially–irregular settlement sites. Although sites occupied early in the sequence would have been recognised as timemarks and accorded special place–value in the narrative of their social group, the community focus remained the microregion itself, as a segment of the landscape identified with a single social group. The small size of any microregion population implied breeding network connections with several other microregions, and the wider structures of social reproduction were based on small–scale, long–distance exchange of pottery and lithics.

In the mature farming phase of the Late Middle and Late Neolithic periods, tells began to emerge on a small number of occupied flat sites. The process of tell formation is a good example of the process of 'becoming', since the formation of a physically distinctive monument would have taken many generations. Rather than being constructed as part of a long–term plan, tells imply a generation–by–generation commitment by one particular social group to a place and its ancestral values, as well as a series of weaker attachments to the tell by occupants of neighbouring flat sites. Thus, a dialectical sense of becoming can be identified: the emergence of a tell and the emergence of a stronger group identity than usual among microregion groups. The significance of ancestral time and the cyclical progression of continued settlement can be contrasted with the shorter–term flat sites and even the 'pseudo–tells' as a measure of group identity. It is tempting to associate this dialectic with a third process – the emergence of dominant kinship units, which controlled social reproduction through control of the timing of tell ritual. In contrast to the earlier Neolithic, with its vernacular landscapes and attachment to the microregion, the Late Neolithic occupation of tells brought a new sense of central place, not so much economic as symbolic. The landscapes of the Late Neolithic were focussed more inwards, on the tells, rather than outwards from sites to their constituent microregions. The new symbolic order was emphasized by the double centrality of tells – the centre of the tell itself and the tell at the core of a network of peripheral sites.

In periods of the Copper Age characterised by the use of flat cemeteries, a new notion of place–value emerges, which stresses the direct spatial relationship between the newly–dead and the ancestors. Removed from the domestic arena to a different place, the newly–dead can be used in different strategies, enabling the living to move away from the traditional values of the tell community (Chapman 1994; in press b and c). The cemetery embodies the episodic time of sequence in burial of the newly–dead and the cumulative time of duration in the formation of stable ancesteral relations. In a vernacular landscape of small farms, the cemetery acts as a focus for the timing of social relations relating to mortuary ritual and exchange – a public symbol of the political landscape which is so clearly distanced from the vernacular in the opposition of domestic and mortuary.

The opposition between mortuary and domestic arenas is exaggerated still further in the Late Copper Age by the construction of prominent barrow cemeteries in landscapes where settlement evidence is almost invisible. The fusion of traditional tell–based place–values and ancestral mortuary values in the monumental barrow is based upon the physical similarity of tells and barrows and leads to a quantum leap in social power. The dispersion of barrows and farms across the landscape leads to a social identity related more to mortuary places than to easily–identifiable microregions; the permanence of the barrows is a symbolic denial of the temporary, seasonal style of settlement.

The notion of timemarks – places where significant social action occurs – is a valuable concept for landscape studies, for it introduces a focus on the social frameworks of cyclical time which run through the lives of human communities. Monuments and narratives are mutually supportive. It is the grand events of the past – the initial settlement of tells and the abandonment of cemeteries – which frame the narratives which people use to construct those landscapes in which the quotidien events of the *habitus* reside.

Acknowledgements

I am happy to acknowledge the financial support for the ongoing *Upper Tisza Project* (1991 –5): the National Geographic Society, the British Academy, the University of Newcastle upon Tyne and the Society of Antiquaries of London, the Research Committee of the University of Newcastle and the Prehistoric Society. It has been a source of great strength to have received support for these bodies from David Harris, John D. Evans, Anthony Harding, Jimmy Griffin, Bernard Wailes and Greg Johnson. I am more than grateful to all my co–workers on this project for discussing and criticising these ideas, the most important of whom are the late Sandor Bökönyi, to whom this paper is dedicated, Robert Shiel, Istvan Bona, Pal Raczky and Jozsef Laszlovszky.

Bibliography

Bailey, D.W., 'The living house', 19 – 48, in R. Samson (ed), *The Social archaeology of houses* (Edinburgh: Edinburgh University Press, 1990).

Barrett, J.C., 'The monumentality of death', *World Archaeology* 22/2 (Oxford: Oxbow, 1991) pp. 179–189.

Bender, B. (ed.), *Landscape: politics and perspective.* (London: Berg, 1993).

Bognar–Kutzian, I., *The Copper Age cemetery of Tiszapolgar–Basatanya.* (Archaeologia Hungarica 42; Budapest: Akademiai Kiado, 1963).

Bognar–Kutzian, I., *The Early Copper Age Tiszapolgar Culture in the Carpathian Basin.* (Budapest: Akadémiai Kiadó, 1972).

Bohannan, L., 'Political aspects of Tiv social organisation', in J. Middleton & D. Tait (eds)., *Tribes without rulers* (London: Routledge, 1958) 33–66.

Bökönyi, S., *History of domestic mammals in Central and Eastern Europe* (Budapest: Akademiai Kiado, 1974).

Bourdieu, P., *Outline of a theory of practice.* (Cambridge: Cambridge University Press, 1977).

Bradley, R., *The passage of arms. An archaeological analysis of prehistoric hoards and votive deposits.* (Cambridge: Cambridge University Press, 1990).

Buttimer, A. & Seamon, D. (eds)., *The human experience of space and place* (London: Croom Helm, 1980).

Chapman, J., *Clusters of sites or sites of clusters ? The Bekes II survey in eastern Hungary.* (Unpublished paper read to NUARS, Bradford, 1981).

Chapman, J., 'Meaning and illusion in the study of burial in Balkan prehistory', 1–45, in A. Poulter (ed), *Ancient Bulgaria Volume 1.* (Nottingham: University of Nottingham Press, 1983).

Chapman, J.C., 'From 'space' to 'place': a model of dispersed settlement and Neolithic society', 21–46, in C. Burgess, P. Topping & D. Mordant (eds), *Enclosures and defences in the Neolithic of western Europe.* (International Series 403; Oxford: BAR, 1988).

Chapman, J. C., a, 'The Early Balkan village', *Varia Archaeologica Hungarica* II (1989), pp. 33–53.

Chapman, J., 1991. The creation of social arenas in the Neolithic and Copper Age of South East Europe: the case of Varna', 152–171, in Garwood, P., Jennings, P., Skeates, R. & Toms, J. (eds) *Sacred and Profane.* (Oxford Committee for Archaeology Monograph No. 32; Oxford: Oxbow, 1991).

Chapman, J.C., 1994. 'Social power in the Iron Gates Mesolithic', in J.C. Chapman & P. Dolukhanov (eds) *Cultural transformations and interactions in Eastern Europe.* (Worldwide Archaeology Series 5; Aldershot: Avebury).

Chapman, J.C. 1994a The living, the dead, and the ancestors: time, life cycles and the mortuary domain in later European prehistory. 40 – 85, in Davies, J. (ed) *Ritual and remembrance. Responses to death in human societies.* Sheffield: Sheffield Academic Press.

Chapman, J. in press a, 'Landscapes in flux: introduction'. To appear in Chapman J. & Dolukhanov, P. (eds)., *Landscapes in flux* (in press).

Chapman, J. in press b, 'Social power in the early farming communities of eastern Hungary – perspectives from the Upper Tisza region'. To appear in Kurucz, K. (ed). *The Neolithic of eastern Hungary* (Nyiregyhaza: in press, 1995).

Chapman, J. in press c, 'Changing gender relations in the prehistory of eastern Hungary'. To appear in Moore, J. M. & Scott., E. (eds)., *Invisible people and processes: writing gender and children into European prehistory* (Leicester: Leicester University Press).

Chapman J. & Laszlovszky, J. 1992. *The Upper Tisza Project 1991: report on the first season.* Archaeological Reports 1991 (Durham & Newcastle upon Tyne):10–13. Durham: University of Durham.

Chapman, J. & Laszlovszky, J. 1994. *The Upper Tisza Project – September 1993 season, Archaeological Reports 1993* (Durham & Newcastle upon Tyne):1–7. Durham: University of Durham.

Chapman J. & Laszlovszky, J. 1993. *The Upper Tisza Project: the September 1992 season.* Archaeological Reports 1992 (Durham & Newcastle upon Tyne):13–19. Durham: University of Durham.

Chayanov, A.V., *The theory of peasant economy.* (Homewood, Ill.: Richard D. Irwin for the American Economic Association, 1966).

Cosgrove, D., *Social formation and symbolic landscape* (London: Croom Helm, 1984).

Ecsedy, I., 'Neolitische Siedlung in Devavanya, Katonafoldek', *Mitteilungen des Archäologischen Instituts der Ungarischen Akademie der Wissenschaften* 3 (1972), pp. 59–63.

Ecsedy, I., *The people of the Pit-Grave kurgans in Eastern Hungary.* (Fontes Archaeologici Hungariae; Budapest: Akadémiai Kiadó, 1979).

Eliade, M., *The myth of the eternal return* (London: Routledge, 1955).

Eliade, M., *Myths, dreams and realities.* (London: Fontana, 1960).

Fabian, J., *Time and the Other: how anthropology makes its object* (New York: Columbia University Press, 1983).

Fairbairn, A., *Archaeobotanical investigations at the Late Neolithic and Bronze Age tells of Polgar-Csoszhalom and OPolgar-Kenderfold,* unpub. internal report to the Upper Tisza Project, 1994.

Forman, R. I. T. and Godron, M. *Landscape ecology* (New York: J. Wiley & Sons, 1986).

Fortes, M., 'Time and social structure: an Ashanti case study', 54–84, in Fortes, M. (ed) *Social structure: essays presented to A. R. Radcliffe-Brown.* (New York: Russell, 1949).

Gillings, M. 'GIS and the Tisa flood plain: landscape and settlement evolution'. To appear in *The impact of Geographic Information Systems on archaeology: a European perspective* (New York: Taylor & Francis, 1995).

Goody, J., 'Time: social organisation', *International Encyclopaedia of Social Sciences* 16 (1968), pp. 25–42.

Gosden, C. *Social being and time* (Oxford: Blackwell, 1994).

Gregory, D. & Walford, R. (eds)., *Horizons in human geography* (London: Macmillan, 1989).

Hegedus, K. & Makkay, J., 'Veszto-magor. A settlement of the Tisza culture', 85–104, in Raczky, P. (ed), *The Late Neolithic in the Tisza region.* (Budapest-Szolnok: Szolnok County Museums, 1987).

Horvath, F., 'Hodmezovasarhely-Gorzsa. A settlement of the Tisza culture', 31–46, in Raczky, P. (ed), *The Late Neolithic in the Tisza region.* Budapest-Szolnok: Szolnok County Museums, 1987).

Howell, S., 'Of persons and things: exchange and valuables amongst the Li of eastern Indonesia', *Man* (N.S.) 24 (1989), pp. 419–438.

Jackson, J. B., *Discovering the vernacular landscape* (New Haven: Yale University Press, 1984).

Jankovich, B.D., Makkay, J. & Szoke, B.M., *Bekes megye regeszeti topografiaja.* (Magyarorszag Regeszeti Topografiaja 8; Budapest: Akademiai Kiado, 1989).

Kalicz, N. & Raczky, P., 'The Late Neolithic of the Tisza region. A survey of recent archaeological research', 11–30, in Raczky, P. (ed), *The Late Neolithic in the Tisza region.* (Budapest-Szolnok: Szolnok County Museums, 1987a).

Kalicz, N. & Raczky, P., 'Berettyoujfalu-Herpaly. A settlement of the Herpaly culture', 105–125, in Raczky, P. (ed), *The Late Neolithic in the Tisza region.* (Budapest-Szolnok: Szolnok County Museums, 1987b).

Kopytoff, I., 'The cultural biography of things: commoditization as process', 64–91, in Appadurai, A. (eds) *The social world of things.* (Cambridge: Cambridge University Press, 1986).

Kosse, K., *Settlement ecology of the Körös and Linear Pottery cultures in Hungary* (British Archaeological Reports I–64; Oxford: BAR, 1979).

Lambek, M., 'Exchange, time, and person in Mayotte: the structure and de-structuring of a cultural system', *American Anthropologist* 92 (1990), pp. 647–659.

Lazarovici, Gh. 1989. 'Das neolitische Heiligtum von Parta'. *Varia Archaeologica Hungarica* II: 149 – 173.

Lynch, K., *What time is this place?* (Cambridge, Mass.: MIT Press, 1972).

Mauss, M. *The gift.* (London: Routlege, Kegan & Paul, 1974).

Meier-Arendt (ed) *Bronzezeit in Ungarn. Forschungen in Tell-Siedlungen an Donau und Theiss.* Frankfurt-am-Main: Museum für Vor- und Frühgeschichte – Archäologische Museum Szolnok, 1992).

Moore, W. E., *Man, time and society* (New York: J. Wiley, 1963).

Mosko, M. 'The developmental cycle among public groups', *Man* (N.S.) 24 (1989), pp. 470–484.

Parkes, D. & Thrift, N., 'Putting time in its place', in Carlstein, T., Parkes, D. & Thrift, N. (eds)., *Timing space and spacing time Volume 1: Making sense of time* (London: E. Arnold, 1978), 119–129.

Parkes, D. & Thrift, N., *Times, spaces and places. A chronogeographic perspective* (Chichester: J. Wiley, 1980).

Patay, P., *Das kupferzeitliche Gräbereld von Tiszavalk-Kenderfold.* Fontes Archaeologici Hungariae; Budapest: Akademiai Kiado, 1978).

Pred, A., *Place, practice and structure. Social and spatial transformations in South Sweden: 1750 – 1850* (Totowa, N.J.: Barnes & Noble Books, 1986).

Raczky, P. (ed), *The Late Neolithic in the Tisza region.*

(Budapest–Szolnok: Szolnok County Museums, 1987a).

Raczky, P. 1988, *A Tisza–Videk Kulturalis es kronologiai kapcsolatai a Balkannal es az egeikummal a neolitikum, rezkor idoszakaban* (Szolnok: Szolnok County Museum).

Raczky, P., 'Polgar–Csoszhalom'. To appear in Kurucz, K. (ed), *The Neolithic of eastern Hungary* (Nyiregyhaza:in press, 1995).

Ray, K., 'Material metaphor, social interaction and historical reconstructions: exploring patterns of association and symbolism in the Igbo–Ukwu corpus', 66–78, in Hodder, I. (ed), *The archaeology of contextual meanings*. (Cambridge: Cambridge University Press, 1987).

Rowlands, M.R., 'Book review of Bradley, R. The passage of arms. An archaeological analysis of prehistoric hoards and votive deposits. (Cambridge: Cambridge University Press,1990), *European Journal of Archaeology* 1 (1993), pp. 205–7.

Sahlins, M.D., *Stone age economics*. (Chicago: Aldine, 1972).

Samson, R. (ed), *The Social archaeology of houses*. (Edinburgh: Edinburgh University Press, 1990).

Shackle, G. L. S., 'Time, choice and uncertainty' in Carlstein, T., Parkes, D. & Thrift, N. (eds)., *Timing space and spacing time Volume 1: Making sense of time* (London: E. Arnold, 1978), 47–55.

Sherratt, A., 'The development of Neolithic and Copper Age settlement in the Great Hungarian Plain: Part 1: The regional setting, and Part 2: Site surveys and settlement dynamics', *Oxford Journal of Archaeology* 1/3 (1982), pp. 287–316 and 2/1 (1983), pp. 13–41.

Sherratt, A., 'Early agrarian settlement in the Körös region of the Great Hungarian Plain', *Acta Archaeologica Hungarica* 35 (1984), pp. 155–169.

Sorokin, P. A. & Merton, R. K., 'Social time: a methodological and functional analysis', *American Journal of Sociology* 42/5 (1937), pp. 615–629.

Stevenson, A., 'Vegetational analysis, in Chapman, J. (ed)., *The Upper Tisza Project. Report to Research Committee* (Newcastle upon Tyne: unpublished report, 1991), 36–38.

Stockdale, E., 'Tiszavasvari – deak halom', in Chapman, J. (ed)., *The Upper Tisza Project. Report to Research Committee* (Newcastle upon Tyne: unpublished report, 1991), 48 – 51.

Thompson, E.P., *Customs in common* (xxx:xxx, 1991).

Tilley, C., *A phenomenology of landscape* (Oxford: Berg, 1994).

Tringham, R. & Krstic, D. (eds), *Selevac – a Neolithic village in Yugoslavia*. (Monumenta Archaeologica 15; Los Angeles: University of California Press, 1991).

Tuan, Yi–Fu., 'Space and place: humanistic perspective' *Progress in Geography* 6 (1973), pp. 211–252.

Tuan, Yi–Fu., *Space and place. The perspective of experience* (London: E. Arnold, 1977).

Tuan, Yi–Fu., 'Space, time, place: a humanistic frame', in Carlstein, T., Parkes, D. & Thrift, N. (eds)., *Timing space and spacing time Volume 1: Making sense of time* (London:E. Arnold, 1978), 7–16.

Wilk, R.W. & Rathje, W.L., 'Household archaeology', *American Behavioral Scientist* 25/6 (1982), pp. 617–639.

Worsley, P. M., 'The kinship system of the Tallensi: a re-evaluation', *Journal of the Royal Anthropological Institute* 86 (1956), pp. 37–75.

Young, M. & Ziman, J., 'Cycles in human behaviour', *Nature* 229 (1971), pp. 91–95.

Dancing in Space: Rock Art of the Campo Lameiro Valley, Southern Galicia, Spain.

George Nash

'Some of the figures were so faint that they could only be seen in flood-lighting. But then they, too, became distinct'

(Gustaf Hallström 1938)1:1

Introduction

When Gustaf Hallström wrote these words, he was referring to a well-used technique by which rock carvings [or petroglyphs] could be 'read' using powerful flood-lighting. The lighting would not only illuminate the 'readable' designs but would also help to interpret damaged or unclear designs. What he and others had failed to consider was that the rock art, when first utlilised, may have also relied on an artificial light source in order to be read?

Applying this principle, I wish to discuss in this paper the symbolic significance of positioning and subsequent interpretation of six rock carving sites (thirteen separate panels) in Galicia, northern Spain. Moreover, I want to place an emphasis on the importance of reading individual designs and figures on a chosen number of panels under certain light conditions. All the designs are incised onto exposed smooth granite rock outcrops. The six rock carving sites, part of a much larger group, are situated in an isolated valley of the Campo Lameiro region, approximately 20 kilometres north-east of the nearest coast and the provincial city of Ponteverdra (Map 1). The northern part of the valley is surrounded by a small but dominant mountain range – Monttillon de Arriba. Monte Cregos (789 mts O.D.), the highest peak, is located directly north of three of the more impressive rock carving sites within the group (4, 5 & 6).

The designs from all the panels fall into five generic groups: zoomorphic and anthropomorphic figures, spirals (and concentric circles), cup and hoof marks, and wheeled crosses. Each group is sub-divided into distinct stylistic forms. However, throughout Galicia, the dominant designs are concentric circles, wheeled circles and in some cases complex geometric designs. On a recent visit to this area in August 1992, I photographically recorded at night some of the more spectacular panels, using an artificial light source (50 watt video light) and high speed transparency film (1600 A.S.A.).

Geographical Distribution (Map 2)

The thirteen rock carving panels for discussion form part of a much larger rock carving area both within and outside the valley. The spatial distribution of the Campo Lameiro group may be extended 40 kilometres westwards either side of the Rio de Ponteverdra. In all, well over 450 rock art sites are located throughout Galicia. This number will now have increased due to the recent landscape survey carried out by University of Santiago de Compostela (1992). The Campo Lamerio valley has one of the highest concentrations of naturalistic rock art in Galicia. Panels of similar design and complexity also exist in Portugal; these may be considered as part of the same rock art tradition to those in Galicia.

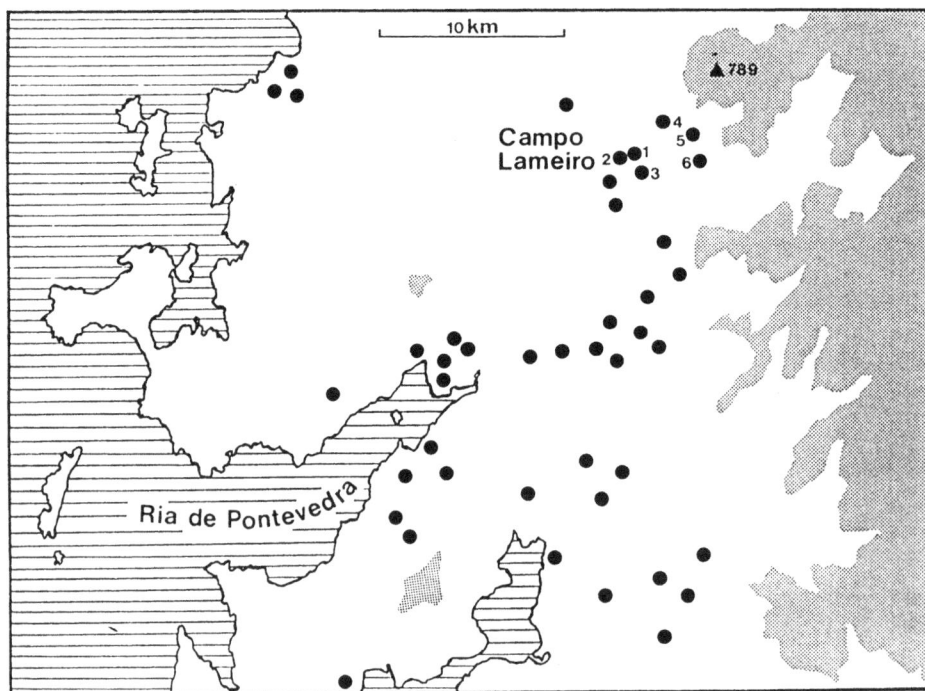

Map 1. The spatial distribution of Petroglyphs in Southern Galicia.

46

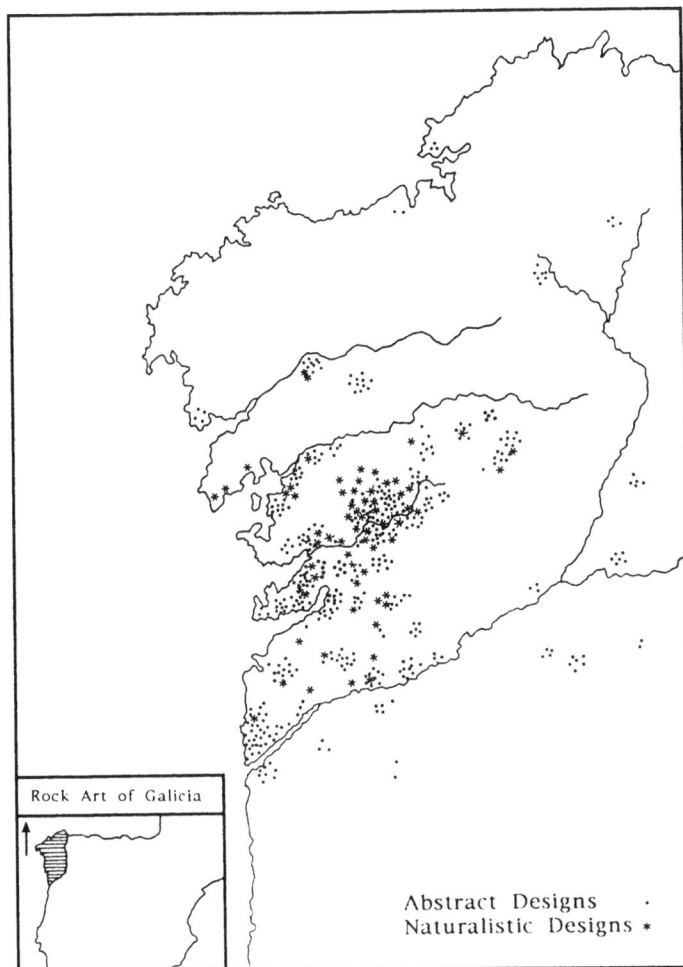

Map 2. The spatial distribution of abstract and animal carvings in Galicia (after Pena Santos & Vazquez Varela 1979).

rock art and earlier, megalithic burial practices), the economy remains mainly that of hunting and gathering, similar to that of the symbolic mechanisms used during the latter phases of the Danish Ertebolle. Here, 'proto'-Neolithic influences from the south and west (including pottery and motif decoration) are being used by late Mesolithic communities.

Looking at the Art

For the sake of this paper, I have organised the rock carving surfaces into a clockwise west–north–east numerical sequence. Their order is as follows: 1) Penalba, 2) De Laxe de Rotea de Mendo, 3) Paredes (a,b,c), 4) Canada (a,b), 5) Parada (a,b) and 6) Fentans (a,b,c,d,e). Nearly all the panels are sited on open, rocky outcrops within the valley slope areas (or what I would term, an intermediate slope zone), except that is, for the Fentans group. Here, five large panels are located on a small valley plateau and away from the northern part of the Campo Lameiro valley. The position of each panel within the slope zone appears to segregate the rich fertile valley floor from the hostile environment of the mountains. All the panels are sited on the edges of domesticated land, between 300 and 500 metres O.D.

The valley floor has a rich, deep alluvial base soil. Today, the land has been divided into small elongated field systems. The predominant crop grown within the valley, indeed the whole region, is grape. Within the intermediate slope zone, recent eucalyptus plantations intrude into the deeper, more fertile soils. In addition to eucalyptus planting, small herds of goat and cattle are grazed especially on the poorer soils on the valley slopes, usually during the summer months (similar to the alpine grazing system). The soil structure within the slope zone is predominantly thin and well drained. In many cases, the soil has been completely eroded to reveal smooth rock granite outcrops. Rock outcropping occurs throughout the intermediate slopes and highland zones. The slope areas, the mountains and the valley floor establish three very distinct geographic zones. All can be theoretically segregated into economic, political, social and symbolic environs (Fig. 1).

Reading the Panels

Whilst examining a selected number of panels in both daylight and at night, I experienced a number of different visual sensations. The available light source was invariably crucial to these experiences. Under daylight conditions, both individual figures and complete panel surfaces appeared flat and difficult to decipher, especially when exposed to direct sunlight.

Another factor restricting a visual interpretation is that many of the surfaces have been exposed to both human and environmental disturbance over the past 4000 years. Despite this, however, nearly all the panels (with the exception of Canada 4b) fairly well preserved. The state of preservation is important to any visual analysis. I would add that the angle of each rock carving surface and the manipulation of certain light sources is also important. By applying a

Elsewhere, in Scandinavia (west and northern Sweden and coastal Norway), northern Britain, Ireland and western France, similar rock art exists. Chronologically, it appears to date from the late (South–West European) Neolithic to the late Bronze Age. However, any precise dating is nonetheless a problem. All are locally sited in marginal agricultural areas. Their location appears to take into consideration nearby streams and highland zonation. In the Campo Lameiro valley there are very few domesticated animal scenes, with the exception of the horse and rider at Parades (3a). It would appear that the more mundane existence of an agricultural/herding society was not important to the inhabitants and artists of this valley. This being the case, two explanations could be considered for their commission. Firstly, a 'history' is being created which draws on the experiences of an earlier and perhaps more symbolic and ritualistic economy – a common link with the ancestors. One can also argue that agriculture, and more importantly, animal husbandry, may not have been an attractive alternative to well–established hunting, fishing and gathering during the Neolithic and Bronze Ages. Therefore, one can envisage a type of small–scale mixed economy existing in this area, hence the depiction in all areas of large hunting animals such as red deer (and, in Scandinavia, reindeer and elk). Despite the mechanisms for domestication being firmly in place (the

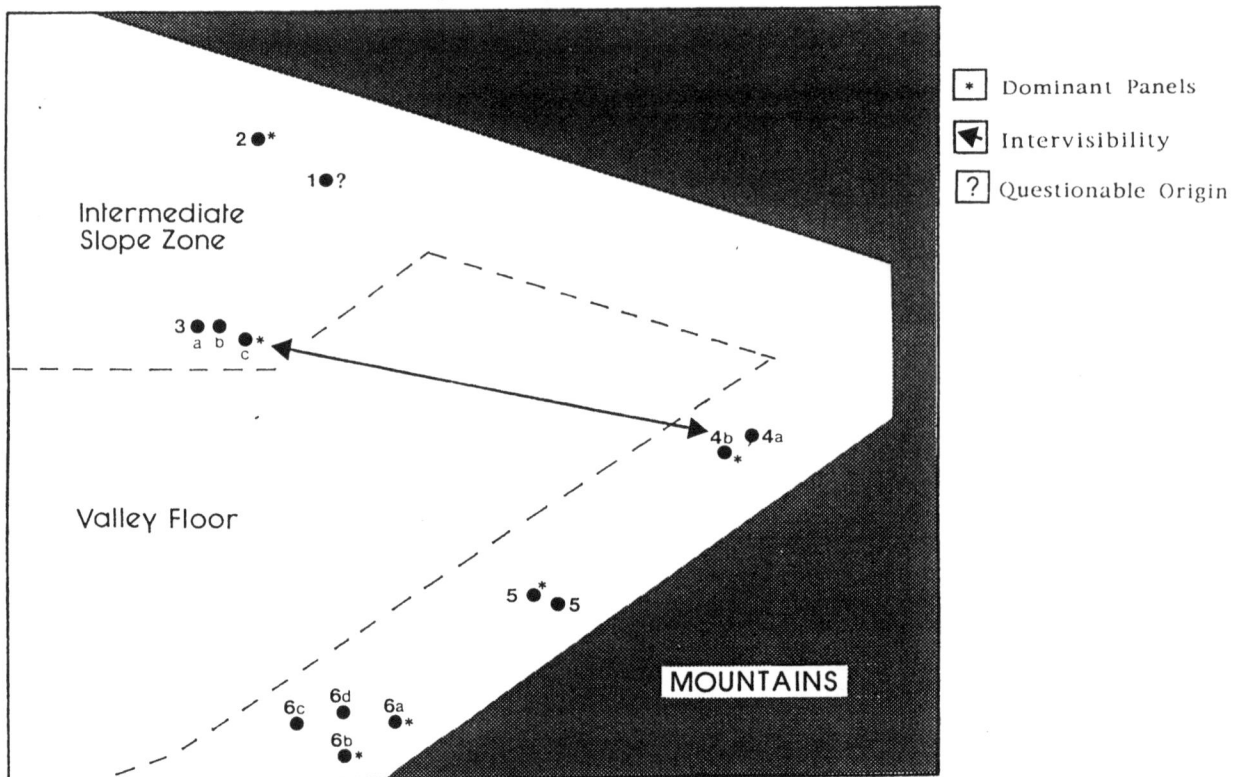

Figure 1. A diagrammatic map of the Upper Campo Lameiro Valley.

controlled light source at night, each panel conveys a totally different sensation than if observed in daylight. In manipulating the light source, by possibly simulating a fire, incised shadows are cast, thus elevating the designs. Obviously, the angle of each rock carving surface is fundamental to illuminating the designs. By angling the light beam, each figure, each design, comes 'alive', thus revealing an animated vibrancy that is certainly absent from the same rock carving surface seen in daylight. Moreover, when exposed to an angled light source, the panels possess an expressive totality that creates a complex and striking visual image. But, how were these panels arranged? In constructing these images, all thirteen panels conform to the following set of rules: i) each rock carving surface has a dominant central motif or figure, ii) all thirteen panels are dominated by either humans or animals (at Canada 4a and 4b deep incised cup-marks and complex spiral/concentric circles dominate), iii) in all cases, the central figure is surrounded by smaller, less significant multiple designs. These secondary designs are strategically distributed around the central figure. Beyond these, cup-marks and hoof marks complete the rock carving surface – the design field, iv) finally, all panels are angled so that either low sunlight or fire will animate the figures and designs, thus creating a stronger visual impact than if seen in daylight.

However, a problem exists with the archaeology. In this region, there has been very little excavation around the rock carving surfaces. In order to reinforce my argument that these rock carvings were only meant to be seen at night, I looked at three excavations undertaken between 1982 and 1991 around rock carving panels in Bohuslan, south-west Sweden. Here, at Braland, Jorlov and Karlenby there was clear evidence of small fires around the base of the rock

carving surfaces. Associated with the fires were small sherds of burnt pottery, clay, quartz worked and unworked flint (Yeats 1991). At Dalsland, another rock carving site in Bohuslan, a stone 'pavement' had been constructed at the base of the rock carving surface. Again, there was evidence of charcoal and burnt quartz (Svensson 1985).

By applying this approach to panels in the Campo Lameiro valley, I would argue that each becomes a clear visual narrative, with a beginning, a middle and an end. The narrative can be 'read' in a number of ways. Firstly, one can start at a given point and process around the panel to its termination. Equally, the narrative could begin with the central dominant figure and end with the smaller peripheral designs. In addition, more narratives, or a continuation of the same theme, may be traced in design groups on other surfaces close by. This idea would certainly apply to the Fentans group (6a–6d). Here, each rock carving panel appears to be thematically related. Thus, each visual narrative performs only part of the act and stories are created within stories. The larger the carving surface, and the more surfaces there are, the more stories are created. By processing from one panel to another, the spectator (the audience) becomes part of the performance in that one has to move (or process) around each panel in a particular way, thus establishing a relationship between the performance (in this case the carvings) and the audience. The enhancement of fire provides both the audience and the performance with the stimulus of creating a visual narrative. This is fundamental if the carvings are to be utilized under night-time conditions. Obviously, the rock carving panels vary in size and form. The more extensive and complex panels can not all be read at once (and therefore understood, if seen as a total design group). Therefore, I would suggest the panels are sub–

divided into smaller, more readable groups or design fields.

The design structure on each panel can depict the following spatial characteristics. Firstly, the central, and in many cases the largest and visually more dominant design, may well be perceived as being the first carving on each panel. Secondly, in all cases, the dominant figure is located centrally on the rock surface. Finally, from the initial design, other secondary designs would have been applied. Each design thereafter could be executed at a specific time. Alternatively, the complete panel could have been commissioned as a single act. This establishes a narrative that is both spatially and sequentially applied.

In order to attempt any interpretation, observation in varying degrees of light, especially during darkness using both available natural and artificial light, is necessary. For instance, the panel narrative becomes the only visible 'body' when direct light falls onto the surface. The availability of an artificial light source appears to transform the rock carving surface into a solitary entity which fixates one's cognitive perception exclusively onto the carvings; everything else behind and at either side of each panel is propelled into darkness. This, above all, creates a rhetoric that is both a visual and symbolic semiotic experience. Whilst in use, during the European Bronze Age, the rhetoric of the art may have been gender encoded or used by particular stratified members/groups within a chieftain/clan society. Similar gender/stratified restrictions are common in many contemporary societies.

The Symbolism of Art as a Social Language

'Art' can be considered as a major communicator between both neighbouring clans and individuals in Aboriginal society. For example, the iconography of the Walbiri portrays clan identity that is structured by a patrilineal system (decent through the male line). The Walbiri occupy an area of semi–arid desert in Northern Australia. Clan festivities and settlement within the clan area are segregated according to gender. Body adornment and clan ceremonies are, according to Munn (1973), divided into four main groups: a) family groups b) women's camps c) men's encampments and d) men's secret groups. Each group possesses a distinct set of rules which usually exclude other groups within the clan. For example, sand stories (pictorial inscriptions made in the sand. Fig. 2) occur only in family and women's encampments, but can be observed by all clan members. This visual narrative, a series of simple, yet symbolic abstract depictions, relates to daily activities such as camp scenes, hunting and foraging. Body painting used in women's camps is more controlled and restrictive. Ceremonies (and body adornment) known as 'Yawalya' allow women to exercise rites over individual designs. Although regarded as trivial by men, these designs are powerful and, above all, confined and exclusive to women. Furthermore, they act as a control for sex, health, child rearing and fertility. Although having a variety of meanings, the design structuring ranges from simple elongated circles to complex multiple designs, each telling a story displaying a cultural scene that involves productivity and growth within

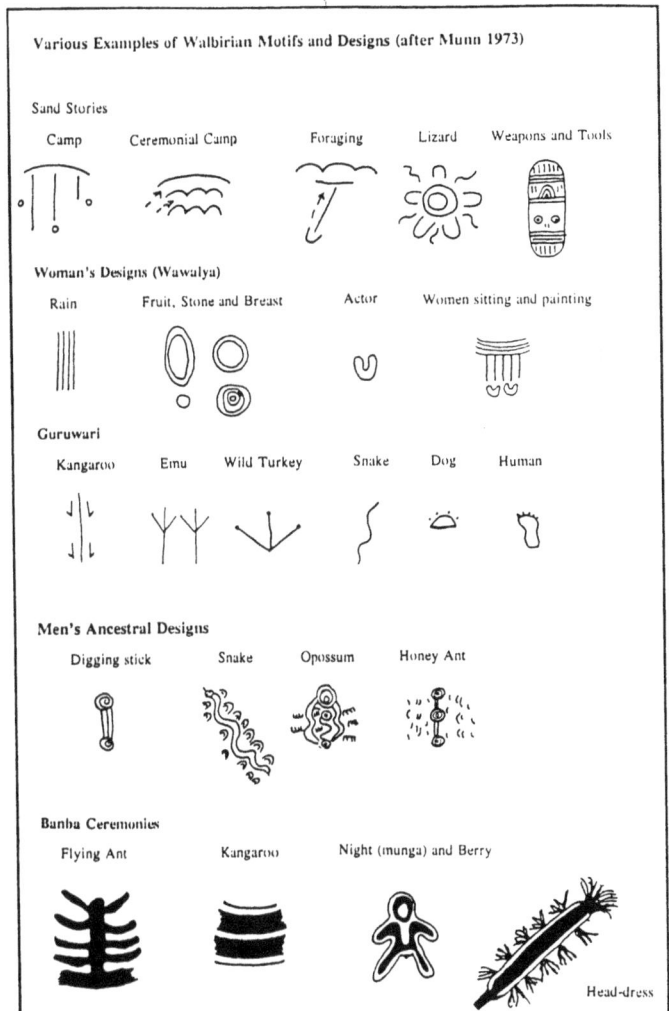

Figure 2.

the clan. The more complex designs depict scenes of food–gathering and eating. Body adornment is also used in men's ceremonies. Designs known as 'Ilbindji' are used to entice and control women. The most secret of Walbirian designs is 'Guarwari'. Used by men in secret ceremonies on the body, headdress decoration and shields. They are also drawn bark–boards. The ceremonies are conducted away from the camps, usually at important ancestral meeting places. Hidden from women, the designs are destroyed after the ceremony, thus making them restrictive and exclusive. Each design is complex and may be allocated to each individual present. The ceremonies can represent a number of special occasions within the Aboriginal calendar, the most important of these being initiation and 'banba' (fertility) rites. Here, boys experience the secrets of the 'Gurawari' and the initiation to manhood. The designs themselves, although personalized, relate to land ownership, territorial rites and relationships with other neighbouring clans. In all cases the designs are revered and considered most powerful. This power, generated from the designs ensures reproduction (fertility), clan bondage and identity.

When drawn onto the body, the designs act as a link between

the individual (the mortal) and the ancestors. The ancestors are derived from dreams which are passed from clansman to clansman. Designs are used to build up pictures (and stories). Each picture, although graphic in structure, can portray a number of aspects concerning ancestral mythology. So the designs do, in fact, create an ambiguity and can be interpreted by different clansmen over long periods of use.

The idea that art may be restrictive or secret can be related to the Galician rock art. The position of each panel within the landscape presents an interesting dichotomy. In one respect, all rock carving panels are above the valley floors. One might assume, therefore, that they are sited in order to be seen. However, due to the fact that much of the intermediate slopes are extensively covered by rock outcrops, the visibility of even the most prominent panels is poor. One must therefore assume that the location is purposely, rather than haphazardly, chosen. If this is so, each panel creates a strategic as well as a symbolic 'statementing' within the landscape. By using the valley slopes for the siting of panels, one is creating a barrier between the mountains which could be regarded as dangerous and mysterious, and the safety, knowledge and familiarity of the valley floor. Furthermore, by locating each site within rocky outcropping, the panels become hidden, commanding a ritual and secret knowledge restricted to certain members of a, by then, well-ordered, stratified and hierarchic society. By positioning each panel in this way, one is imposing a number of symbolic (and political) statements on the landscape; and signifying the link between what is known and what is unknown.

In addition to the restrictions of visual knowledge from the valley floor to the intermediate slope zone, the intervisibility of each panel is also restrictive. Many of the more complex sites appear to be hidden away on secluded ridges or, in the case of the Fentans group, on a high valley plateau. The only direct intervisibility is between the panels at Canada (4a and 4b) and Paredes (3a, 3b and 3c). Inter-panel visibility appears to be the most obvious feature pertaining to site identity, especially within a landscape whereby one rock outcrop is similar to another. All panels within a site group are visible.

The rock carvings at Paredes (3a, 3b & 3c), Parada (5a & 5b) and Fentans (6a, 6b, 6c, 6d & 6e) are positioned in order of design complexity. For example, the concentric circles and animal designs at Fentans 6a and 6b are on surfaces overlooking Fentans 6c and 6d. Although all the panels possess both animals, anthropomorphic figures and complex concentric circles, the more complex panels are sited only on one side of the valley plateau. All five panels face towards the northern part of Campo Lameiro valley. None of the surfaces is orientated towards another. The position of the rock carving surfaces appears to suggest that these act as processional territorial makers, either for the performance of ceremonial rites of passage between the panels or, more plausibly, as a termination point for animal herding (with the possible incorporation of hunting magic). Both would have involved the symbolic and ritual movement and control of space.

Semiotics of Performance and Display: A Theoretical Perspective

Many analogies have been drawn between prehistoric art and the various art forms of contemporary non-western hunter/gatherer societies. Recently, Tilley (1994) has applied the cosmology of North-West Territories Aborigines to the phenomenology of landscape, with reference to the siting of megalithic monuments in south-west Wales and the Black Mountains. Other contemporary analogies have focused upon the Mbuti pigmies, the !Kung (San) Bush people (Lewis-Williams 1989) and North-West American Coastal Indians (Levi-Strauss 1962). Arguably, this approach is convenient in that it detracts from the problems of a limited artifact assemblage.

One of the main themes which this paper covers is the idea that the application and use of rock art is bound up within a wider ritual performance. This approach represents not only the performance itself, but other components, such as dress, gesture, song, place and oral tradition. However, can performance be related to the *act* of carving/painting, and is this act part of the performance? Both painting and carving on portable and static surfaces used in many contemporary non-western hunter/gatherer societies are bound up in ritual and symbolism, despite the fact that these acts consume large amounts of time and energy. They do, nevertheless, form part of a complex socio-symbolic unit. Other forms of visual expression, too, are treated in the same way, for example, dance, drama, mime, poetry and song. These forms of visual expression involve social, political and religious organisation. Within most tribal societies, this organisation is controlled by one person and conforms to a series of strict rules. Each act within the performance is bound up in ritual. Munn (1977, 1983) recognises a symbolic process in the preparation, construction and exchange of (Gawa) canoes on the island of Kiriwana in the Trobriand Islands, Melanesia. Munn refers to each of these construction phases as a 'conversion plane'. At each stage the canoe changes its form, shape, identity and symbolic meaning, from the initial felling of the tree (the natural) through to production (the raw material) to initial exchange of the canoe (maker to user) and eventually on to the (Kula) main exchange system. Likewise, the preparation, application and adoption involved in applying paint or of carving onto a static surface may be regarded as a series of conversion planes. At each stage, the nature of the design, the surface and the artist may change.

Changes to the Rock Panel

The Conversion Plane (adapted from Munn 1977)

1. Rock surface (the natural)

2. Preparing the surface (the synthetic)

Liminal Space {

3. Application to the surface (humanising the surface)

4. Use and reuse of the surface (creating a history)

Leroi–Gourhan (1968) has suggested initiation rites may have played an important role in the execution of Palaeolithic cave art. Young boys may have undergone 'rites of passage' into manhood via a liminal space (i.e. chosen areas of the cave) during production of a cave painting. Marshank (1975) argues that social stratification within the cave is required in order for the cave wall designs to be fully understood. Liminal space would be located away from the main habitation areas – usually deep within the passage system. Not surprisingly, there is a wealth of Palaeolithic cave art within these areas. For example, at the cave of Pech Merle, Cabrerets, Lot in south–western France, Leroi-Gourhan (1968) recognised the painted designs were sequentially structured according to location. The paintings portray a wide range of subjects, mainly segregated according to animal type. Mammoth designs are located at least 1000 metres away from the cave entrance, within a large cavern. Bear, too, were painted deeper within the cave system – approximately 1100 metres from the entrance. Other caves appear to be organised in a similar way. Leroi-Gourhan (ibid.) concluded that mammoth, bison, horse and hand prints occupied the central part of the system; while bear, humans, chamois (wild goat), reindeer and red deer were located in the peripheral zones. Each of these areas was well away from the main occupation areas. Within the liminal space, a state of *limbo* would have existed while each participant, neither boy nor man, produced the 'art'. Again, the performance – the initiation – is segregated into three distinct 'planes'; boy – *limbo* – man.

So too, execution of the art: the virgin surface, the sketched design and finally, the painting. As the painting nears completion, so the painter approaches adulthood. Both the artist and the art 'come of age'. As stated earlier, they create and establish history.

With reference to tribal ritual, each element of performance, when integrated with other components, creates an homogenous whole. Each motif becomes part of an overall deign sequence. However, can any one of these individual components, such as dance, prose or gesture, constitute a performance? Bowra (1962:51) outlines a chronology of performance. He suggests 'rhythmical action' precedes words. Sensory expression, created through the movement of dance, gesture or simple chanting, could well have been enough to constitute an 'event'. The absence of scale and landscape on rock carvings may establish a semi–visual (restrictive) language. Semi–abstract stylistic anthropomorphs and geometric forms are present alongside complex naturalistic representative designs on a number of the Campo Lamireo panels. Absent from the panels however, is landscape – is this yet another necessary omission? Similar to the absence of words during performance, visual coding on rock art is important in the transmission of messages/meanings to certain people. Messages and meanings created (*written*) by artists and performers alike appear to portray control. The audience, the attendance, the congregation and the voyeur alike can only observe. Therefore, reading, comprehension and visual experience can be the only input. Each element constitutes an experience for both the performer and the audience. The omission of any

one element compels the audience to create their own personal experience, similar to that of the encounter with theatre – the audience creates its own narrative, its own scenario, its heroes and villains. Each narrative requires syncopation and the element of surprise. This relies upon timing. Each actor (a single component) forms part of the performance, so, for the audience, timing is important. The actors, although being part of, and playing to the audience, nevertheless, form a metaphysical space between what is mundane and what is special (and supernatural). The manipulation of masks, make–up and dress exaggerate and extenuate the detachment of the zones of audience and performance. The actor is no longer a mere mortal, he/she/it has become different, immortal, divine and godlike. Bowra remarks

"they are witnessing something which belongs to a different order of being"

(1962:53)

Syncopation and Rhythm

I have so far discussed the importance of dance as part of a complex performance package. Associated with dance is music, poetry (prose), chanting and body rhythm. All are bound–up with ceremonial ritual activity. But what of daily life? It would appear that even the most mundane tasks are bound up in ritual and symbolism. The majority of tasks rely on visuality and audibility. Paula Brown (1978:49–51) has highlighted the social and ritual importance of body and dress–decoration within the highland tribal groups (the Telefomin, Star Mountain and Balin Valley areas) of central Papua New Guinea and Irian Jaya (Indonesia). Male body-decoration in the form of tattooing is more exaggerated and is strategically placed over the body to establish rank and position within the group. Dress and body–piercing, too, create visual ranking. Brown (ibid.) suggests only the public areas of the body are treated in this way, the body acting as a signifier to communicate social position – a public message. This message is semiotic. Here, a visual language, including body–gesture is applied, replacing the language of speech (Barthes 1967: 25). Equally, these signs are prevalent during ceremonial dance and ritual display. They, along with armbands, legbands, neck bands, wigs, feathered head-dresses and ornamental necklaces made of shell, bone, pig's tusk, dog's teeth, snake's skin, leaves, flowers and fern, form part of a complex visual package. Barthes (ibid. 27) distinguishes this as costume and not clothing. Costume semiotically represents a language, while clothing represents speech. It would appear that subtle idiosyncratic differences exist between the two. Obviously, one could argue that the differences dependent upon the intensity of visual display, in that language is more prominent in costume than clothing. Messing (1960:558–60) has suggested that a language of gesture exists within the way in which clothes are worn. 'The non–verbal language of the Ethiopian toga' explores how the toga (*shamma*) creates a series of expressions which project messages from the wearer to the onlooker. The way in which the *shamma* is worn determines rank and status.

Equally, Saussure (1916 [1966] – *Course in General Linguistics*) suggests there is a distinct difference between language and speech. Language is a collective discourse that is recognisable between individuals. Underlying language, is a set of well–defined and universally familiar rules. For instance, nodding one's head to say 'yes' (affirmative) or shaking the head from side to side indicating 'no' (negative) generally crosses the barrier of speech. Barthes (1967) uses the garment systems. Here, garments can either complement other garments or oppose them. Although a coat is a coat, a raincoat possesses a different meaning and application from a waistcoat. One can therefore see a difference between, say, complex concentric circles, simple circles and cupmarks.

The replication of certain designs, in particular concentric circles or red deer indicates a possible set of universal rules – language. The way in which these are applied to the panel may indicate a speech. By speech, I refer to the way in which certain designs are arranged – a type of 'hieroglyphic' language (e.g. musical notes). Language and speech are inextricably linked. Tilley writes that material culture (in this case, rock carvings from Nämforsen, northern Sweden) articulates a language, or more precisely, a speech (based on a generative language). He states

'So far I have made the basic point that material culture, speech and writing all share the same qualities but that communication through speech is more direct. They involve different transformations of the same materialist practice of spacing, differentiation, articulation. In other words all these practices are structured in precisely the same way through breaking up space, creating and establishing difference, articulating and rearticulating units'.

(1991:16)

Tilley also discusses rock art as a book with pages (1991:29). He attempts to read it. Tilley becomes the onlooker, the audience, and places his own personal interpretation on it. However, is the reader qualified to make the correct interpretation? One could argue that *art is ambiguous*. The text is constructed by the audience. If this is the case, does the artist, the performer, convey the message he/she wants? Tilley's paradigm, a systematic 'visual' requirement by the onlooker, establishes a receiver–only approach. If a general language of symbols, signs and images is being conveyed by the artist, then the audience need make no personal interpretation. Nevertheless, Tilley does re–address the problem of the meaning/ understanding of certain non–recognisable images. Can we as onlookers (archaeologists) read the (Tilley's) full text. The answer must be 'no'! For example, Hallström (1938) recognises nearly 2100 figures on the Nämforsen panels. Of these, 370 cannot be fully identified. Therefore 17.6% of the text is missing – the narrative is incomplete, it cannot be fully read. Can a crime book be fully understood, if the plot is missing? Like the plot, images on the rock panel may have been either completely destroyed, vandalised, defaced or they may lie undiscovered.

This approach is all well and good if the art is executed at one point in time. However, what of 'art' that is performed as a series of events. Indeed, what of 'art' that is executed on the same panel surface over an extensive period of time when possibly the social, economic and symbolic ideology may have changed? Here, can the meaning stand the test of time? Is the narrative, the performance at any moment in time transmitting different meanings? If so, then panel designs may confuse and distract the onlooker. I, as art prehistorian, can only hypothesise of the meaning rock art, I create my own narrative. In order to make each panel (the narrative) flow, a structured grammar of designs must be present (Bowra 1962). The presence of grammar, plus changes in meaning over time, establish a structured history. Not surprisingly, the older the panel and the greater the number of changes in style and form, the more 'history' the panel creates. Likewise, portable art too can create its own history.

For example, a history is formed from shell armlets (*mwari*) and necklaces (*soulava*) which circulate within the 'Kula' exchange system around the Trobriand Islands, Melanesia. First observed by Malinowski in 1922, and later discussed by Campbell (1983:229–247) and Weiner (1983: 147–170, 1989), each jewellery component – the cowrie shell (*buna*), the string (*utuna*) and black banana seeds (*botoboto*) – forms part of a complex and powerful display. As exchange items circulate, they begin to acquire a history. They are regarded as more valuable the longer they remain in circulation (Mauss 1923). Exchange however, is not the only mechanism present; there is also a need to establish power relations among (male) participants (Weiner 1983). Apart from exchange meetings, 'kula' gifts are on full display during ceremonial ritual activities. It would appear that the control, manipulation and display of 'history' establishes individual power, as well as group (tribal/clan) authority. However, during ceremonial festivities, in particular, organised dance, when group cohesion is at its strongest, there exists a contradiction and accompanying this, an isolated rhetoric, in that individual performers are signifying themselves as 'power players'. There emerges a need to create disharmony and individual isolation within the group. This takes the form of a narrative, usually between the forces of good and evil; powerful participants usually act out these roles. Likewise, the components that make Kula valuables, establish a narrative, a history, and 'plays' on purity, magic and structured opposition, usually between male and female. Colour–symbolism is crucial for each component. Campbell (1983: 229–247) has recognised body–symbolism as being paramount when a necklace or armlet is made. The criteria for a successful exchange are based, not only upon colour, but also upon texture, weight, size, number of components and age. Campbell (ibid.) has stated that both *'vaiguwa'* and *'mwari'* are gender–encoded (men wear armlets, women necklaces). On a more complex level, the components that make up *'mwari'* and *'vaiguwa'* are symbolically encoded. *'Mwari'* components symbolically and metaphorically reproduce parts of the male body, while *'vaiguwa'* manipulates tree terminology. The use of tree terminology corresponds with the fact that most of the components derive from plants, for example, black banana seeds (*'botoboto'*).

The terminology used for *mwari*, although pertaining to the body, does in fact focus mainly on male body parts. The frontal edge of the *'mwari'* shell is referred to as *'pwala'* or testicles. Each component on *'mwari'* and *'vaiguwa'* is named, ranked and possesses a personal history. The number of *'bunakudula'* (small cowrie shells) suspended around the 'dabala' (forehead) determines the status and rank of both the owner and the shell valuable. The more shells present, the greater the rank and history (up to six *'bunakadala'* may be suspended, and added to over time). Likewise, additions noted by Hallström [Norway] (1938) and, more recently, Beltrán [Levantine Spain] (1982:24) and Nash [Sweden] (1996) reveal a series of rock carving and painting panels possessing a history. All three regions show changes in style and design, repainting (in different colours) and alteration to motifs, in particular, zoomorphic designs. Likewise, additions visible on the Laxe da Rotea de Mende (2) show at least two clear changes in design/ideology. The transmission of change is seen with the defacement of earlier naturalistic zoomorphic carvings by small geometric designs. The two sets of designs show no direct symmetrical composition. However, when separated, a design sequence becomes more probable. One can argue that the new designs are merely an act of vandalism towards the 'old order'. However, one can say also that both sets of designs are creating a chronology, an historical sequence that establishes a beginning (the original carving), a middle (the point of transition) and an ending (the act of defacement). Defacement of the 'old order' appears to be a unique act within the panel assemblage of Galicia. In producing new rock art, it would seem more obvious to carve on a new rock surface than on an older 'used' surface. One can possibly see a chronological build-up of designs on a series of panels, rather than on the same panel. Although the defacement of earlier (or later) abstract geometrics does not superimpose the zoomorphic designs, the artist(s) appears to be creating harmony rather than dominance.

Performance and Rock Art: Construction and Use

Bowra (1962:28–36) has recognised a similar construction to the art of ritual performance using the media of song and dance. Many of the ideas concerning repetition, melody and harmonisation may be applied to the overall (sequential) design-structuring of rock art. For example, rock art, dance and song used in contemporary hunter/gatherer societies incorporate a beginning, a middle and an end (the narrative). In addition, both sets of media also possess a series of structured repetitions. Repetition allows the composition to flow. The more simple the repetition, the more recognisable the song becomes. Simple repetitive tunes are also easier to pass down to later generations. The simple repetitive rhythm can, however, contain complex prose and elaborate syncopation. It is these components, and not the rhythm, that change through time (Bowra 1962). The sequential designs incorporated onto the Galician panels are also repetitive. They, too, change their morphology over time, but not their overall structure. Elaboration occurs according to the ranking of designs, geographic location and panel positioning (see above). Individual designs, although simplistic, do, nevertheless, create a complex picture. Usually, the panel

structuration is organised in a linear form. Each design is fluid, in that it may be adapted and added to over time.

At the carved panel of De Laxe de Rotea de Mendo (Plate 3), within the northern reaches of the Campo Lameiro Valley, two female deer are positioned between the antlers of the stag, the largest and most dominant design of the panel. Within this assemblage, female deer are, in all cases, present alongside stags. They appear in groups of three, usually below or at the side of larger stags. The positioning of the two female deer may imply possible herding, control or possession. Indeed, the ambiguity of such designs may well indicate the social control within Bronze Age society itself. Similar sequential structuring involving red deer exists elsewhere. This probably includes structural opposition, whereby animals represent humans or, importantly, gender (Tilley 1991).

Bowra (1962) outlines a series of rules concerning the various components used to construct tribal dance, song and poetry. The melodic/harmonic components, along with rhythmical prose, establish a rhetoric encompassing the whole group. This act, above all, establishes group cohesion and bonding. It binds men with women, and juveniles with adults. Song, dance and prose are accomplished by a recognised repetitious melody. Many songs are performed with instruments, in particular drums (percussion), string and wind. This set of instruments has been adapted by many hunter/gatherer societies, especially, Australian Aborigines, Kalahari bush-people (!Kung), north-west Coastal (Canada) Indian groups and Arctic Eskimos. Singing is usually accompanied by dance. Both the rhythmical sounds (achieved by accented song) and drums harmonise (syncopation) with dancing. In addition to singing and instrumental accompaniment, supporting actions, such as the clapping of hands, stamping of feet and chanting, add to the overall parody. Thereby a 'theatre of performance' is in operation. The performance usually takes the form of a story and involves a select or chosen strand within the tribal group. Social and political stratification, as well as gender encoding, are the primary traits underlying performance needs.

Dance not only involves the movement of the body but may also embrace facial and body gesture. The men of the Wodaabe nomads from southern Niger (Sahel) celebrate former births and marriages through dance (*yaake* and *geerewol* dances). The *geerewol* dance usually takes place in front of prospective female partners. Men are judged on how 'beautiful' they are (Maybury-Lewis 1992:104). In order to attract the right girl, facial gesture is of paramount importance (van Offelen 1983:483). The whiteness of teeth and eyes, plus a shaved hairline, are the main deciding factors. Secondary to facial gesture are head-dress (Turban), jewellery, dress and make-up. These may be regarded as enhancements to the act. Eyes, teeth and forehead are refined with strategic make-up around the chin, cheeks and bridge of the nose. Make-up achieves 'a complete look'. Young women will watch the performance from a given distance, outside a ring of dancers. Only the most 'beautiful' men can compete in the more powerful dance, the *geerewol*, and are judged by unmarried women – who, in turn, have been chosen for their 'loveliness'. They too, perform subtle facial gestures, usually by using their eyes in 'scrutinising glances'. Male participants, in order to hold the girls' attention, will contort their faces, exposing more vigorously their teeth, chin and eyes.

The ritual of dance using facial gesture is indeed complex. The face is the main focal point of the body. Art, although static, draws upon many of the codes of display. One can see that the prime reason for display is harmonisation – the need to belong, the need to be identified. Rock art creates an identity for the artist, the user and group as a whole. Art distinguishes the group from other groups and establishes regionality. Cultural regionality is evident, with identical designs present throughout Galicia. The high concentration of rock painting panels from the Campo Lameiro Valley and the coastal plains, west of Pontevedra, appear to display similar clan/group affinities. The representation, particularly identical designs of red deer and concentric circles, is replicated throughout. Themes appear to share a stylistic and sequential structural affinity with neighbouring panels. The figures and designs are all of a standardised form, e.g. barbed antlers, female red deer between male deer antlers and multiple circles. The artists' pecking is both simple and well–orchestrated and suggests an impressionistic approach to at least four panels within the upper valley sequence. But

why replication? One could argue that panels, certainly within the upper valley, were commissioned by the same artist. Alternatively, the designs may represent clan identity and were shared by a number of artists (a 'school') within the clan/tribal group.

The Performers–Humans, Deer, Spirals and Cupmarks

By far the most impressive sites include panels possessing both humans and red deer. In many cases, these designs are accompanied by large, complex spiral designs (or concentric circles). Spirals are always positioned just above deer and it could be argued they are dominant over them (in particular stags). Characteristically, stylised stags possess, in all cases, inverted barbed antlers (on panels 2, 3c, 5b, 6a and 6d). The stags from these five surfaces are standardised in both style and form, suggesting a possible chronological continuity in rock carving technique. The stags and hinds may represent a structural opposition, whereby deer represent humans. At the rock carving site at Namforsen in north–east Sweden, Tilley (1991) has suggested similar oppositions. Here, boats and elk symbolise both male and female respectively. By engendering animals in this way, duality is created between male/female and deer/humans. Moreover, the animal becomes more than just a provider of meat, it acts and performs human emotions. By utilising the panels at night, such performances become part of these emotions.

Appendix 1
Presence/Absence of Designs on each Panel

Designs	1a	2a	3a	3b	3c	4a	4b	5a	5b	6a	6b	6c	6d
Humans		X	X+						X	X *		X	
Animals	X? *	X *	X+		X *		X *	X *	X *	X	X *	X *	X *
Concentric		X				X *	X *	X	X	X	X	X	X
Cupmarks				X		X	X	X	X	X	X	X	
Hoofprints										X			
Dagger										X			
Wheeled Cross		X							X				

* Denotes the dominant/central design or figure on each panel
? The figure from this panel, a large snake has questionable origins. It has been suggested that it is contemporary to other designs within the valley
+ At Parades 3A, the central design is of a horse and rider

Appendix 2
Panel and Site Intervisibility

	1*	2a	3a	3b	3c	4a	4b	5a	5b	6a	6b	6c	6d
1*		-	-	-	-	X	X	-	-	-	-	-	-
2a	-		-	-	-	-	-	-	-	-	-	-	-
3a	-	-		X	X	X	X	-	-	-	-	-	-
3b	-	-	X		X	X	X	-	-	-	-	-	-
3c	-	-	X	X		X	X	-	-	-	-	-	-
4a	X	-	X	X	X		X	-	-	-	-	-	-
4b	X	-	X	X	X	X		-	-	-	-	-	-
5a	-	-	-	-	-	-	-		X	-	-	-	-
5b	-	-	-	-	-	-	X			-	-	-	-
6a	-	-	-	-	-	-	-	-		X	X	X	
6b	-	-	-	-	-	-	-	-	X		X	X	
6c	-	-	-	-	-	-	-	-	X	X		X	
6d	-	-	-	-	-	-	-	-	X	X	X		

* The single snake figure at Penalba is of questionable origin. It is believed that this figure dates from either the Late Iron Age or Early Middle Ages

Acknowledgements

This paper is the result of a visit to Galicia in August 1992. In the company of Christopher Tilley, I spent many long hours visiting the sites and sampling the local wine. I would like to thank Tim Yeats for his comments and, above all, encouragement in writing this paper.

Bibliography

Anati, E. (1964) 'The rock–carvings of Pedra das Ferraduras at Fentans (Pontevedra)', in Ripoll (ed.) *Miscelanea and homenage al Abate Henri Breuil (1877–1961) Tomo I*, 123–35.

Anati, E. (1976) *Evolution and Style in Camunan rock art*, Capo de Ponte: Centro Camuno di studi Preistorici.

Barthes, R. (1977) *Image–Music–Text*, London. Fortana. (Translated by S.Heath).

Beltrán, A. (1982) *Rock Art of the Spanish Levant*. Cambridge. Cambridge University Press.

Bowa, C.M. (1962) *Primitive Song*. London. Wiedenfeld & Nicolson.

Bowra, C.M. (1962) *Primitive Song*, 28–56. Weidenfeld & Nicolson, London.

Bradley, R. (1993) *Altering the Earth*, the 1992 Rhind Lectures, Society of antiquaries of Scotland Monograph Series No.8, 22–44.

Bradley, R., Criado Boado, F. & Fadregas Valcarce, R. (1994) 'Rock art research as landscape archaeology: a pilot study in Galicia, north–west Spain' in *World archaeology* Volume 25, No.3 374–390.

Brown, P. (1978) *Highland Peoples of New Guinea*. Cambridge. Cambridge University Press.

Campbell, S. F. (1983). Attaining Rank: A classification of Kula Exchange Valuables in J. W. Leach & E. R. Leach (eds), *The Kula: New Perspectives on Massin Exchange*, 229–247. Cambridge. Cambridge University Press.

Criado Boado, F. & Penedo Romero, R. (1993) 'Art, time and thought: a formal study comparing Palaeolithic and postglacial art'. *World Archaeology Vol. 25 No.2*.

Hallström, G. (1938) *Monumental Art of the Stone Age in Northern Europe 1*. Stockholm.

Leach, E. R & Leach, J. W. (eds). (1983). *The Kula: New Perspectives on Mass in Exchange*. Cambridge. Cambridge University Press.

Leroi-Gourhan, A. (1982) *The Dawn of European Art: An Introduction to Palaeolithic Cave Painting*: Cambridge. Cambridge University Press.

Levi-Strauss, C. (1962) *Totemism*, (Translated by R.Needham). London. Penguin Press.

Lewis–Williams, J.D. (1983) *The Rock Art of Southern Africa*. Cambridge. Cambridge University Press.

Lewis–Williams, J.D. (1989) 'Southern Africa's place in the archaeology of human understanding' *Suid–Afrikaanse Tydskrif vir Wetenkap*, Vol.85. 47–52.

Lopez Cuevillas, F. (1943) 'Las inscultures del "Outeiro da Cruz"', *Boletin del Museo Arqueológico Provinvial*, Vol. 1. 95–101.

Lopez Cuevillas, F. (1951) 'La clasificasión tipológica del arte rupestre del noroeste hispánico y una hipótesis sobre la cronología de alguno de sus tipos' *Zaphyrus* Vol. 11. 73–81.

Mauss, M. (1990) *The Gift: The Form and Reason for Exchange in Archaic Societies*, London (reprint) Routledge. Translated by W.D. Halls.

Munn, N. (1963) 'The Walbiri Sand Story' *Australian Territories* 3, 37–44.

Munn, N. (1973) *Walbirian Iconography*, Cambridge. Cambridge University Press.

Munn, N. (1976). The Spatiotemporal transformations of Gawa Canoes. *Journal de la societe des Oceanistes No 3*, 39–53.

Munn, N. (1983). Gawan Kula: Spatiotemporal control and the symbolism of influence in J. W. Leach & E. R Leach (eds). *The Kula: New Perspectives on Massin Exchange*, 277–307. Cambridge. Cambridge University Press.

Nash, G.H. (1993) 'Symbols in Space: Rock Carvings of the Campo Lameiro Region, Southern Galicia, Spain'. *Unpublished paper* presented at TAG conference held at the University of Durham, 14th–17th December 1993.

Nash, G. H. & Yeats, T. (1995) *'The Culbone Stone: Christian Icon or Prehistoric Symbol'?* Unpublished.

Nash, G.H. (1995b) *The Landscape Brought Within: A Re-evalluation of the Rock Painting Site at Tumleshed, Torslanda, Goteborg, West Sweden*. Megalith and Social Geography Symposium Transactions, Falkoping, Central Sweden

Nash, G.H. (1996a) 'The symbolism and mechanisms for island–mainland interaction: doing Kula in the Danish Mesolithic' in K.Brown & M.Patton (eds.) *The Archaeology of Islands*: Oxford. BAR International Series.

Nash, G.H. (1996b) *A Structural Analysis of Decorated Mesolithic Artifacts from Denmark*: Oxford. BAR International Series.

Obermaier, H. (1925) 'Die bronzezeitlichen Felzgravierungen von Nordwest Spanien (Galicien)', *IPEK*.

Pera Santos, A. & Vazquez Varela, J.M. (1979) *Los Petroglifos Gallegos*, La Coruna: Edicios do Castro.

Phelan, P. (1993) *Unmarked: The Politics of Performance*, London. Routledge.

Sobrino Buhigas, R. (1935) *Corpus Petroglyphorum Gallaeciae* Seminario de Estudos Galegos, Santiago de Compostela.

Sobrino Lorenzo Ruza, R. (1952) 'Origen de los petroglyphos gallegos atlanticos', *Zephyrus*, Vol. III, 125–49. Salamanca.

Sobrino Lorenzo Ruza, R. (1956) 'Ensayo sobre los motivos de discos solares en los petroglifos gallegos atlanticos', *Zephyrus*, Vol. III, 11–19. Salamanca.

Tilley, C. (1991) *Material Culture as Text: The Art of Ambiguity*, London. Routledge.

Tilley, C. (1994) *A Phenomenology of Landscape: Places, Paths and Monuments*, Oxford. Berg.

Vazquez Seijas, M. (1945a) 'Aportacion a la Provincia de Lugo al Corpus Petroglyphorum Gallaeciae', *Boletin de la Comision Provincial de Monumentos*

Historicos y Artisticos de lugo, Vol. II, 75–81. Lugo.

Yeats, T. (1991) *The Writing Machine: Rock Art and the Concept of the Body in the Bronze Age of Goteborgs och Bohus Lan, Sweden,* Cambridge University. Unpublished Thesis.

Plate 1. The Campo Lameiro Valley looking north.

Plate 2. Parades - Horse and rider - Image of the Bronze Age.

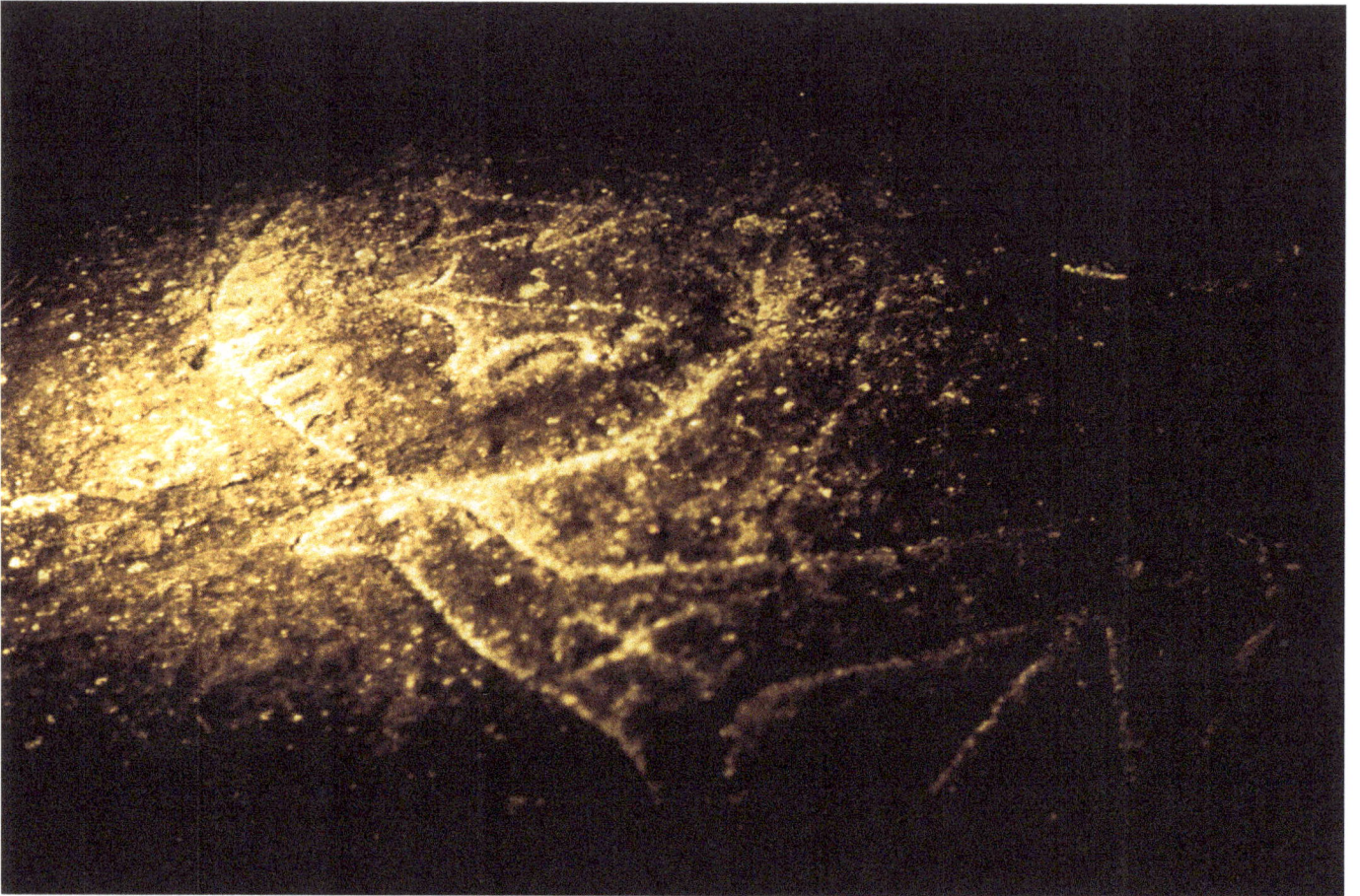

Plate 3. De Laxe de Rotea de Mendo - Male stag and female red deer.

Plate 4. Fentans - Concentric circles and red deer.

Towards a Phenomenology of Building: the Neolithic Long Mound at La Commune–Sèche, Colombiers–sur–Seulles, Normandy

Trevor Kirk
Department of Archaeology
Trinity College, Carmarthen

The act of building: constructing monuments, society and subjectivity in Neolithic Normandy

Throughout the twentieth century the Neolithic monuments of Atlantic Europe have been variously interpreted in terms of cultural diffusion (Childe 1925), processualist reconstruction of social structure, economy and territorality (Renfrew 1973, Chapman 1981), the identification of deep–seated structuring principles (Hodder 1984) and the mediation of Neolithic power relations (Tilley 1984). Though far from an exhaustive summary of the interpretive frameworks applied to date, all of the above approaches view the act of building as an index of technological capacity which is realised through the application of social, cultural or economic convention. Technology in this sense implies the exercise of either human will or cultural codes upon material resources in order to effect a result which is beneficial to the individual, interest group or society. The benefits of technology may be plural and shifting and may variously accrue within the fields of economic practice, social relations or political and ideological power. For example, a tomb may be used to symbolise and mediate territorial claims, to legitimate social inequalities among the living or to negotiate cosmological relationships between the living and the dead. Though previous interpretive approaches to Neolithic monuments differ in the accent which they lay upon ethnicity, ecology, societal systems, cultural codes or power relations there is a tendency for all to adopt a Cartesian standpoint which presupposes an independence of human consciousness and action from the material and social world in which people live. In this view people in the past adopted positions of detachment from the world, objectively assessing possibilities for shaping the material and cultural world. Appropriate courses of action were selected through reference to established frameworks of knowledge. The relationship of people with the world is understood to be an epistemological one; one grounded in people's detached knowing of the world. In this paper I wish to adopt a different position which takes as its starting point Heidegger's proposal that technology and in particular the act of building entails *involvement* with the world rather than detachment from it (Heidegger 1977a and 1977b). Technology (*techné*) arises from audition and response between people and the material world. Technology is a bringing–forth (*poesis*) of possibilities which arises from the mutual recursive interactions between people, their peers and materiality (Heidegger 1977a, 293–4; Gosden 1994, 109; Foucault 1986).

I hope that this paper will contribute to the development of a phenomenology of building within archaeological interpretation (Richards 1993, Thomas 1993, n.d., Tilley 1994). I shall use a detailed case study, the construction of the Commune–Sèche Neolithic long mound in Normandy to examine the act of building as a form of technology which entails more than an imposition of conscious thought upon the material world. Rather, building and thinking are inseparably bound to one another within the human practice of *dwelling* or *Being–in–the–world*:

> Building and thinking are, each in its own way, inescapable from dwelling. The two, however, are also insufficient for dwelling so long as each busies itself with its own affairs in separation instead of listening to one another. They are able to listen if both – building and thinking – belong to dwelling, if they remain within their limits and realize that the one as much as the other comes from the workshop of long experience and incessant practice
>
> (Heidegger 1977b, 338–339)

To think and to form an understanding of the world demands a unity of mind, emotion, memory, perception, bodily movement, action and materiality. People and materiality inhabit history; they carry forward and constitute themselves in relation to biographies replete with the dispositions of *habitus* (Bourdieu 1977), an awareness of personal and group history, and a repertoire of meanings arising from actions which have already taken place within locales. Both people and places develop biographies. A person's experience of places, things and human relationships lies at the heart of her/his identity. The biography of a place arises from the actions, experiences, perceptions and interpretations of people who inhabit, have inhabited or will inhabit that space. The constitution of place and identity therefore lies in the co–presence of people and place, in the sentient experience of place by people (Merleau–Ponty 1962). Human action embraces the material world, internalising landscape and resources in the process of subjective constitution. Modelling archaeological residues as a detached record of human action should, in my view, be replaced by an appreciation of the unity of agency and materiality in the historically–located constitution of both the human condition and landscape (Barrett 1994, Patrik 1985, Tilley 1994). As against the Cartesian *union* (the coming together) of subject and object, humanity and the material world are a single and inseperable *unity* (Kwant 1963, 13). Neither humanity nor materiality exists outside of the dialectic in which they are mutually constituted. People not only produce meanings that illuminate and lend order to the world but human identity and subjectivity are in part constituted in the encounter through which the world becomes known.

Towards a biography of place: La Commune–Sèche Neolithic long mound, Normandy

In this paper I shall investigate the Commune–Sèche Neolithic long mound as both the medium and outcome of successive actions through which place, subjectivity and social relations were constructed, contested, reproduced and transformed (Kinnes 1975, Evans 1988, Bender 1993, Tilley 1994). The locale presents a range of potentialities on which people may have drawn and, in the process, imbued the locale with meaning and also situated and defined the relationship of the subject to the landscape and society (Tuan 1978). As the locale was rethought and remodelled, so the possibilities of human involvement with that locale were transformed.

The Commune–Sèche long mound occupies a low limestone ridge overlooking the narrow valley of the river Seulles, one of a series of minor river courses transecting the limestone plateau of the Plain of Caen. The trapezoidal cairn measures at least 65 metres in length, from 17 metres to 8 metres in width and survives to a maximum height of 3 metres (Fig. 1). The long mound incorporates one stone–built chamber (a second chamber having been recorded in the nineteenth century – de Caumont 1830). The internal structure of the mound features a series of bays probably demarcated by ephemeral wooden shuttering and each containing a rubble and/or earthen fill which contrasts that of each of its neighbours. It is with the biography of this place that I shall be concerned here.

Building as involvement with the world

The act of building the Commune–Sèche long mound created a new sense of place through the creative re–structuring of cultural meanings already situated within the landscape. The matrix of the mound draws together a variety of materials from different locales within the landscape, locales with associated mythological, cultural, political and economic significance and meaning. Each bay of the mound contains a

fill of rubble and/or earth which is different in character to that of all neighbouring bays (Figure ???). The repertoire of materials effectively comprises:

a) *Turf* – probably derived from the immediate environs and deposited either as a low core at the base of the mound or as turf stacks up to 1.4m in height.

b) *Limestone nodules, blocks and plaquettes* – these three distinct forms of local limestone are either combined within bays or are explicitly sorted to avoid mixing within bays. These limestone elements may also be deposited with or without a soil matrix.

c) *Large limestone slabs* – a non–local material used either in the construction of revetments or conspicuously consumed within the matrix of the mound (for example, Structures 245, 392 and 553).

d) *Alluvial sand* – occurs in only one instance as a lens sealed within the fill of the bay located between Structures 83 and 84.

Using these materials to build the mound manifested the interconnection of people and landscape. The act of selecting material for deposition may have represented a set of original statements generated as people drew creatively upon the myths and meanings associated with the locales from which those materials derive. In this respect the act of building does not seek to establish a universally agreed sense of place, a place from which unambiguous meanings may be

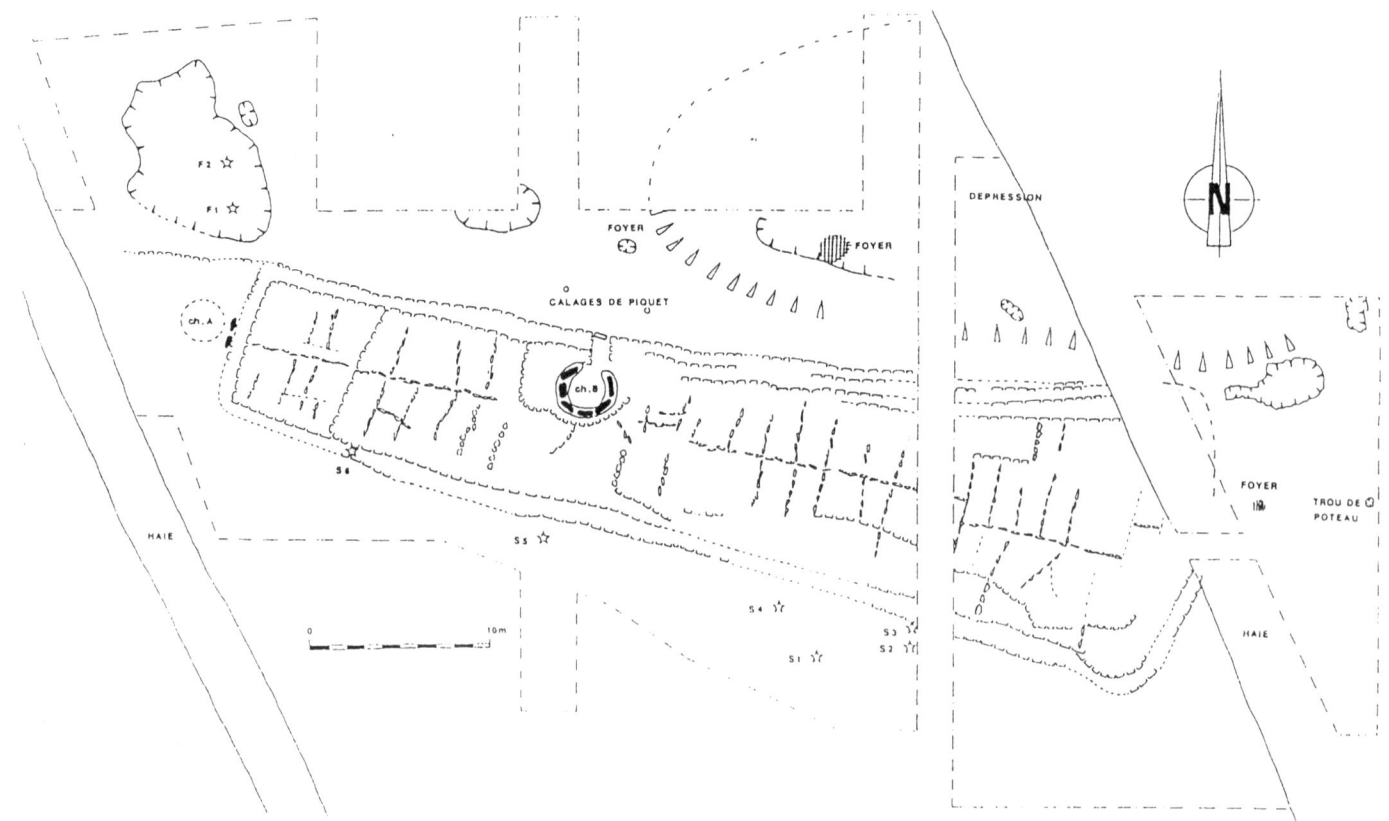

Figure 1. Plan of La Commune–Sèche Neolithic long mound (after Kinnes and Chancerel 1994, figure 2).

read. Rather, people drew upon possibilities of meaning located within the landscape to produce potentially original, even contradictory and conflicting meanings through the act of building. The process might be described as the invocation of existing cultural codes and meanings within the lifeways and actions of individual human agents (Bourdieu 1977, Giddens 1979). This understanding of agency acknowledges the creativity of people and the diversity of agencies (plural) and experiences produced through *being-in-the-world*. MacGregor (1994, 80–82) has recently noted that in many archaeological studies too great an emphasis is placed on the role of routine in the constitution of agency (for example, Leone 1984 and Shanks and Tilley 1987). In this view structuration risks becoming a theory of reproduction which focuses insufficient attention on the ability of people to explore the diverse possibilities for action presented by the physical and social world with which they are involved. I read MacGregor's argument as a call for greater sensitivity to the different experiences, knowledges and understandings produced by the diverse forms of involvement of people with the world. Pursuit of the human agent, a unified and stable subjectivity, might be productively replaced by an exploration of *agencies*, which I take to mean the diversity of actions and meaning produced by people drawing upon different forms of *habitus* and also the fluidity of meaning produced by individuals as their relationships of involvement with the world unfold as they pursue pathways through the social and physical world. Building the Commune–Sèche long mound may have presented people with an opportunity to reaffirm or transform their attachment to the landscape by creating novel forms of engagement with constructional materials (turf, earth, limestone rubble and slabs) and the meanings which they connote. The narrative form of the landscape traditionally experienced as a set of pathways, locales, myths, actions and human relationships was now re-written and re-negotiated in the act of building. This act was, of course, inherently political. As Chris Tilley has recently reminded us,

> The experience of ... places is unlikely to be equally shared and experienced by all, and the understanding and use of them can be controlled and exploited in systems of domination – a consideration strikingly absent in virtually all phenomenological theory and one that constitutes a major theoretical void (Tilley 1994, 26).

The act of building the Commune–Sèche long mound was probably laden with political power–play as claims and counter–claims to knowledge and understanding of the monument were played out through acts of building and perception of the locale. However, we must attempt to clarify here the nature of building as an interlacing of discursive knowledge (tradition, memory, cosmology, ritual) and a practical knowledge of 'how to go on' (bodily movement, perception, involvement with the world) (Bourdieu 1977, Giddens 1979). Turning first to discursive knowledge Barrett (1988, 31; 1994, 77–81) argues that ritual may act as a medium for unifying diverse forms of discursive knowledge to form a dominant reading of the cultural order. Ritual creates 'truths' about the nature of the

social world often through reference to the 'other worlds' of ancestors, spirits and deities. Building La Commune–Sèche might therefore be interpreted as a set of ritual practices invoking traditions, memories and myths about the landscape as inhabited by ancestors and 'other world' spirits. These forms of discursive knowledge are woven together to form a set of dominant though contestable interpretations of the world. However, as Gosden (1994, 88–90) has pointed out the execution of ritual and the formation of dominant readings may be constituted in no small part through non–discursive practices as the physical world is experienced through the sentient body. Indeed building the Commune–Sèche long mound would have entailed the routine adoption of bodily positions and forms of engagement with the physical world through which an understanding of the mound, its constituent materials and their origins and meanings may have been produced. The acts of building discussed in this paper should therefore be seen as the product of an interplay between discursive and non–discursive forms of action and knowledge.

The cultural codes upon which people draw in building, though far from prescriptive, are nonetheless important as they represent personal memories and cultural traditions in relation to which people construct their identities. The act of building the Commune–Sèche long mound is interesting in this respect in that a regular pattern of bays is not only defined but overspill from one bay to another is carefully avoided. As my earlier comments on the nature of agency would suggest there exists no strict grammar whereby the selection of an appropriate fill is determined (turf? limestone nodules? blocks? a combination of materials?) nor a fill's spatial relationships with other fills (should turf be kept separate from limestone?). Rather, building entailed the creative interconnection of people with landscape, tradition and memory. Nonetheless, the regular shape and size of the bays coupled with a strict avoidance of overspill between bays does imply a common set of building principles upon which the community drew. The building project(s) may therefore have acted as a unifying factor occasioned by periods of temporary co–operation between segments of an otherwise fragmented social group (Edmonds 1993, 109–111). Indeed, the biography of La Commune–Sèche may have been constituted through the cycles of seperation and aggregation in which Neolithic groups were probably involved, cycles relating to herding, crop management, hunting, gathering, resources acquisition (water, flint, timber, fuel), ritual and exchange[1].

However, the act of building is ostensibly an act of interpretation. Construction of the Commune–Sèche long mound evoked meanings already located within the locale

---

[1] The generally fragmentary and heterogenous nature of the pot sherds does not imply formalised strategies of structured deposition, though sherds from a single VSG vessel with applied button decoration deposited at the north-west end of the mound may be an exception. The duration of deposition is also open to question. Though VSG and Cerny are traditionally interpreted as chronologically successive post-Bandkeramik cultural groups (Constantin 1985, Constantin and Demoule 1982), no chronological (stratigraphic) relationship can be demonstrated between VSG and Cerny artefact distributions at La Commune–Sèche. However, the recovery of both arefact styles from an homogenous sealed ground surface allows for the contemporary use of both styles. The association of VSG and Cerny artefact styles with distinct socio-cultural groups may not, therefore, be secure.

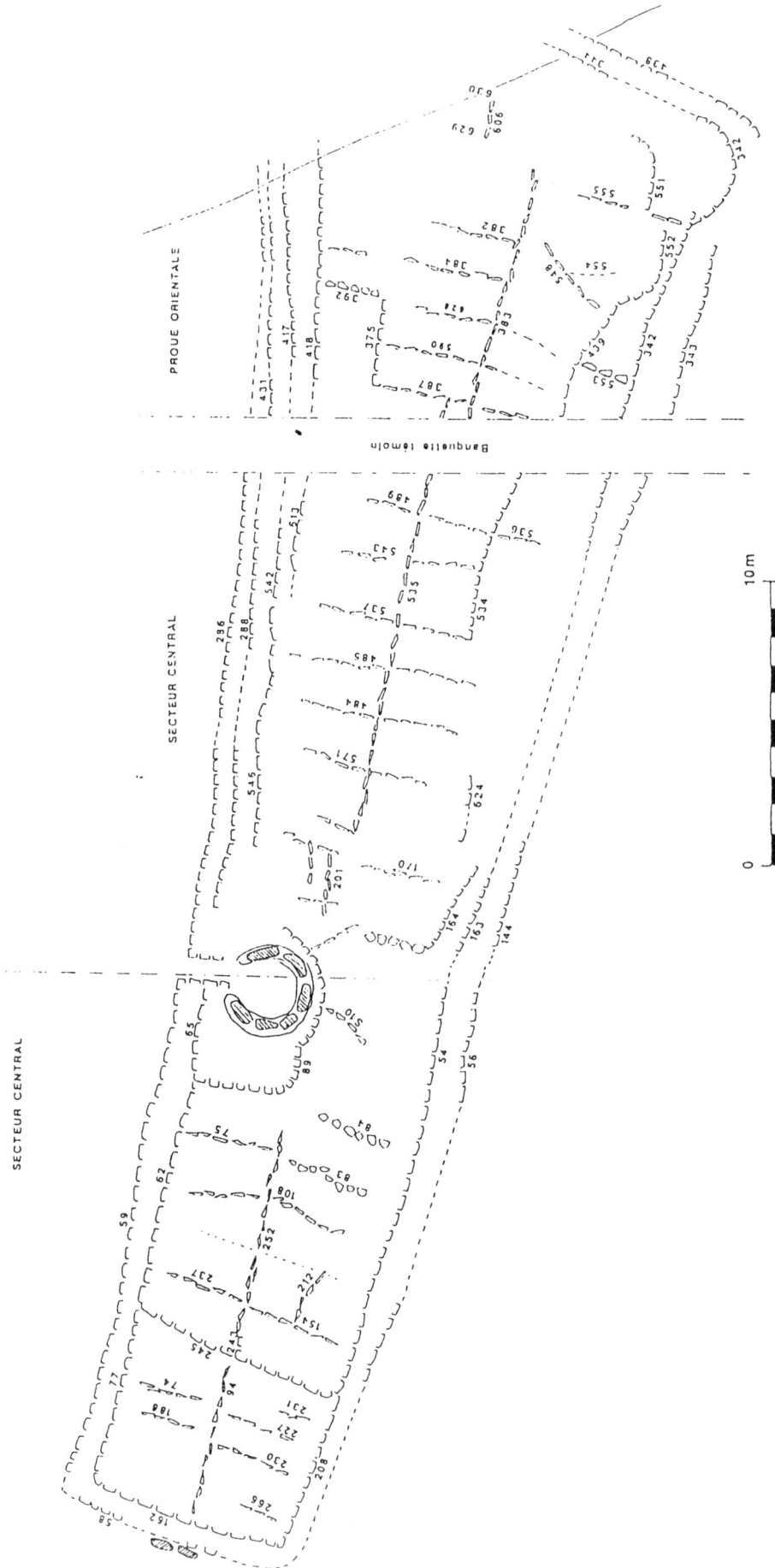

Figure 2. Plan of the key structures within the Commune–Sèche long mound (after Kinnes and Chancerel 1994, figure 5).

and landscape yet drew from them possibilities and nuances not previously realised. Building brought forth a new narrative form within which some locales, traditions, memories and meanings were situated centre stage through people's use of these cultural resources, while other locales were consigned to the wings for want of human use of these places and their possibilities of meaning (de Certeau 1984, Part III; Tilley 1994, 28–29). Building is therefore a political act in the sense that it seeks to presence certain meanings at the expense of others. However, that is not to say that a unanimous or unitary understanding is imposed. Rather, consumption or comprehension of the locale is, like the act of building, a strategic act embedded within networks of power (Thomas n.d., Chapter 4).

These networks of power may have been mediated in part through differential experience of the act of building. Indeed, I have already noted the originality of experience and meaning produced by individual acts of selection and deposition of building materials within the various bays of the mound. A number of further observations also suggest that the experience of building was not only paramount but that the action be experienced in different ways by those people involved. First, the mound revetments are built in short sections, often in starkly contrasting building styles and with little attempt to tie one section into the next. The entire fabric of the cairn is therefore inherently unstable. Indeed, it is not unreasonable to suggest that the cairn was designed to decay rapidly. The pristine state of the mound was therefore of minimal interest. Rather, the act of building may be seen as the key to understanding the significance(s) with which the mound was initially imbued. Indeed, it should be further noted that the strategy for building the revetments was primarily geared to marking the limits of the bays which lay

behind them rather than the establishment of a stable architectural structure (Kinnes and Chancerel 1994, 4). Symbolic reference to discrete episodes of building appears to have been more important than the construction of a stable piece of architecture.

The lack of evidence for repair and maintenance of the mound might also be interpreted as an indication of the primary importance of the initial acts of building. In this respect it is interesting to note that during the lull between the 1971 and 1989 seasons of excavation the site had reverted to 'une veritable jungle impénétrable' (Kinnes and Chancerel 1994, 50). If repair and maintenance were not part of the Neolithic project of building, then a similar reversion to scrub or copse may have occurred soon after completion of the mound. Again, the importance of the locale appears to reside in the act of construction.

It is also worth noting that certain key constructional elements were immediately and quite deliberately hidden from view. Structures 245, 375 and 439 comprise free-standing dry-stone wall features (Fig. 2). Though constructed with a degree of care which might imply the preparation of structures destined for public view, it appears that these structures were planned from the outset to be internal features sealed by the matrix of the surrounding cairn. The impression is one of deliberate secretion of structures produced by discrete and unusual episodes of construction in which relatively few people participated. Traces of burning half-way up the northern (external) face of Structure 375 (Fig. 3) may indicate a formalised act to mark the sealing of the structure within the body of the mound. Cultural meanings, emotions and experiences associated with the act of building and encountering the structure were

Figure 3. Structure 375 at La Commune-Sèche (after Chancerel and Kinnes 1992).

formally closed down. One set of possibilities opened up by the locale could no longer be accessed via personal experience of the place. To understand the locale was now to enter into a spoken discourse about the place as it once was. This shift of discursive field (from the realm of personal experience to the establishment of speaker–listener relationships) may have facilitated the negotiation of positions of dominance based upon the ability to recall the original act of construction. The authority of this discursive field may have endured beyond the life–span of the builders through the institutionalised monitoring of access to traditional accounts of past events. The network of meanings created and maintained through the act of building was therefore interlaced with the politics of mediating position and status within society.

Pits: the northern structured deposits

To the north of the long mound a series of Neolithic pits were excavated into the limestone bedrock (see Fig. 1). A variety of material deposits (flint, pottery, burnt stone, human bodies) were laid down before and/or during the back–filling of these pits. Though the precise chronological relationship between the pits and long mound is unclear, the upper pit fills tend to comprise pitched limestone slabs which may represent collapsed cairn revetment. If, as has already been argued, the cairn was subject to rapid decay, then the pits may be broadly contemporary with the building of the mound. The absence of silt deposits or turf horizons between the pit fills and overlying cairn collapse would also imply a minimal lapse of time between the act of pit digging/back–filling and the decay of the mound.

The positioning of the pits is such that they may have acted as mnemonics designed to prompt the adoption of certain bodily positions from which the mound was to be encountered and interpreted. The general configuration of the pits demarcates a narrow linear space along the northern flank of the mound. So long as the pits were open (or indeed invoked within oral tradition) approach to the mound (or its proposed site) from the north would have entailed movement between the pits and an internalisation of their symbolic content. That content may have related in part to the way in which the pits were positioned to commemorate selected acts of mound construction and the biographies of action which they evoke. The clearest instance of this phenomenon is represented by a shallow scoop excavated directly opposite the entrance to Chamber B. Excavated into the limestone bedrock and packed with burnt limestone blocks this small pit is also associated with two post–holes (see Fig. 1). The configuration of these features suggests that access to the chamber may have involved stepping over or around the pit before passing between the two posts, one placed either side of the chamber entrance. The invocation of fire – a phenomenon with the power to transform materials from one state to another, for example raw to cooked, cold to hot, whole to fragmentary (Lèvi–Strauss 1986) – may represent a symbolic reference to the transition from life to death which was monitored and sanctioned within the confines of the chamber. A unity of bodily presence, architectural features and traditional symbolism therefore produced a

choreographed procedure (Richards 1993) whereby experience and understanding of the chamber was mediated. It may not be unreasonable to suggest that this approach from the north also took in the site of La Fougère (located c.600 metres to the north) (Fig. 4). La Fougère has produced unusually large numbers of polished axe and schist bracelet (Kirk 1992, Jean Barge: pers.comm.) and may have been a venue for monitoring and sanctioning access to novel resources at the centre of Earlier/Middle Neolithic networks of exchange, kinship and political alliance. La Fougère may therefore have been keyed into a ritual pathway linking a number of sites including the Commune–Sèche long mound.

The invocation of fire as a metaphor for the transition between life and death may also be glimpsed in the rituals taking place within Chamber B. The deposition of burnt human bone within the chamber may connote a desire to mediate the passage from life to death through the execution of ritual practices designed to produce a social sanctioning of the event. The architecture of the mound limits physical access to these practices and the pit arrangments limit the range of possibilities for approaching, experiencing and interpreting the site. Engagement in the fields of discourse and power within which these mortuary practices operated therefore depended on people's involvement with the built landscape and the sedimented layers of cultural meaning which it embodies. Accessing arcane knowledge and mediating relationships with the ancestors, processes whereby power, identity and subjectivity are likely to have been constituted, occurred in and through people's involvement with the physical world. *Being–in–the–world* entails an inseparable fusion of people, power, discourse and place.

If the small pit, posts, mound and chamber are architectural elements combined to elicit or encourage preferred modes of experiencing the locale then what of the other pits to the north of the long mound? Are they too designed as mnemonics to bodily movement, experience, perception and understanding? For example, does the positioning of the north–west pit serve to commemorate (or anticipate?) construction of the western cairn extension and the meanings, myths and experiences which that event produced? Similarly, the building of Structure 375, already identified as a novel constructional event, may be commemorated by the placing of a single scraper on the clean limestone base of a small pit situated immediately to the north of Structure 375. Even the north–east pit may act as a marker or reminder of the formal eastern limit of the cairn.

It is also notable that the two smallest pits (those adjacent to Chamber B and Structure 375) are no more than shallow scoops excavated into the limestone bedrock. Though an overburden of topsoil may have been removed (the depth of which is unknown due to subsequent soil creep and intensive ploughing) the act of digging appears to have been considered complete once bedrock had been reached. With bedrock in sight deposits of burnt stone and a flint scraper were laid down and the pits backfilled. Engagement with the limestone substrata, one of the sources of material for construction of the cairn, may have been considered

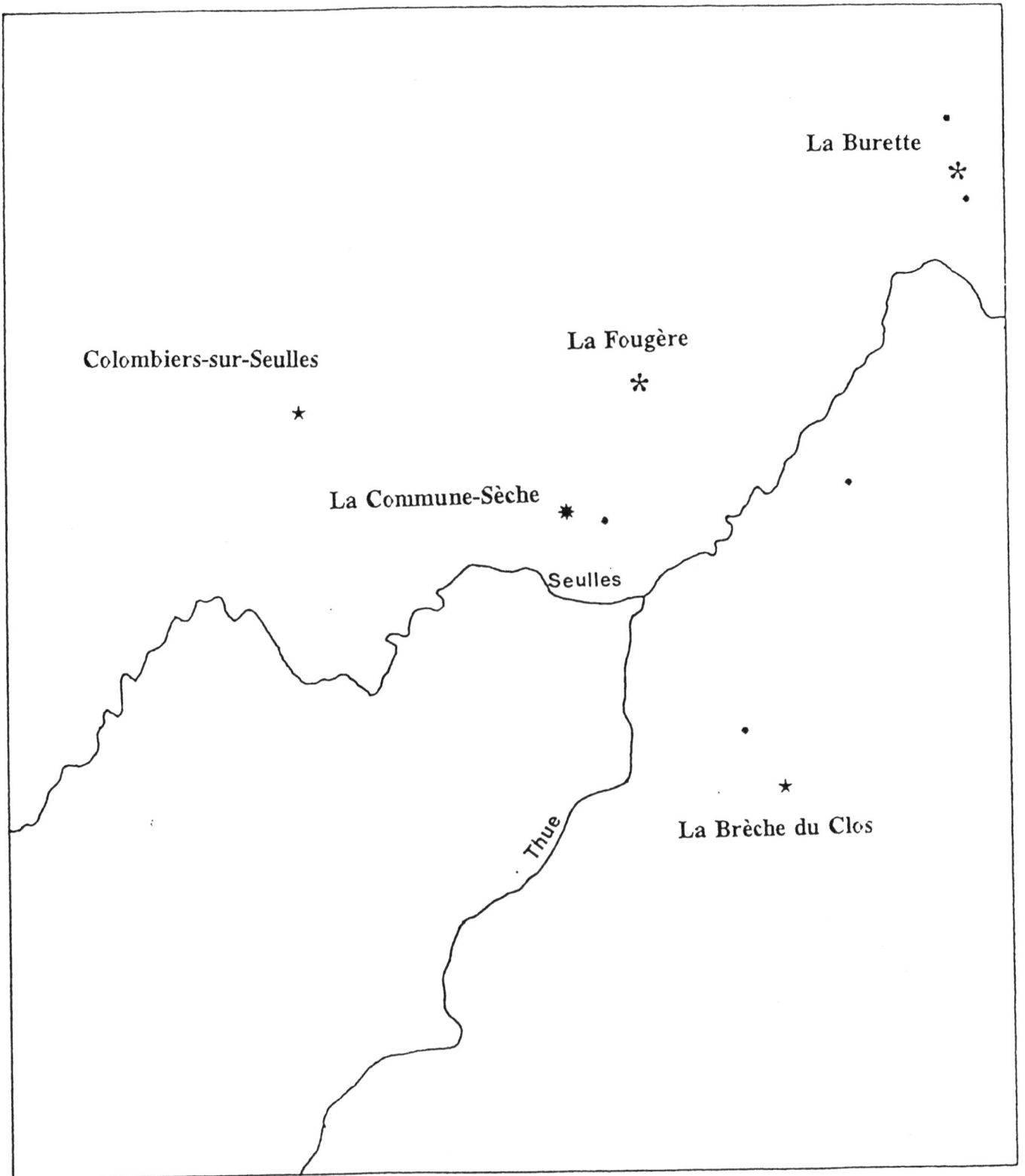

Figure 4. The landscape setting of La Commune–Sèche long mound showing Mesolithic and Neolithic sites. Scale 1:25,000 (source: author).

* ✷ – Neolithic long mound   ★ – possible Neolithic linear enclosure
* ✳ – Neolithic flint scatter   • – Mesolithic flint scatter

symbolically significant and may have enabled people to confirm or rethink their attachment to the locale.

Structured deposits are not extensive within the northern pits, though their content may be significant. In addition to the examples already described, the main deposits comprise a hearth setting, two crouched burials, three tranchant arrowheads, one backed flint knife and a handful of abraded sherds (Kinnes and Chancerel 1994). The symbolic content and composition of these deposits might be summarised as representing fire, the dead and 'rubbish'. Though wary of promoting a scheme of structuralist reductionism, one might be tempted to view these deposits as a medium for negotiating the transition from life (daily refuse) to death (crouched burials) via socially sanctioned rites of passage (represented by the transformative properties of fire). The juxtaposition of complete articulated bodies outside the mound and fragmented cremated remains within Chamber B may also be seen as a set of metaphors for the passage from living agent to ancestral spirit (though the absolute contemporaneity of the two deposits is not assured).

Human bone: the southern structured deposits

To the south of the long mound pits are replaced by six deposits of human bone (S1–S6) (see Fig. 1). It is difficult to access the precise nature of the deposits due to extensive post-depositional disturbance. However, a degree of variation seems likely in, for example, the contrast between collections of long bones (S4) and possible partial articulation (S5). The bones are generally deposited within the lower levels of collapsed rubble from the mound. The deposits appear to have been laid down soon after the onset of mound decay. Following deposition the human remains may have been summarily covered by limestone slabs before being fully sealed by further episodes of cairn collapse. S6 differs in the sense that it is deposited between the southern revetments of the monument. However, if – as has been argued – the mound was subject to rapid decay, then all six deposits would have been laid down within the limits of the mound as it was then experienced and perceived (that is to say as a rubble massif with indistinct and constantly shifting boundaries). Indeed, the deposition of ancestral remains may have been a ritual procedure whereby the changing configuration of the mound was sanctified and its meaning reaffirmed or transformed. Deposits of human bone and pottery in association with the rubble collapse from passage graves at Condé-sur-Ifs and Vierville (Dron and Le Goff 1993, Chancerel et al 1986) may indicate that ritual authorisation of the cultural significance of decaying monuments was repeatedly practised in Neolithic Normandy.

The human bones in deposit S5 are associated with a scatter of animal bone (species to be confirmed), a vase with an internal perforated lug, two tranchant arrowheads and two retouched flint flakes (Kinnes and Chancerel 1994, 37). Despite post-depositional disturbance it is perhaps not unreasonable to view these artefacts as a coherent structured deposit. The selection of pottery, animal bone (domesticated or wild?) and hunting equipment may reference the economic activities and production processes enacted elsewhere in the landscape and with which the building and physical encounter of the monument was articulated.

The north/pit:south/human bone opposition may also reflect an adherence to a common set of building principles. Operating within the code or being aware of its use may have served to unify people's otherwise diverse experiences of the locale. Also, a strictly codified north/south differentiation of space may have fostered a sense of familiarity and belonging within people returning to the locale as part of a temporal passage through the landscape. Experience of the monument

may have been organised around activities such as the seasonal movement of cattle herds, pursuit of wild resources and raw materials, and the maintenance of social ties.

Pathways in time and space: the Mesolithic landscape

So far I have considered the major constructional events carried out at La Commune-S che during the Neolithic. However, the Commune-S che long mound was constructed within a landscape already redolent with meaning arising from people's involvement with the physical and social world. I have already suggested that building allowed people to creatively re-assess the myths and meanings associated with the locales from which the materials of the mound were derived. By looking back to the Mesolithic and Early Neolithic landscape the processes for producing meaning through human involvement with the world might be more clearly stated.

Surface survey in the Colombiers-sur-Seulles region indicates that Late Mesolithic activity centred on the valley corridors (Kirk 1992) and especially the limestone ridges and valley slopes which overlook and give access to the river courses (see Fig. 4). From these vantage points late hunter-gatherer communities may have monitored and tracked animals attracted to the water courses below. Two Middle/Late Mesolithic microliths sealed beneath the Commune-S che long mound (Kinnes and Chancerel 1994, 40) suggest that this locale, situated on a low ridge directly overlooking the river Seulles, may have been embedded within a network of traditional pathways via which the landscape was experienced. These pathways were among the spatial media through which life was enacted. Pathways along the river corridors were inseparable from the human actions which imbued them with meaning and which were in turn lent direction and form by the possibilities opened up by the landscape. Many of the social and economic activities of late hunter-gatherer groups are likely to have been shot through with the temporality (tradition, history, memory, myth) and spatiality (locales, pathways) of landscape. For example, information about the availability of food may have been gleaned and then disseminated through people's use of pathways. In this context I take information to mean both knowledge deriving from personal experience of place and also the meanings traditionally associated with locales. Thus, the act of finding food may have drawn closely upon existing conceptions of the fecundity of certain locales. The landscape therefore opened up possibilities for the structuring and execution of economic activity. In a similar vein, traditional pathways along the river corridors may have offered access to the river pebbles which were the major source of flint for local Mesolithic communities (Kirk 1992). In addition to the inseparable tie between the potentialities presented by landscape and the development of economic strategy, Late Mesolithic pathways may also have facilitated flows of information about the location of other groups and the timing or reporting of ritual, ceremony or exchange transactions. In short, the dynamic forces of fragmentation, rivalry, temporary collaboration and assistance which characterise intra-band and inter-band relations may have been enacted through people's engagement with time–spaces replete with their own biographies, meanings and potentialities.

The consolidation of locale in the Early Neolithic

During the fourth millennium b.c. key pathways along the river corridors were supplemented by the establishment of important locales on the flat limestone plateaux extending to both north and south. The pattern is not simply one of expansion beyond the narrow river corridors (though let us not forget that the plateaux may have been important hunting and gathering grounds during the Mesolithic) but, perhaps more importantly, locales became increasingly differentiated. Five locales appear to have been especially favoured: La Burette, La Fougère, La Brèche du Clos, Colombiers–sur–Seulles and La Commune–Sèche (see Fig. 4). Though the absolute chronology of these sites is presently uncertain, La Brèche du Clos and Colombiers–sur–Seulles probably represent variants of the Passy–style linear enclosure generally associated with post–Bandkeramik (Middle Neolithic I: Cerny) groups, while the remaining sites have yielded Middle Neolithic I (Cerny and Villeneuve–Saint–Germain) artefacts and/or Middle Neolithic II (Chasséen) material (Kinnes and Chancerel 1994, Kirk 1992, Antoine Chancerel and Jean Barge: pers. comm.) Despite a weak chronological framework, the locales established during the earlier part of the Neolithic are characterised by either acts of building (La Brèche du Clos, Colombiers–sur–Seulles and La Commune–Sèche) or the production, processing, use and deposition of material culture (La Fougère and La Burette). Most notably the latter sites have yielded unusually high numbers of polished axes and schist bracelets. Indeed these locales may have been situated at the heart of the procedures for monitoring and sanctioning access to these novel resources at the beginning of the Neolithic.

It is, however, the act of building in which I am mainly interested here. In particular I want to return to La Commune–Sèche and the constructional acts which transformed both the physical landscape and possibilities of human interpretation during the course of the Neolithic[2]. The architecture of the Commune–Sèche long mound appears to reference a set of earlier social practices involving the deposition of Middle Neolithic I pottery, blade–based flint artefacts and fragments of schist bracelet. Preliminary analysis has revealed a distinct spatial patterning in the distribution of this material culture (Kinnes and Chancerel 1994). Cordon decorated pottery, blade–based flint tools and fragments of schist bracelet, artefacts conventionally attributed to the Villeneuve–Saint–Germain (VSG) cultural group, are sealed beneath the western end of the mound (Fig. 5). This artefact distribution is distinct from that of Cerny pottery which clusters further to the east (Fig. 6). Though the precise nature and time–scale of Middle Neolithic I activity is subject to debate[3], the architecture of the long mound

draws upon the possibilities of meaning presented by the existing landscape. Extensive turf clearance was followed (or accompanied) by episodes of burning, including an ephemeral hearth marking the eastern extent of the VSG artefact distribution. The mutually exclusive distribution of VSG and Cerny artefacts is effectively recalled and commemorated within events which immediately precede the construction of the long mound. Furthermore, the architecture of the mound references the Middle Neolithic I landscape through the location of Chamber B (see Fig. 5 & 6). The previously unbounded Middle Neolithic I locale is redefined in a fashion which produces ambiguous and multiple possibilities of experience and understanding. The act of sealing part of the locale beneath the long mound transforms, even terminates some traditional methods of experiencing and understanding the locale. Yet the construction of the chamber, an enclosed space to which access was strictly monitored, may have revived or redirected the cultural meanings associated with the locale. An open space to which access appears not to have been limited was transformed into an enclosed space which may have been experienced only periodically and by a limited number of people. The events occurring within the chamber are little understood, but appear to have included the deposition of considerable quantities of human bone (de Caumont 1830, Chancerel *et al* 1992, 22). The cultural significance of the locale may therefore have been sanctified by ancestral authority.

Conclusion

In this paper I have mainly focused on those acts of building through which people in the Neolithic expressed and lived out their interconnection with the material world. I have argued that the biography of La Commune–Sèche was produced through the creative involvement of people with place[4]. Building has been viewed as a fusion of the discursive political strategies whereby people negotiated positions of status and the non–discursive practical knowledge, a 'feel for the game' (Bourdieu 1990) through which the act of building was experienced via the sentient human body which is the living bond attaching us to the world. The sense of involvement or belonging with the world produced through building was not unitary or self–evident. Rather, the meaning(s) of place were produced through the situated practices of individual agents and interest groups.

---

[2] The linear enclosures at La Brèche du Clos and Colombiers–sur–Seulles were recently identified through aerial photography and have not yet been subject to detailed field assessment (Jean Desloges: pers. comm.). Extensive discussion of these sites is therefore not possible at the present time.

[3] Neolithic sites in Normandy have yielded very limited faunal assemblages, pollen samples and plant macrofossils. Evidence comes almost exclusively from passage grave sites and the post–Bandkeramik ground surfaces which they seal. Recent excavations of passage graves and buried ground surfaces

at Ernes, Condé–sur–Ifs, La Hoguette and La Commune–Sèche have yielded evidence for cattle, pig, sheep, dog, hazelnuts and wheat (Caillaud and Lagnel 1972, Dron 1989, Dron and Le Goff 1993, Kinnes and Chancerel 1994, San Juan and Dron 1987). However, the small sample sizes and formalised contexts of deposition preclude a detailed reconstruction of Neolithic economic practices in Normandy.

[4] The biography of La Commune–Sèche is, of course, still being written as people continue to experience and interpret the site. However, more recent encounters, actions and interpretations of the site arising from tourism and heritage visiting, the act of excavation, World War II military activity, post–medieval quarrying and farming, and traditional folklore must await a future paper.

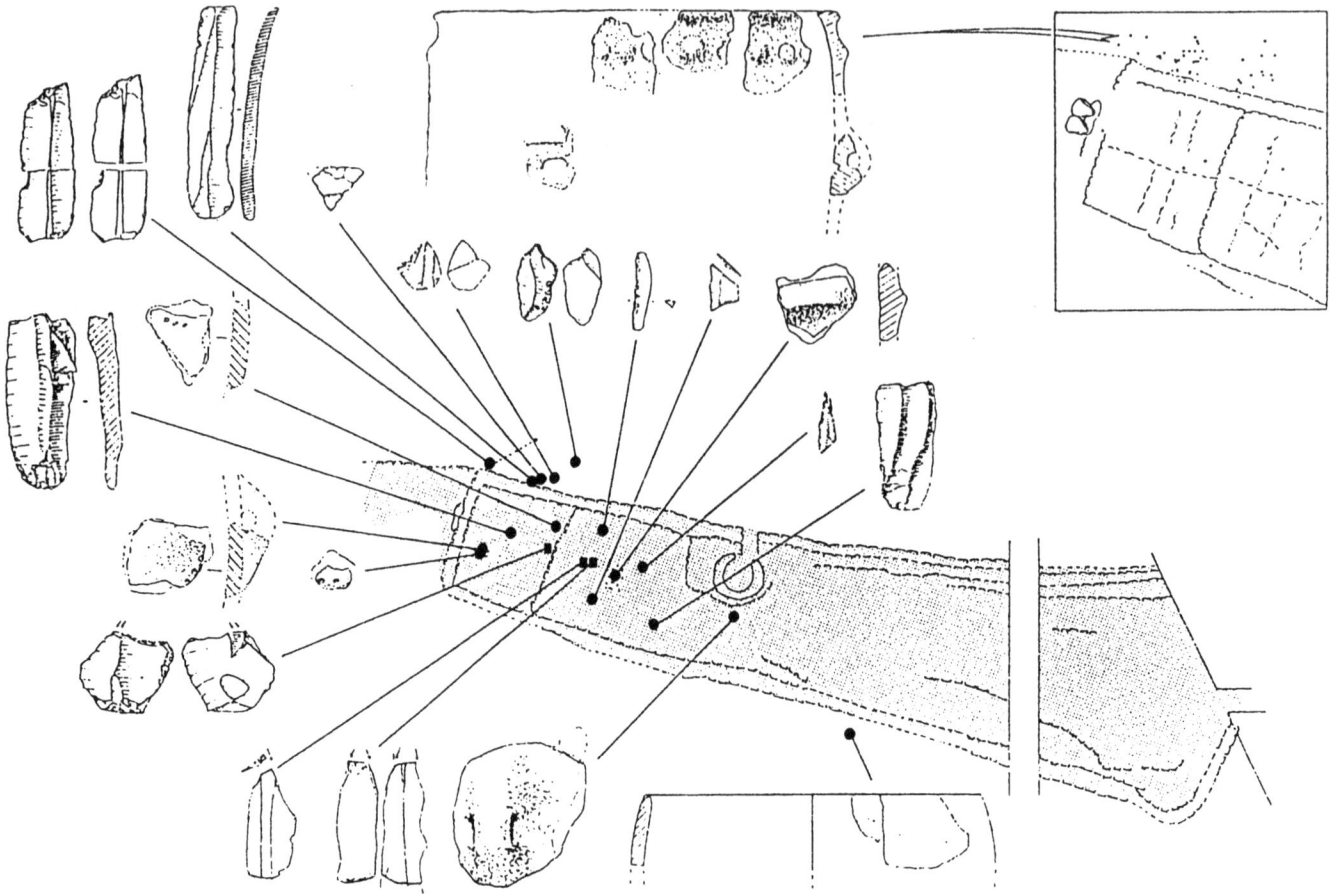

Figure 5. Distribution of Villeneuve–Saint–Germain (VSG) style artefacts at La Commune–Sèche. Dots – artefacts from the sealed Neolithic ground surface, squares – artefacts from redeposited ground surface within the mound.
The inset shows the distribution of sherds from a single large VSG vessel (after Kinnes and Chancerel 1994, figure 48).

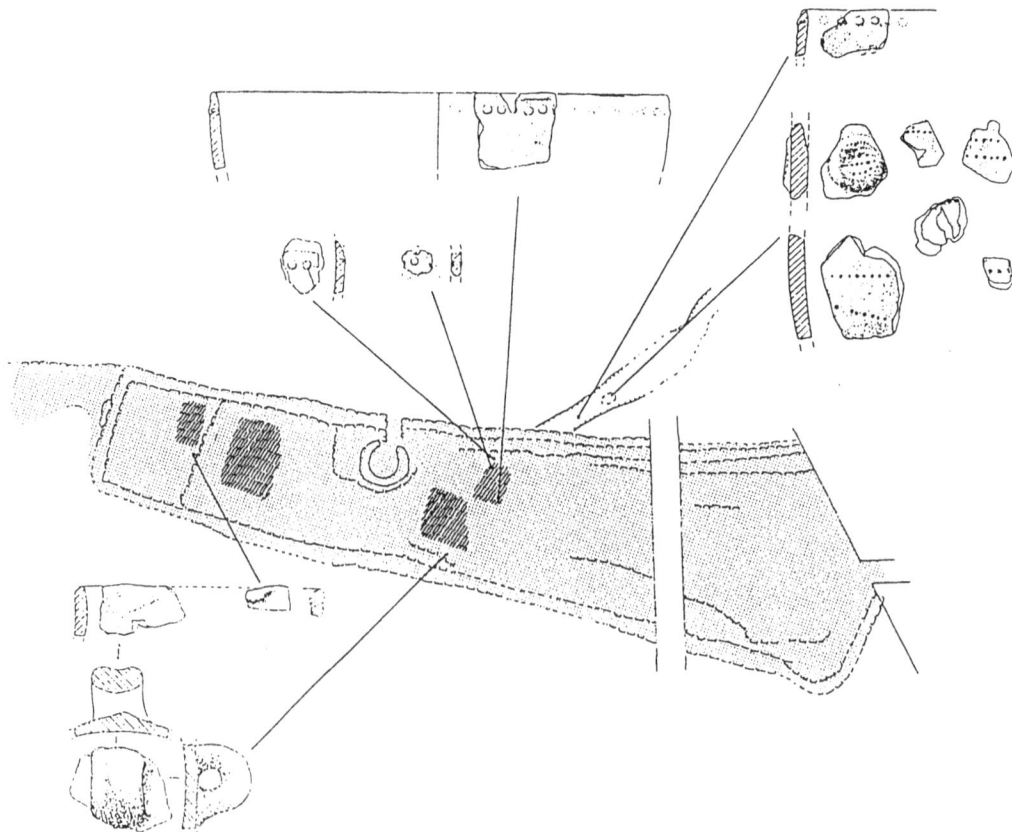

Figure 6. Distribution of Cerny style artefacts at La Commune–Sèche.
Shaded areas – redeposited ground surface within the matrix of the mound (after Kinnes and Chancerel 1994, figure 49).

Acknowledgements

Thanks to Ian Kinnes and Antoine Chancerel for allowing me access to unpublished material from the Commune-Sèche long mound excavation. I am also indebted to all those people who worked on the site with Ian, Antoine and myself between 1989 and 1994. Your dedication to the task in the face of driving rain, howling gales and unexploded World War Two munitions was little less than miraculous.I am grateful too to Jean Desloges, Jean Barge and Jean-Luc Dron for sharing their detailed knowledge of the prehistory of the Plain of Caen. Thanks also to Julian Thomas for permission to refer to a draft copy of his book, *Time, Culture and Identity*.

Bibliography

Barrett, J., 1988. 'The living, the dead and the ancestors: Neolithic and Early Bronze Age mortuary practices', in J. Barrett and I. Kinnes, (eds.), *The Archaeology of Context in the Neolithic and Bronze Age: Recent Trends*, pp.30–41, University of Sheffield.

Barrett, J., 1994. *Fragments from Antiquity. An Archaeology of Social Life in Britain, 2900–1200 B.C.*, Oxford, Blackwell.

Bender, B., (ed.), 1993. *Landscape. Politics and Perspectives*, Oxford, Berg.

Bourdieu, P., 1977. *Outline of a Theory of Practice*, Cambridge University Press.

Bourdieu, P., 1990. *In Other Words*, Cambridge, Polity Press.

Caillaud, R. and Lagnel, E., 1972. 'Le cairn et le crématoire néolithique de La Hoguette à Fontenay-le-Marmion (Calvados)'. *Gallia Préhistoire* 15(1), 137–185.

Chancerel, A. & Kinnes, I. (1992) 'Colombiers-sur-Seulles: Tumulus de la Commune-Seche'. Rapport de synthese de fouille pluriannuelle, 4 eme annee de recherche, MS, Caen, Service Regional de l'Archeologie de Basse-Normandie.

Chancerel, A. & Kinnes, I. (1993) 'Colombieres-sur-Seulles: Tumulus de la Commune-Seche'. Rapport de synthese de fouille pluriannuelle, 5 eme annee de recherche, MS, Caen, Service Regional de l'Archeologie de Basse-Normandie.

Chancerel, A., Kinnes, I., Lagnel, E. and Kirk, T., 1992. 'Le tumulus néolithique de la Commune-Sèche à Colombiers-sur-Seulles (Calvados)'. *Colloque Interrégional sur le Néolithique, Vannes 1990 (Révue Archéologique de l'Ouest, Supplément No. 5)*, pp.17–29.

Chancerel, A., Verron, G. and Pradat, J., 1986. 'La chambre A du tumulus néolithique de Vierville (Manche)'. *Actes du Xème Colloque Interrégional sur le Néolithique, Caen, 1983 (Révue Archéologique de l'Ouest, Supplément No. 1)*, pp.267–269

ChancerelChapman, R., 1981. 'The emergence of formal disposal areas and the 'problem' of megalithic tombs in prehistoric Europe', in R. Chapman, I. Kinnes and K. Randsborg, (eds.), *The Archaeology of Death*, pp.71–81, Cambridge University Press.

Childe, V.G., 1925. *The Dawn of European Civilisation*, London, Kegan Paul.

Constantin, C., 1985. *Fin du Rubané, Ceramique de Limbourg et Post-Rubané. Le Néolithique le Plus Ancien en Bassin Parisien et en Hainaut*, Oxford, British Archaeological Reports, International Series, S273.

Constantin, C. and Demoule, J-P., 1982. 'Le groupe de Villeneuve-Saint-Germain'. *Helinium* 22, 255–71.

De Caumont, A., 1830. *Cours d'Antiquités Monumentales de la France, Tome I, Ere Celtique*, Paris.

De Certeau, M., 1984. *The Practice of Everyday Life*, Berkeley, University of California Press.

Dron, J-L., 1989. *Le Site Néolithique d'Ernes dans le Calvados. Rapport Intermédiaire 1989*, MS, Caen, Service Régional de l'Archéologie de Basse-Normandie.

Dron, J-L. and Le Goff, I., 1993. *La Bruyère du Hamel, Condé-sur-Ifs (Calvados). Rapport Pluriannuel (1990–1993)*, MS, Caen, Service Régional de l'Archéologie de Basse-Normandie.

Edmonds, M., 1993. 'Interpreting causewayed enclosures in the past and the present', in C. Tilley, (ed.), *Interpretative Archaeology*, pp.99–142, Oxford, Berg.

Evans, C., 1988. 'Acts of enclosure: a consideration of concentrically-organised causewayed enclosures', in J. Barrett and I. Kinnes, (eds.), *The Archaeology of Context in the Neolithic and Bronze Age: Recent Trends*, pp.85–96, University of Sheffield.

Foucault, M., 1986. *The Use of Pleasure. The History of Sexuality*, Volume 2, London, Viking.

Giddens, A., 1979. *Central Problems in Social Theory*, London, Macmillan.

Giddens, A., 1984. *The Constitution of Society*, Cambridge, Polity Press.

Gosden, C., 1994. *Social Being and Time*, Oxford, Blackwell.

Heidegger, M., 1977a. 'The question concerning technology', in D.F. Krell, (ed.), *Martin Heidegger: Basic Writings*, pp.283–317, London, Routledge and Kegan Paul.

Heidegger, M., 1977b. 'Building, dwelling, thinking', in D.F. Krell, (ed.), *Martin Heidegger: Basic Writings*, pp.319–339, London, Routledge and Kegan Paul.

Hodder, I., 1984. 'Burials, houses, women and men in the European Neolithic', in D. Miller and C. Tilley, (eds.), *Ideology, Power and Prehistory*, pp.51–68, Cambridge University Press.

Kinnes, I., 1975. 'Monumental function in British Neolithic burial practices'. *World Archaeology* 7, 16–29.

Kinnes, I. and Chancerel, A., 1994. *Colombiers-sur-Seulles: Tumulus de la Commune-Sèche. Rapport de Synth se de Fouille Pluriannuelle, 6ème Année de Recherche*, MS, Caen, Service Régional de l'Archéologie de Basse-Normandie.

Kirk, T., 1992. *A Field Survey of Neolithic Activity in the Communes of Colombiers-sur-Seulles, Banville and Amblie, Calvados, France: Results of a Second Season*, December 1992, MS, Caen, Service

Régional de l'Archéologie de Basse-Normandie.

Kwant, R.C., 1963. *The Phenomenological Philosophy of Merleau-Ponty*, Pittsburgh, Duquesne University Press.

Leone, M., 1984. 'Interpreting ideology in historical archaeology: using the rules of perspective in the William Paca Garden in Annapolis, Maryland', in D. Miller and C. Tilley, (eds.), *Ideology, Power and Prehistory*, pp.25–35, Cambridge University Press.

Lèvi-Strauss, C., 1986. *The Raw and the Cooked*, Harmondsworth, Penguin.

MacGregor, G., 1994. 'Post-processual archaeology: the hidden agenda of the secret agent', in I. Mackenzie, (ed.), *Archaeological Theory: Progress or Posture?*, pp.79–91, Aldershot, Avebury.

Merleau-Ponty, M., 1962. *The Phenomenology of Perception*, London, Routledge and Kegan Paul.

Patrik, L.E., 1985. 'Is there an archaeological record?' *Advances in Archaeological Method and Theory* 8, 27–62.

Renfrew, C., 1973. 'Monuments, mobilisation and social organisation in Neolithic Wessex', in C. Renfrew, (ed.), *The Explanation of Culture Change*, pp.539–558, London, Duckworth.

Richards, C., 1993. 'Monumental choreography: architecture and spatial representation in Late Neolithic Orkney', in C. Tilley, (ed.), *Interpretative Archaeology*, pp.143–178, Oxford, Berg.

San Juan, G. and Dron, J-L., 1987. *Ernes (Calvados). Fouille d'un Cairn Néolithique. Rapport 1987*, MS, Caen, Service Régional de l'Archéologie de Basse-Normandie.

Shanks, M. and Tilley, C., 1987. *Re-Constructing Archaeology*, Cambridge University Press.

Thomas, J., 1993. 'The hermeneutics of megalithic space', in C. Tilley, (ed.), *Interpretative Archaeology*, pp.73–97, Oxford, Berg.

Thomas, J., n.d. *Time, Culture and Identity. An Interpretive Archaeology*, MS.

Tilley, C., 1984. 'Ideology and the legitimation of power in the Middle Neolithic of Sweden', in D. Miller and C. Tilley, (eds.), *Ideology, Power and Prehistory*, pp.111–146, Cambridge University Press.

Tilley, C., 1994. *A Phenomenology of Landscape. Places, Paths and Monuments*, Oxford, Berg.

Tuan, Yi-Fu, 1978. 'Space, time, place: a humanistic frame' in T. Carlstein, D. Parkes and N. Thrift, (eds.), *Making Sense of Time: Timing Space and Spacing Time*, Vol. I, pp.7–16, London, Edward Arnold.

From Settlements to Monuments: Site Succession in Late Neolithic and Early Bronze Age Jutland, East Denmark

I J N Thorpe
School of Humanities, King Alfred's College, Winchester

Introduction

The project which forms the core of this paper is the Thy Archaeological Project, or TAP for short (Fig. 1). TAP began in 1990, and is due to run until 1998. Thy is the Northwest part of Jutland, bordered to the west by the North Sea and to the east and south by the Limfjord, as far from Copenhagen as it is possible to be while still remaining in Denmark. TAP was specifically set up to be a landscape project – examining this particular area over a long timescale. We are concerned with the development of the landscape of southern Thy from the Late Mesolithic (c. 4000 BC) up to the eighteenth century, when the great landed estates were broken up and the land was shared out among the peasants, who moved house from small villages to live among their new fields. (See Bech *et al.* 1996 for a fuller account of TAP, and De Marrais *et al.* 1996 for a summary of general developmental trends in Neolithic to Early Bronze Age Thy).

Project background

TAP began as a tri-national project – Danish, British and American – with Danish colleagues from the National Monuments Agency and local museum at Thisted, with two of TAP's five co-directors (Dr Kristian Kristiansen, subsequently appointed as Professor of Archaeology at Goteborg in Sweden, and Jens-Henrik Bech, the local museum inspector) and a workforce mainly from Århus University in Jutland. The British contingent has come from University College London, directed by Professor Mike Rowlands and myself. The American team primarily hail from the University of California, Los Angeles, under the leadership of Professor Tim Earle, now at Northwestern University, Evanston, Illinois.

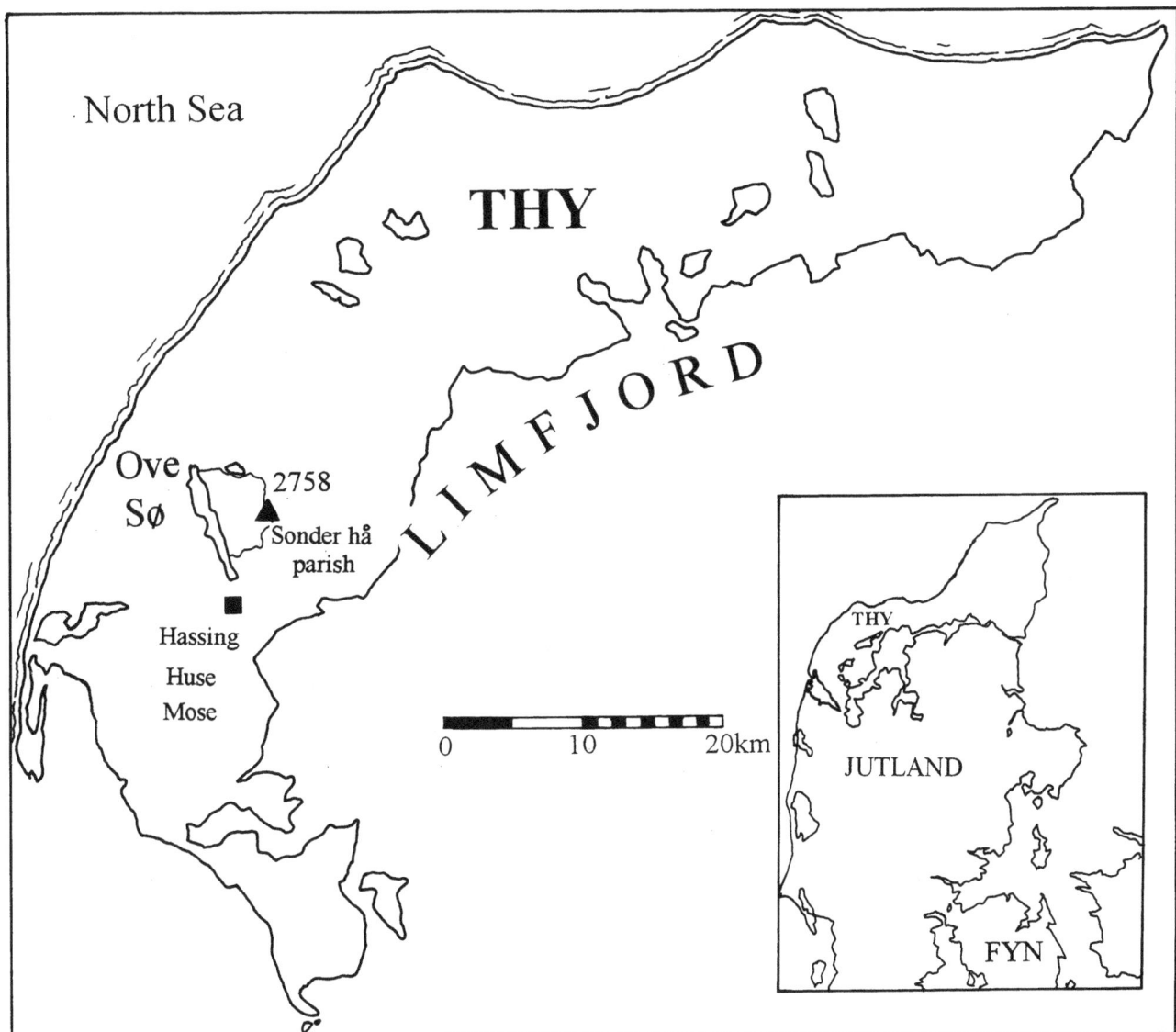

Figure 1. The location of Thy.

71

The original impetus behind TAP came from Kristian Kristiansen, who was situated outside the academic world by virtue of being in a government agency, and was perhaps unusual for Denmark in having written extensively on Danish Neolithic and Bronze Age contacts with the wider world beyond Scandinavia. He was therefore in an ideal position to set up a project which was designed specifically to take a rather different approach to that which was the consensus at the time, in particular to attempt to develop new methodologies which would enable a wider range of fieldwork data to be produced and interrogated.

What brought us as a group together intellectually, despite coming from different traditions, is that we shared a basic materialist orientation and doubts over the value of abstract terms such as culture, nature, and society in describing appropriate units of archaeological analysis. To explore the long–term interaction between human cultural and natural processes, and the consequences these interactions have for understanding the construction of economy and social identity, we have adopted the notion of a *cultural landscape* – defined as a physical and visual form through which meanings are created and transformed. This is, however, not to argue that the basic premise that human beings are fundamentally social should be replaced by a more diffuse notion of the cultural landscape as a symbolic representation of the dialectical relationship between human action and a physical environment. It is the tensions between, and resolution of, these symbolic, political, and economic views of historical process that constitutes a principal area of concern of our project.

Achieving a practical synthesis requires us to specify the interpretive goals of TAP. As objects and processes for investigation, we have recognised three major complexes: the variable and changing availability of resources, the economic relationships of production and exchange, and the sociopolitical and ritual actions that constitute social groups. These phenomena can be considered interactive processes, the shifting dialectical relationship between which rejects simplifying assumptions of order, totality or dominance.

In terms of the variable and changing availability of resources, landscapes are ordered by the material and symbolic value of different resources, topographies, and the relationship of these to political institutions. As part of our research we are plotting the local availability of flint, amber, clays, good quality soils and other resources . Such resources were realised (made available) by human technology and no necessary *determination* flows from nature to technology or vice versa. The interpretation of landscape as a cultural artefact specifies that nature has value in proportion to its cultural significance. But, because the long–term consequences of cultural practices went beyond the intentions of the people involved, the notion of environment outside the cultural landscape defines a sphere of biological, topographic, geological and climatological *resistances* to conceptual ordering. In Thy such processes are dramatically represented by the transformation of the landscape through climatic change, human exploitation of mineral and agricultural resources, the podsolisation of soil (creating

large scale heathlands), the development of peat during the Bronze Age, and the replacement of woodlands by farmlands, pasture and heath. To document these dynamic developments TAP is affiliated with a project developed by the Danish Geological Service to undertake multi–level pollen analyses to reconstruct regional and local changes in the plant communities of Thy (Andersen 1992–3; 1996; Andersen & Rasmussen 1994).

Why choose Thy? A number of different factors came into play here. First, the use of raw materials distinguished Thy from the rest of Denmark. Amber washed up on coast from ancient undersea forests has been harvested and turned into ornaments of various kinds since the Mesolithic (Beck & Shennan 1991). Flint was mined at a number of sites in Jutland (Becker 1959; 1980), and it is clear that in the Late Neolithic in particular Thy was a real centre of flintwork production, especially of fine daggers. This has resulted in a very clear concentration of early flint daggers of lanceolate form in North Jutland (Vandkilde 1990). In both these cases high quality raw material was locally available; there are also, however, a large number of items of early metalwork (axes, daggers, swords, ornaments) deposited in graves and hoards in Thy (Vandkilde 1990). This is despite Thy being the part of Denmark furthest from the copper, tin and gold sources of Central Europe.

Second, there is the clear possibility, arising from these observations on raw materials and imported items, that the inhabitants of Thy used the North Sea to make contact with other groups within and beyond the present Danish border. Trade along the North Sea coast to Germany was extremely important in Medieval Thy and there is no good reason to suppose that this was not continuing a prehistoric tradition.

Third, pollen analysis of a small bog (Hassing Huse Mose) in Southern Thy suggested that the area sampled (taken as a 10 km circle around the sample point for the purposes of pollen analysis) had a different agricultural history to the rest of Denmark. The most significant point of divergence was a major tree clearance phase at the beginning of the Late Neolithic, around 2600 BC, rather than during the Early Bronze Age (Andersen 1992–3). This preliminary indication has been confirmed by a second regional pollen diagram from Ove Sø (Andersen & Rasmussen 1994), a large lake in the centre of southern Thy, spot samples taken from the buried soil below several round barrows of Bronze Age date (Andersen 1996), and a pollen diagram from the Gjævhul peat deposits on the North Sea coast (Liversage and Robinson 1992–3).

Finally, Thy contains numerous large and rich barrows (Bech *et al.* 1996), with a clear concentration of some 1800 barrows in the study area, which is the 10 km circle around Hassing Huse Mose – an area of 314 km². The distribution is not uniform, but much of this variation in numbers may relate to later patterns of land use (Bech *et al.* 1996). Many of these are impressive mounds of considerable size, which demonstrate a significant labour input. They also demonstrate the cutting of turf on a large scale to construct the mounds, for the mound material is not derived from a surrounding ditch, but heaped up and retained by a stone kerb. A number of barrows also have a primary stone cairn of small boulders.

Our area of study lies between the North Sea and the Limfjord, with wind–blown sand deposits on the North Sea coast, built up into substantial dunes, a large lake in the middle (Ove Sø), which was joined to the sea several thousand years ago, and a rolling landscape of moraine soils, intensively farmed today. So within the study area there are contrasts between the North Sea coast, the inland Limfjord coast and the zone between them, and between high and low ground, and also between lighter and heavier soils (clays and sands), and for the Neolithic and Bronze Age possibly between areas of more or less barrows. By adopting this relatively small area as the core of the project it can be situated within the concept of the micro–region as a building block of archaeological research (seen at a finer scale again in the notion of the community area – Kuna 1992; Neustupny 1992).

Methodology

The existing archaeological knowledge of Thy has been obtained in a similar way to the rest of Denmark. Amateur collections have provided very large numbers of high quality stray finds of flintwork; barrow diggings in the last century and rescue excavations in more recent times have produced many fine bronzes, amber and flintwork from graves, although few skeletons (due to acid soils). Rescue excavations have also revealed house sites, which have been dealt with by stripping away the topsoil over large areas to reveal the post–holes of houses (with the house form itselfused as an indicator of date, together with a relatively small amount of associated finds). This has created a series of very good house plans, but only produces a few finds in association except in rare cases where floor levels survive (Rasmussen 1992–3). Material in the ploughsoil has been assumed to be out of context and removed from its original association with household activities, and therefore of little archaeological value.

This standard way of dealing with sites has become almost fixed by the very high labour costs within Danish archaeology, which mean that hand digging topsoil is almost never financially feasible. While this method has produced excellent general period maps of settlement, there has been little opportunity to investigate questions of micro–variation between sites or even houses (although see Rasmussen 1992–3). Such differences may not have existed, in which case nothing is lost by removing the ploughsoil, but this can certainly not be assumed to be the case without investigation. This methodology can also be seen to have resulted in a privileging of the house as an indication of settlement, and indeed in the development of a concept of the 'proper' house. This makes it more difficult to investigate those sites which do not fit the standard pattern. Thus if houses can not be identified on a site then it may well be argued that it represents an original settlement with houses that has been completely degraded by agricultural activity, rather than a different kind of activity area to the standard settlement, one

which did not require houses. Equally, if the houses which are recovered do not conform to type then the first possibility explored is always that the post–holes have been missed, and sometimes explanation may not move beyond this point.

How are sites located? Much is reported by the public, for the general interest in archaeology in Denmark is extremely high, as demonstrated by the tens of thousands of subscribers to the popular magazine *Skalk*, making it a pleasure to work there. The high quality of Neolithic and Bronze Age flintwork, especially in the larger axes, daggers and sickles, has led to the emergence of a network of private collectors, who vary from the farmer interested solely in his own land to German enthusiasts. Although their collections are not comprehensive, they can undoubtedly be used to pinpoint areas worthy of controlled fieldwalking or trial trenching (see Bech et al. 1996 for a detailed consideration of the value of private collections). Fieldwalking surveys that have been carried out by archaeologists (mostly in advance of roadworks or construction) tend to be topographically based (e.g. Olausson 1987–8). They are focussed on examining places in the landscape where settlements should be (on gentle slopes for example), and are highly successful in predicting the presence of material of particular periods in particular locations, as well as very good at spotting stray finds. Areas deemed to be less likely settlement locations may be examined only in a cursory fashion, or ignored completely if time is short, given the low likelihood of significant quantities of material being discovered. Such a procedure does, of course, tend to reinforce existing views of the settlement pattern, and renders the discovery of use patterns of marginal landscapes through fieldwalking evidence unlikely. Material recovered in the ploughsoil through fieldwalking is also only used as a very general guide to where sites might be below the topsoil, to be followed up by machine trenching. This is because it is believed within Danish archaeology that ploughsoil finds have been so churned up and shifted around by ploughing that they can not be used in any meaningful analysis. So Danish archaeology in Thy, as elsewhere, has been highly successful in many ways, but increasingly may tend towards finding more of the same, rather than being set up to record a total landscape.

We have therefore designed and carried out an archaeological field investigation in three Thy parishes – Sønderhå, Nørhå, and Heltborg. Our analysis so far focusses on just one parish, that of Sønderhå, where our survey work is furthest advanced, and where the bulk of our investigations into Late Neolithic and Early Bronze Age sites through small–scale excavation have been undertaken. Contrasts between the three parishes through time are already apparent, but it would be misleading to attempt here more than a few generalised comparisons before equivalent databases have been established.

So what have we actually done? TAP has undertaken a four stage approach to topsoil finds, with excavation representing a fifth level of investigation (for a more detailed discussion of TAP methodology see Bech et al. 1996).

First we have contacted private collectors and farmers in order to see their collections and catalogue them, and to persuade them not to *stop* collecting but to record their finds more systematically, ideally on a wall map immediately on entering the house. There seemed no point in attempting to persuade collectors to give up collecting, particularly on their own land, and experience has shown that they are more likely to find securely datable objects than the TAP fieldwalkers, who will locate a surface scatter of flint accurately, but may not be able to date it on their single visit, while the local collector will probably already possess a number of datable finds from the location.

Second, TAP has undertaken systematic fieldwalking at two levels of detail. We have focussed on a particular period in each March fieldwalking season, and have thus targetted particular kilometre squares, walking all available fields within those at 10 m intervals. We walk as a group, keeping together, marking all diagnostic finds with flags and alerting team members to the presence of lesser finds, so that concentrations of surface material will be noted. Although it would be technically feasible to collect all archaeological material, time constraints and museum collection policy ruled this out. When a concentration of material is found, then that is quickly scanned by the whole group for datable material. If the site is not of the date with which we are primarily concerned that season then diagnostic finds are bagged and its location is noted for future reference. If the site is of the date we are concentrating on that year then we set out a series of 50 x 50m blocks laid out on a North–South grid (using the Universal Transmercator system – Cole 1992) covering the site and an area beyond the edge of the scatter. Within these blocks we walk lines running North–South at 10 m intervals more slowly, recording the numbers of flint flakes (but not keeping these) and the position of each flint tool, piece of pottery, etc, along with any soil marks. While this work is proceeding a sketch is drawn of each field in which the blocks are walked, recording their postion relative to field borders, etc., any other scatters of material, and any stray finds, for example axes, which generally occur off–site. If no blocks are walked then a sketch is made recording concentrations and stray finds.

Of course, some fields can not be walked because they are not ploughed, for example permanent pasture and areas of woodland. Here we have developed the technique of shovel-testing, first used in the United States of America (Shott 1989), but little seen in Europe. In the TAP version of the method a grid of 50 x 50m squares is laid out, and a small amount of topsoil (twenty litres) is removed from the centre of the square and sieved through a standard size mesh. Although only a tiny percentage of the topsoil within a 50 x 50m square is examined using this method, it has proved to be a highly effective way of locating Late Neolithic and Bronze Age flint scatters, which are extremely dense concentrations of material. A similar but more intensive method (to take into account the lower densities of material in the topsoil) is now being used in two large scale British landscape projects at Shapwick in Somerset (see Smith & Thorpe 1996) and Clarendon in Wiltshire.

The next stage of activity on a site which will be the scene of an excavation is to carry out further work on the ploughsoil, which would normally be machined away once excavation began. A series of 2 x 2m squares are laid out within the same 50 x 50m blocks as for the fieldwalking, at least three squares to a block. Using an earthmoving machine the topsoil is removed from the squares and moved to a central location within the field. A standard sample size of four hundred litres of soil is then sieved from each square, using a mechanical finds sorter, which we had built by a local blacksmith. One person fills twenty bucketfuls of soil and heaves them into the machine while the other sorts through the rocks and potsherds shaken out by the machine onto a mesh–topped table. The idea is to obtain a large enough sample to see if patterns of activity can be detected in material now in the ploughsoil. The results have demonstrated that significant concentrations of material do survive in the ploughsoil, with up to 300 pieces of struck flint being recovered from a 400 litre sample. It is also clear from the TAP results that concentrations of lithic material in the ploughsoil can be tied to houses. At the Early Bronze Age site of Thy 2788 counts of over 200 flakes came from squares which proved to lie directly above and just to the North of a small rectangular house structure associated with cooking pits, while the count from squares some fifty metres from the house fell to below fifty flakes (see Bech *et al.* 1996 for further details). This would seem to confirm the general observation that tillage does not displace lithic material more than a few metres (e.g. Clark and Schofield 1991). It is also significant that fieldwalking and ploughsoil testing do not correlate particularly well, in so far as ploughsoil testing recovers larger numbers of undiagnostic flakes relative to tools, while fieldwalking is more successful in producing pottery.

Finally, excavations are undertaken on a selection of sites, attempting to cover the variability noted in the ploughsoil examinations, with the excavation designed to follow on from all the previous stages of activity. The types of sites investigated so far include settlements, burial sites and field systems. In each case sampling has been undertaken for palaeobotanical remains as well as to produce more reliable artefact density counts in order to facilitate comparisons between and within sites.

Preliminary results

Some general results are clear from a preliminary examination of the results of fieldwalking and recording of private collections from 1991–5. We can compare two areas – the inland lake–side parishes of Sonderhå & Norhå and Heltborg parish on the Limfjord. Both private collections and our own fieldwalking show Mesolithic concentrations on the coast and by small inland lakes, some of which were once joined to the North Sea. A similar pattern applies for the Early and Middle Neolithic. In the Late Neolithic (starting with the Single Grave Culture) there is a clear shift inland, with substantial settlements established on hilltops and barrows constructed mainly on hillsides. In the Early Bronze Age settlements and barrows switch location, so settlements move to hillsides, also becoming smaller, and barrows to hilltops. In the Late Bronze Age and into the Iron Age this move downslope of settlement continues, so that by the Roman Iron Age most settlement sites are on fairly low-lying damp ground and are artificially built up (Bech 1985).

The period for which the most information is available at present is the Late Neolithic to Early Bronze Age, as this has naturally been the focus of our barrow excavations, but also the majority of settlements located and subsequently investigated in detail have so far fallen within this date range. For the Late Neolithic and Early Bronze Age private collections and fieldwalking have between them revealed a substantial number of concentrations of material in the ploughsoil, by now amounting to some 50 distinct sites. Over a dozen of these have been excavated on varying scales. A definite change in the character, as well as the siting, of settlements seems to take place from the Late Neolithic to Early Bronze Age. In the Late Neolithic both hamlets and single houses exist within short distances of each other, the hamlets producing extremely dense and large lithic concentrations in the ploughsoil. The post-built rectangular house walls are difficult to detect, with the size of the post-holes showing the houses to be of very flimsy construction. It does appear as though the major clearance phase detected at the beginning of the Late Neolithic (Andersen 1992–3) had permanently altered the environment, leaving few trees behind. The other major feature of Late Neolithic houses is the presence of a sunken floor in most cases. A very good match has been shown to exist between the ploughsoil material and that from excavations, showing that to machine away the ploughsoil risks losing a major element of the site material, that which is not retained in pit fills or the sunken floors of houses. In the Early Bronze Age all identified sites are single houses, although sometimes situated quite close to other Early Bronze Age houses, therefore represented in the ploughsoil by smaller lithic scatters. In the Early Bronze Age there are also rectangular timber houses, rather larger than in the Late Neolithic. This does not appear to represent an improvement in timber supply, however, as surviving Early Bronze Age timbers (as at Bjerre – Bech 1991) are of extremely poor quality. There thus seems to have been no significant recovery in the local timber supply.

The sunken floors of the Late Neolithic structures have proved to be highly productive, producing large numbers of artefacts and ecofacts (although, not, unfortunately, animal bones) from both primary floor levels and subsquent fill deposits. These elongated depressions were excavated in a chequer-board pattern of 2 x 2m squares, with undiagnostic finds and samples recorded in 1 m squares within the larger unit, and diagnostic finds given three-dimensional point proveniences. The volume of soil removed during excavation was recorded, in order to facilitate the comparison of densities of artefacts across and between house floors. One additional way in which we have attempted to examine these deposits is to use the heavy fraction from botanical samples left over after flotation. These samples have nothing removed beforehand, so they represent a pure unsorted sample. This allows for very detailed analysis, with concentrations of flaking debris allowing the identification of flintworking areas within houses, even though larger flakes may show no such concentration – this suggests that larger material was tidied away. Other samples have produced possible dust from amber working. These samples also provide an extra more rigorous dimension of comparison between structures. Preliminary analysis suggests that this emphasis on comparison between structures is a profitable approach. For example, House I within the hamlet of Thy 2758 has overall high flake counts, debris from pressure flaking and a large number of dagger fragments; the single house structure at Thy 2756, within sight of Thy 2758, has low flake counts, little debris from pressure flaking and a high proportion of arrowheads.

One surprise has been the discovery of substantial amounts of Beaker–influenced ceramics in and around these Late Neolithic sunken floor buildings. More highly decorated Bell Beaker drinking cups and jars were found along with less well made horizontally banded vessels which appear to have been used for storage and cooking (see Bech *et al.* 1996). Such Beaker–influenced pottery has been found before in Northern Jutland (e.g. Jensen 1972; Asingh 1987; Liversage and Robinson 1992–3), but our work shows it to be the standard ceramic type on settlements at the end of the Late Neolithic in southern Thy, as Liversage suspected (1987). This is extremely surprising because Southern Jutland has almost no Beaker related material. A similar distribution pattern also emerges from the study of metalwork of Late Neolithic Period I, which has a real concentration in North Jutland around the Limfjord (Vandkilde 1990). This material shows connections with western Europe, specifically Holland, in terms of style and raw material. Further Beaker–related influences are represented by the production of type I flint daggers, which seem to copy tanged copper daggers, in North Jutland (Vandkilde 1990), in the production of V–perforated amber buttons in Thy and in the higher degree of use of arrowheads as gravegoods in North Jutland (Rasmussen 1990). The degree of linkage between North Jutland and western European Beaker developments suggests that Thy, at least, was a fully connected part of the Beaker network.

Did the exchange of amber and flint draw Thy, and thereby Northern Jutland as a whole, into wider North European exchange networks, from which the rest of Denmark was excluded, or excluded itself? It is unlikely that the exchange of amber and flint with foreign partners was necessary to the maintenance of the social fabric in Thy, and it may therefore be that pre–existing developments in the Single Grave period, during which the dramatic transformation of the landscape began, had already produced a more outward looking society in Thy before the Late Neolithic. Unfortunately, the archaeological record of Thy, as elsewhere in Denmark, for the Single Grave period is largely confined to burials. To fill this gap in the settlement record is one of the major remaining aims of TAP.

Settlements, fields and barrows

We have also investigated some twenty five ploughed over barrows, mostly round in form, with a few long barrows. Unusually, the majority of long barrows are of Early Bronze Age date in Thy. Why there should have been this revival of an ancient form of barrow burial at this particular time is not clear, although it is hoped that analysis of the gravegoods of burials below long barrows compared to those accompanying round barrow burials may throw some light on the problem. All barrows excavated by TAP have been examined for surviving burials or grave goods, preserved settlement traces and for buried soils preserved below the mound. Few well preserved burials have been detected, due to ploughing having completely removed all but a residual trace of where the mound had been in many cases. A number of burial deposits have been salvaged, however.

More interesting is the observation through excavation that many hilltop barrows of Early Bronze Age date can be shown to cover Late Neolithic domestic material. To this may be added barrows which are protected and therefore unavailable for excavation, but which are still being eroded by agricultural activity, particularly grazing cattle – in several cases the turves making up the mound contain flintwork of Late Neolithic character.

The most significant observation, however, was that in nearly all the cases where the barrow mound was relatively well preserved there were ard marks preserved below the mound. Moreover, in most instances these were found to be cutting through a Late Neolithic occupation surface, often related to

houses, as at Thy 2758, where House III lay below the Early Bronze Age round barrow (Fig. 2).

This evidence from Thy can be used to throw some light on the debate over the interpretation of ard marks below burial mounds. These were first recognised in Denmark in the 1930s as humus–filled grooves in the subsoil, and interpreted as furrows left by the use of an ard share (see Thrane 1989 for a history of research). There has, however, been a continuing debate over the motive underlying the use of the ard in this context. Pètzold (1960) argued that those ard–marks found below Bronze Age barrows represented a part of the burial ritual, but this view has traditionally found little support (e.g. Nielsen 1971). One exception is the rare examples of ard–furrows which encircle barrows, and pre–date the construction of the mound, and are thus seen as a stage in the construction ritual of the barrow (Thrane 1989), presumably one in which the sacred area was marked out from the rest of the landscape.

A generalised interpretation of ard marks as ritual in nature, forming part of the funerary ceremony, has been revived by Rowley–Conwy (1987) and supported by Tarlow (1993–4), despite being dismissed by Thrane (1989) and the negative response by Kristiansen (1990). Rowley–Conwy's case is based on two main sites, the Middle Neolithic passage grave of Lundehøj on the island of Møn (Ørsnes 1956) and the circular mark below the Early Bronze Age Hjerpsted round barrow on Jutland (Weill 1975). Circular markings are, as discussed above, generally interpreted as a special case, so this really only leaves a single case, that of Lundehøj. Here the circumstances appear to rule out agricultural activity, as

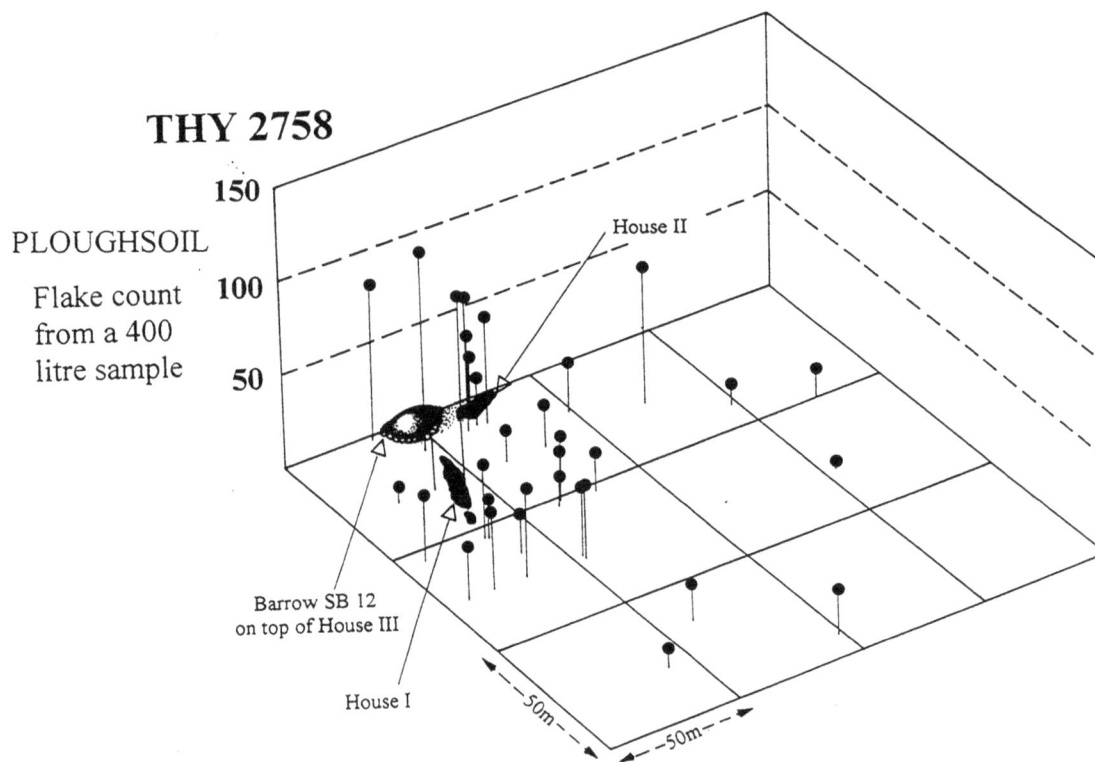

Figure 2. Thy 2758, results of ploughsoil sampling and excavation.

the ard marks are cut into a clay floor which is said to have been laid down after the stone chamber within which it was situated was constructed. The ard marks must therefore, if this stratigraphic observation is correct, be accepted as being produced within the area of the chamber. At this one site, there is therefore, a good case for a ritual episode of use of an ard referring to agricultural cultivation (Tarlow 1993–4). However, as Kristiansen has pointed out vigorously (1990), this is hardly a sound basis for generalisation. Rowley-Conwy has also brought in as a piece of supporting evidence the suggestion by Randsborg and Nyboe (1986) that one of the directions in which the criss–cross ard marks run is always parallel to the alignment of the grave, thus implying a quite direct relationship between the two. However, this observation is not accepted as correct by Thrane (1989), who concludes from his general survey of the material that this is true in several cases, but certainly not in all. Indeed, as Kristiansen notes (1990), there is a tendency for graves to be aligned roughly on compass points, which may be true also of fields and thus possibly of ploughing within those fields.

The alternative point of view, as argued by Nielsen (1971), Thrane (1989) and Kristiansen (1990), is that ard marks below barrows represent traces of traditional farming fortuitously preserved by the subsequent placement of a burial mound above this random fragment of a field. The interpretation of ard marks in general as agricultural in nature has been based on three observations. First, that not all barrows cover ard marks, and that this is true of modern excavations where ard marks have been searched for, as well as older excavations (Thrane 1989); therefore an episode of ritual ploughing can not be a universal feature of burial ceremonies, as Randsborg and Nyboe (1986) implied. Second, that where the ground surface below the barrow into which the ard marks have been cut has been preserved outside the area of the mound, the ard marks are seen to continue beyond the area of the mound (Kristiansen 1990). Third, the ard marks found below barrows appear to be of the same kind as those ard marks discovered in ancient fields (Nielsen 1986), and therefore it can be argued that the simplest course of action is to assume that the same activity brought about both groups of plough marks (Thrane 1989).

A more direct line of enquiry has, however, been employed as part of TAP, which may be said to have answered Thrane's plea (1989) for scientific analysis of these ploughed soil horizons. Three barrows excavated by TAP which proved to cover ard marks have been sampled for pollen (Andersen 1996). These are at Bjergene I (Thy 2758), a round barrow, and Bjergene II (Thy 2453), a long barrow, both of which also covered Late Neolithic settlements, and Damsgård (Thy 2954). At Bjergene II there were clear traces of the presence of plants which grow on bare mineral soils (Andersen 1996). These were barley and several species which today occur as weeds in cultivated or fallow areas – sheep's sorrel, goosefoot and knotgrass. The cultivation of a field at Bjergene II before the construction of the long barrow is clearly indicated. Similar, though less varied, plant communities occur in the buried soils below the Bjergene I and Damsgård barrows, with barley and oats present at Damsgård (Andersen 1996). It is also significant

that in each case pollen analysis also revealed that cultivation had been abandoned in favour of grazing before the construction of the mound, indicated primarily by the presence of ribwort plantain (Andersen 1996). The direct link between ard marks and burial can therefore be shown not to exist in these specific instances. Further pollen analyses as part of ongoing TAP sampling of buried soil horizons should allow further refinement of this picture, but the outlines are already becoming clear.

While the weight of evidence is therefore clearly in favour of the interpretation of the vast majority of ard marks being a consequence of agricultural activity rather than a stage of the burial ritual, we may take a wider view of the matter, following Tarlow's suggestions (1993–4). Those examples of circular furrows being scored around the area later covered by the mound, while not representing the same kind of activity as the criss–cross ard marks of fields, do seem to represent another reference to ploughing, albeit rather more oblique than that seen at Lundehøj. As Tarlow argues, Weill's (1975) view that the roughly circular scorings of the ground at Hjerpsted represent markers for placing kerbstones in the correct position, is possible, but hardly the most likely method if the creation of an accurate circle was what was required. Instead it seems as though a connection was perhaps being made between the soil fertility created through human labour and that to be hoped for from the benificent intervention of the favoured dead. In addition, we may see here the marking off of an area of land for burial by a plough line and a line of stones, just as the edges of fields were marked off by a plough line and a bank and ditch, or perhaps an earth and stone bank. In both cases a clear dividing line has been drawn partly with the aid of an ard. We may also investigate, as Tarlow suggests (1993–4), the reasoning behind the creation of barrows within fields. In some cases this involved the construction of mounds within fields which were still being ploughed, as noted at Diverhøj on Jutland and sites in Schleswig (Asingh 1987). Here the barrow was later enlarged, thus preserving the ard marks running around the earlier mound. In each case these were sites where earlier settlements also lay below the barrow. The taking out of cultivation of this particular piece of land must been both costly and awkward. Other barrows, such those examined by TAP, were within grazed areas, but here as well there may have been a high cost in terms of the loss of valuable land. At Damsgård the high presence of ribwort plantain in the samples from the barrow mound is interpreted as demonstrating heavy grazing pressure (Andersen 1996). Here, too, then, it was not a cost–free decision to set aside land for burial.

One final observation which can be made from the pollen analyses is that they appear to demonstrate the possibility that the turves which make up the barrow mounds were derived from a variety of sources. At Damsgård, for example, although the samples from the mound showed very high amounts of ribwort plantain, that from the buried soil below the mound had less than half the ribwort content. Thus Andersen (1996) concludes that there was a high level of grazing pressure in the area from which the turf sampled in the mound had derived, but only a moderate level of grazing pressure at the site of the barrow itself. The possibility therefore exists that at least some of the turf used to construct the barrow was brought from somewhere else. Similarly, at both the Visby long barrow (Thy 2563) and the Egshvile round barrow (Thy 2554) there was significant variety in the percentage of tree cover in different samples from the barrow mounds, one of the Egshvile samples deriving from an area where birch woodland had been cleared and burnt. While Andersen (1996) adopts the straightforward position that the turves sampled derive from sites around the barrow itself, there is nothing to show that they could not have been derived from a much wider landscape. Further work could clarify this issue, as there are a number of turf mounds in Thy where the conditions of preservation are such that it is possible to sample individual turves. This more detailed examination should produce further evidence that turves had been brought from a number of separate environments to create the mound. This could well have acted as a demonstration of the power of the dead individual in terms of their land holding therefore of the power and wealth of their successor. The size of a burial mound may therefore relate to the wider landscape not just in terms of creating a highly visible monument which involves taking land out of agricultural use, but may also represent a reminder of the way in which the landscape was exploited and controlled by powerful individuals.

Finally, we may examine the overall sequence revealed for a number of barrow locations in Thy and elsewhere. The pollen analyses from TAP barrow mounds (Andersen 1996) show that later enlargements of the mound structure with more turf, presumably associated with further burials, took place in a heavily grazed landscape. This general picture is also seen in the regional pollen diagrams (Andersen 1992–3; Liversage and Robinson 1992–3; Andersen & Rasmussen 1994). A sequence therefore appears to exist here of settlement–>field–>barrow and grazing. This relates to the general change in the use of hilltop locations noted above, from being the focus of settlement in the Late Neolithic to occupation by the dead and grazing animals in the Early Bronze Age.

It appears as though the cultural construction of the landscape, which defines traditions of meaning which are embodied by, and embedded within, the landscape, produced through time a series of cultural constraints on the way in which settlements, fields, grazing land and burial sites were articulated. Circumstances had developed which made certain places within the landscape particularly appropriate as focal points for activities which referred back to previous uses of the same ground. Specifically, the reuse of settlement locations for barrow construction following agricultural activity may have a greater significance than generally believed. Although one could argue that the survival of settlement traces below mounds is merely a fortuitous consequence of the protective mound covering, as suggested for ard marks, settlements are far more durable given the greater depth of associated features and material remains left in the ploughsoil. It seems unlikely therefore that the connection between the two is purely an artefact of site destruction processes. The surface survey and

excavations of TAP show that in a number of cases there are perfectly satisfactory locations for barrows, along the same ridge line, for example, which would have avoided earlier settlement traces, but these were not chosen for mound construction. The large number of preserved barrows which incorporate large amounts of lithic material may also be relevant here, for it is possible that turf and soil from the location of a previous settlement was brought to the burial site because it was accorded a special significance.

What might the connection be, which led to the eventual monumentalisation of particular places in a culturally created landscape? It may be that particular settlement sites were seen as more significant than others. For example, there are some indications from comparative analysis of sunken floor buildings that sites with less material were not later covered by a barrow. It may be that richer sites had a higher place in a political landscape which eventually led to their memorialisation by incorporation within a funerary structure on an ancestral settlement site. An additional factor may have been the greater soil fertility which the presence of an earlier settlement may have possessed, suggesting a conceptual link between fertility and death (Tarlow 1993–4). The two factors could easily have operated in combination.

Whatever the case, it is clear that these local perceptions of the cultural landscape can be investigated through a multi-faceted approach to the archaeological record which operates at several scales. Further fieldwork will enable us to examine these suggestions in more detail. This will involve consideration of the placing of barrows of various kinds relative to earlier and contemporary settlement. A major focus of continuing interest will be the variation between settlements in the Neolithic of Thy, which may have created a long lasting perception of the local landscape which can then be traced in subsequent actions for well over a millennium, until barrows were abandoned and settlements moved down onto the lower ground and became villages.

Acknowledgements

I must thank all my colleagues in the Thy Project, and particularly the Danish for their forbearance with bumptious foreigners who must all too often have seemed to heading down complete blind alleys.

Bibliography

Andersen, S. T. (1992–3) 'History of Vegetation and Agriculture at Hassing Huse Mose, Thy, northwest Denmark, since the Ice Age', *Journal of Danish Archaeology* 11, 57–79.
(1996) 'Pollen analyses from Early Bronze Age barrows in Thy', *Journal of Danish Archaeology* 12.
Andersen, S. T. and Rasmussen, P. (1994) 'Geobotaniske undersøgelse af kulturlanskabets historie. Pollenanalyser fra gravehøj og søer 1993', *Danmarks Geologiske Undersøgelse. Kunderapport* 18.
Asingh, P. (1987) 'Diverhøj – a Complex Burial Mound and

a Neolithic Settlement', *Journal of Danish Archaeology* 6, 130–54.

Bech, J–H. (1985) 'The Iron Age village mound at Heltborg, Thy', *Journal of Danish Archaeology* 4, 129–146.

(1991) 'Et bronzealderlandskab ved Bjerre i Nord Thy. Om arkæologiske udgravninger forund for en planlagt motorbane', *Museerne i Viborg amt* 16, 41–48.

Bech, J–H., Earle, T. K., Kristiansen, K., Rowlands, M., Thorpe, I. J., Aperlo, P., Erdman, D., Kelertas, K., Haack Olsen, A–L. and Steinberg, J. (1996) 'The Thy Archaeological Project. Preliminary report', *Journal of Danish Archaeology* 12.

Beck, C. and Shennan, S. (1991) *Amber in Prehistoric Britain*, Oxford: Oxbow Monograph 8.

Becker, C.J. (1959) 'Flint mining in Neolithic Denmark', *Antiquity* 33: 87–93.

(1980) 'D.K Dänemark: Hov–Bjerre–Aalborg–Hillerslev–Fornaes–Stevns Klint', in G. Weisgerber (ed.) *5000 Jahre Feuersteinbergbau*, Bohum: Deutsches Bergbau Museum, 456– 473.

Clark, R. and Schofield, R. (1991) "By Experiment and Calibration: an integrated approach to the archaeology of the ploughsoil", in A. J. Schofield (ed.) *Interpreting Artefact Scatters: contributions to ploughzone archaeology*, Oxford: Oxbow Monograph, 93–105.

Cole, W. (1992) *Using the UTM grid system to record historic sites*, Washington, D.C.: Department of the Interior, National Park Service.

DeMarrais, E., Castillo, L. J. and Earle, T. (1996) 'Ideology, Materialization and Power Strategies', *Current Anthropology* 37, 15–31.

Jensen, J. A. (1972) 'Myrhøj, 3 hustomter med klokkebægerkeramik', *Kuml*, 61–122.

Kristiansen, K. (1990) "Ard marks under barrows: a response to Peter Rowley–Conwy", *Antiquity* 63, 322–327.

Kuna, M. (1991) 'The structuring of prehistoric landscape', *Antiquity* 65, 332–347.

Liversage, D. (1987) 'Mortens Sande 2 – a Single Grave Camp Site in Northwest Jutland', *Journal of Danish Archaeology* 6, 101–124.

Liversage, D. and Robinson, D. (1992–3) 'Prehistoric Settlement and Landscape Development in the Sandhill Belt of Southern Thy', *Journal of Danish Archaeology* 11, 39–56.

Neustupny, E. (1991) 'Community areas of prehistoric farmers in Bohemia', *Antiquity* 65, 326–331.

Nielsen, V. (1971) 'Spor', Brudstykker, Holger Friis tilegnet, Hjørring: *Historisk Samfund for Vendsyssel*, 73–83.

(1986) 'Ploughing in the Iron Age. Plough Marks in Store Vildmose, North Jutland', *Journal of Danish Archaeology* 5, 189–208.

Olausson, D. (1987–8) 'Where have all the settlements gone? Field Survey Methods for Locating Bronze and Iron Age Settlements in a Cultivated Landscape', *Meddelanden från Lunds universitets historiska museum*, 99–112.

Pätzold, J. (1960) 'Rituelles Pflügen bei den vorgeschichtlichen Totenkult', *Prähistorische Zeitschrift* 37, 189–239.

Randsborg, K. and Nyboe, C. (1986) "The Coffin and the Sun", *Acta Archaeologica* 55, 161–184.

Rasmussen, M. (1992–3) 'Settlement Structure and Economic Variation in the Early Bronze Age', *Journal of Danish Archaeology* 11, 87–107.

Rasmussen, L. Wincentz 1990. 'Dolkproduktion og distribution i senneolitikum', *Hikuin* 16, 31–42.

Rowley–Conwy, P. (1987) 'The interpretation of ard marks', *Antiquity* 61, 263–266.

Shott, M. (1989) 'Shovel–test sampling in archaeological survey: comments on Nance and Ball, and Lightfoot', *American Antiquity* 54, 369–404.

Smith, K. and Thorpe, I. J. N. (1996) 'Shoveltesting at Shapwick: a preliminary report', in C. Gerrard and M. Aston (eds.) *The Shapwick Project: a Topographical and Historical Study – the Fourth Report* (University of Bristol).

Tarlow, S. (1993–4) 'Scraping the bottom of the barrel: an agricultural metaphor in Neolithic/Bronze Age European burial practice', *Journal of Theoretical Archaeology* 3/4, 123–144.

Thrane, H. (1989) 'Danish Plough–Marks from the Neolithic and Bronze Age, *Journal of Danish Archaeology* 8, 111–125.

Vandkilde, H. (1990) 'Senneolitikum ved Limfjorden: Fradominans til anonymitet', in Limfjordspojektet rapport. *Limfjordsegnens kultur–og naturhistorie*, Århus, 109–122.

Weill, S. (1975) 'En høj i Hjerpsted', *Kuml*, 83–98.

Ørsnes, M. (1956) 'Om en jættestues konstruktion og brug', *Aarbøger for Nordisk Oldkyndighed og Historie*, 221–232.

Christian Landscapes of Pagan Monuments. A Radical Constructivist Perspective.

Cornelius J Holtorf
Department of Archaeology, St David's University College, Lampeter

Constructing Megaliths in the Landscape

Geographical studies have shown time and again that landscapes are not only 'natural' but also very much 'cultural' (see Meinig (ed.) 1979; Cosgrove 1989; Bender (ed.) 1993). In order to understand a landscape one has to understand people, because 'any landscape is composed not only of what lies before our eyes but what lies within our heads' (Meinig 1979: 34). There is, however, no one single meaning of landscape. Landscapes are symbolic and they can be interpreted in different ways. In order to understand landscapes we need to know in which context we want to 'decode' them (Cosgrove 1989: 125ff.). Megaliths are in many cases particularly impressive features of landscapes and as such they were appreciated by those who approached them. The fact that these monuments happen to have been built several millenia before the time on which I will focus is only a minor detail of their Being and neither terribly exciting nor particularly important. The issue is how people made megaliths intelligible and how they made sense and use of them in different ways at different times (Holtorf forthcoming (a) and (b)). One could therefore say that megaliths, together with the landscapes as part of which they were received, have continuously been reconstructed, cognitively. Often cognitive constructions did also have an impact on material constructions, through changes and transformations of the actual stones. I will give some examples for this later. But at first, I need to explain why I write of 'constructing' monuments (see also Holtorf 1995).

Constructivism developed from recent approaches within the Philosophy of Science and the Sociology of Scientific Knowledge. Constructivists argue that all knowledge is constructed rather than discovered, and that it is impossible to tell (and unnecessary to know) if and to what degree knowledge reflects an 'ontological' reality. Most radically, this position has been put forward by proponents of 'Radical Constructivism' such as Ernst von Glasersfeld (1987; 1991). They argue that knowledge is both won and validated by 'fitting' to, and 'viability' in the light of, our experiences of the world, i.e. how it makes sense to us and not to what extent it represents an assumed objective reality. Obviously, the viability of knowledge is to a large extent also dependent on contingent social circumstances which partly, though not exclusively, define what does and what does not 'make sense' in a given situation. Radical Constructivism is highly empirical in its approach, yet nothing would be more opposed to it than empiricism.

From a Radical Constructivist perspective, the past as such is not denied, although the conviction is held that as human beings we lack a position from which we could measure the degree to which our accounts represent the 'real past' (Rusch 1987). Similarly, archaeological objects such as megaliths are not disputed in their physical existence but we cannot know any 'inherent' meanings or facts about them. Radical Constructivism claims that we construct knowledge and meaningful understanding according to cognitive and practical (that includes social) viability in the world as we experience it, not according to correspondence to a (past) reality. The same is of course also true for this very argument which attempts no more than to make sense and does not claim to disclose the truth about anything. A Radical Constructivist archaeology holds that (pre) history and (pre) historic objects, in all the different forms they are, or were, seen in and made sense of by different people, are constructions of the respective present.

In this paper, I am concerned with making sense of (cognitive) constructions of prehistoric monuments in the minds of people living in different places and ages. I am constructing constructions, and this is why my endeavour constitutes a 'second order' construction of megaliths. By telling you something about other people's constructions of megaliths, I tell you something about both my own construction of these other constructions and my own construction of the megaliths themselves. This is not to devalue my own approach but to make clear what I do and do not claim about its status. I do not set my own constructions apart from other people's: all are cognitive constructions of experienced phenomena, which try to make sense in their own right. Nothing more.

Christian Landscapes of Megaliths

In the following I will focus on megalithic monuments as they were 'constructed' by the Christian Church, theologians and Christians. What I will attempt is an overview over some major ways in which Christianity made sense and use of megaliths through its representatives and followers.[1] Christians encountered ancient monuments in the physical landscape and made them part of a cultural and symbolic landscape, thus rendering them intelligible. By studying the underlying cognitive constructions of megaliths I aim at transcending the conventional limitations in landscape studies of a narrowly defined time period or geographical area concerned. Surely I do not want to imply that 'Christianity' had a single voice. I also do not want to deny that Christian views on both the pagan past and megaliths must have varied considerably between bishops, various theologians and different sorts of local believers; they also differed from century to century, and from country to country (see e.g. Burl 1979: chapter 2; Dark 1993). This could not have been ignored if my study had been conceived as part of a wider history or sociology of Christianity. But this is not its context. My interest are megaliths and how they were understood long after they had been erected. Christianity provides a wide-spread and distinctive context for such understandings, even though the interpretations themselves were diverse. Studying Christian landscapes of pagan monuments contributes both to a poetics of prehistory and, more specifically, to an aesthetics of megalith receptions.

---

[1] In the remainder of this paper, I will draw heavily (and often unacknowledged) on Daniel 1972; Grinsell 1976: chapters 2–4; Grinsell 1986; and Morris 1989: chapter 2. Consult these accounts for more case-studies and detailed references to the literature.

The main reason why megaliths could be cognitively constructed some three thousand years after their first erection was of course their monumentality. In opposition to many other remains of earlier ages, these stones had not disappeared and were still visible, possibly well known to local people. This is, however, not to say that people had an idea about the actual age or original cultural context of the stones; some may have held them for natural features, most for relatively young and in any case Christian constructions. Often enough, the stones were first and foremost perceived as something hard and permanent which could be re-used for other purposes. Quite a few of the thousands of country churches and stone walls of churchyards may partly have been built out of the large stones that demolished megaliths conveniently supplied (Barber & Williams 1989: 72).

Overall though, Christianity seems mostly to have neglected the old 'pagan' places: 'Given the very large total of both prehistoric stone monuments and medieval churches, the lack of correlation between the two seems conclusive. On the other hand, the very singularity of those cases that are known may invest them with a potential significance' (Morris 1989: 82). In the latter cases, megaliths were not considered as merely building material but as something that is connected to the spiritual and religious sphere. They became part of a mythical landscape and Christian cosmology. The Christian reinterpretations of some prominent prehistoric remains partly reflect the larger 'Christianisation of the landscape' (Roymans 1995).

The Church and its theologians employed (at different times and places, which will be mostly ignored here) two main strategies to deal with prehistoric monuments. One strategy consisted of ascribing these stones to the Devil and consequently treating them as sites of evil. Perhaps because they had played a role in the ritual life of pagan communities, prehistoric monuments appeared as a symbol for paganism as such: 'the god of one religion becomes the Devil of that which replaces it' (Grinsell 1976: 20). It may have been a consequence of such a 'diabolisation' (Roymans 1995: 15) that today a large number of megaliths and other sites in the landscape are named after the Devil (Fig. 1), or connected with him in folklore. At Avebury, Wiltshire, for instance, many stones were carefully buried in the earth, possibly after having been linked with the Devil (Burl 1979: 35–37; cf. Ucko *et al.* 1991: 179f.).

The fact that megaliths in Medieval times have been ascribed to the Devil does not automatically allow an interpretation of the stones as monuments of highly (negative) religious significance. Medieval society was a religious society to a degree which we find difficult to imagine today, living in a (Western European) 'Christian' society ourselves where only a small proportion of people believe in God, even fewer go to church services and the church as institution has hardly any direct political influence at all. Medieval Christianity embraced all aspects of life.[2] Accordingly, something which

Figure 1. Distribution of sites named after the Devil (after Grinsell 1976).

is foreign to this society is foreign also in the religious sense. Supposed sites of ancient pagan practices can thus be determined ad hoc, and there is no need to assume any continuity of prehistoric cults or practices. As Leslie Grinsell writes, 'in many instances 'Devil' traditions ... merely indicate that the monuments to which they relate were constructed by a race unconnected with the present inhabitants' (1976: 21). It is hardly surprising then that the strange old stones of megaliths, which often featured very prominently and monumentally in the landscape, were similarly perceived as something foreign and unwelcome stemming from another time or another world that was unconnected to the present, e.g. the worlds of the Devil or of giants. Similarly, in early modern times prehistoric sites were perceived as directly connected to witchcraft (Grinsell 1973).

How the Christian Church dealt with pagan sites is partly reflected in the edicts of the early Church Councils. The canons of the Councils of Arles (443–452), Tours (567),

---

[2] For a critical view on this old assumption see Susan Reynolds' account of Medieval scepticism (1990); see also Carlo Ginzburg's classic **The Cheese and the Worms** (1992) about the complex worldview of a sixteenth–century miller. Their point, however, makes the argument for a direct religious significance of ancient monuments stronger and not weaker, since many

monuments have quite obviously, for some reason, been linked to the Devil (see. above and fig.1).

Figure 2. The carved stone of St Uzec.

Figure 3. 'Christian over Pagan'.

Nantes (658), and Toledo (681 and 693), among others, contained passages that condemned worshipping at the pagan sanctuaries and encouraged the Bishops and all Christians to neglect, to hide, and even to destroy them, with the threat of excommunication for those who did not obey. A pagan sanctuary in Gaza was completely demolished and its stones were made the paving around a new church erected on the same place, 'where the trampling of Christian feet would proclaim Christ's victory over the heathen past' (Marcus 1990: 154). It is not clear, but quite possible, that in this way also some prehistoric monuments, such as megaliths, were demolished by Christians.

An alternative and much more common strategy employed by the Christian Church was adoption, i.e. 'depaganising' and 'christianising' of the monuments in order to allow a new interpretation in the Christian sense. By the edict of Honorius (408), it was even forbidden to demolish pagan shrines and instead they had to be rededicated as Christian sanctuaries. In a letter sent in the year 601 Pope Gregory had advised King Aethelberht to 'repress the worship of idols' and 'destroy the shrines'; only one month later Gregory had changed his mind (Marcus 1970), when he wrote to Abbot Mellitus on his departure for Britain, that

'we have been giving careful thought to the affairs of the English, and have come to the conclusion that the temples of the idols among that people should on no account be destroyed. The idols are to be destroyed, but the temples themselves are to be aspersed with holy water, altars set up in them and relics deposited here. For if these temples are well-built, they must be purified from the worship of demons and dedicated to the service of the true God. In this way, we hope that the people, seeing that their temples are not destroyed, may abandon their error and, flocking more readily to their accustomed resorts, may come to know and adore the true God. And since they have a custom of sacrificing many oxen to demons, let some other solemnity be substituted in its place, such as a day of Dedication or the Festivals of the holy martyrs whose relics are enshrined there ... They are no longer to sacrifice beasts to the Devil, but they may kill them for food to the praise of God, and give thanks to the Giver of all gifts for the plenty they enjoy'
(Bede 1968: 86f.[I, 30]).

For Walter Johnson there 'is every reason to believe that the ancient 'temples' were megaliths' (1992: 6). But the text is revealing even if Gregory might not have referred here to prehistoric monuments but to former Roman or Saxon cult practices and temples, which is perhaps somewhat more plausibel (Morris 1989: 70f.). Clearly, the Christianisation of megaliths was popular too.

Some menhirs, such as the famous stone of St.Uzec, were embellished with Christian symbols and their top parts were carved out into Christian crosses (Fig. 2; Mortillet 1897). This is, however, not necessarily a transformation into a place of Christian worship since the cross can simply represent a symbolic purification of the formerly pagan site (Fig. 3; cf. Coleman–Norton 1966: 705). Other megaliths became associated in legends with the life of Christian Saints, such as St.Samson and St.Cornely. The Welsh tomb 'Ty Illtud' is decorated with crosses among others and received its name from St.Illtud who might have used it as a hermit's cell (Grinsell 1981). Similarly, St.Guthlac may have lived in a prehistoric chambered long barrow (Shook 1960), although this may have been a Roman tomb. It was also possible to deal with pagan tombs by baptising those buried: St.Patrick supposedly opened a grave and christianised the dead therein. In the case of the chambered long barrow Jack Barrow at Duntisbourne Abbots, Gloucestershire, which had been opened in 1875, the human remains were reburied in the churchyard and surmounted by a Christian cross that had been carved from one of the slabs of the tomb. In the chapel of St.Michel, which was built on top of a passage grave at Carnac, a church fresco from around 1970 can be found; it shows archaeologists excavating a tomb and by that redeeming the soul of Neolithic people who can now find their way to the heavenly Jerusalem (Kaul forthcoming).

Occasionally prehistoric monuments were incorporated into new church buildings built on their places. This brought two advantages beyond the properties of megaliths as building material: a (sometimes imaginary?) continuity of cult at the same location, and simultaneously the assurance that this cult from now on could be none but a Christian one (Kirchner 1955: 669 671). There is also the possibility that the early Church leaders tried to control the special effects caused by underground springs and various natural powers and forces that had been experienced at the prehistoric monuments (Barber & Williams 1989: 74–77). In the Chapelle des Sept–Saints in Plouaret, North Brittany, a mass is still regularly celebrated inside a megalithic tomb around which the church has been erected (Fig. 4; Mortillet 1897). At Confolens, Saint Germain, a megalith was turned into a chapel, and the supporting stones of the 'Dolmen de la Chapelle', as it is called, were replaced by round pillars with carved capitals of the eleventh/twelfth century. A late Neolithic statue menhir, covered only by a baroque wood shuttering, served as an altar stone in the church of Bühel at Latsch (Spindler 1994: 206, 210). At La Hougue Bie on Jersey two Christian chapels of the 12th and 16th century respectively were erected on top of a mound containing a passage grave (Nash, pers. comm.). Other examples of churches built over or using megaliths are to be found on the Iberian peninsula, such as Alcobertas, where a well–preserved dolmen now forms the side–chapel of the church of St. Mary Magdalene (Fig. 5), or the chapel of San Dionísio in Pavía, which is a transformed dolmen. The chapelle of Santa Cruz at Cangas de Onís in North Spain was first built in AD 737 on a mound containing a Neolithic megalith (Blas Cortina 1979). In Rudston, Humberside, a menhir that stood in the middle of a landscape covered with prehistoric monuments of all kind, was first christianised, probably through a cross–head fixed to it (hence *Rudston* – rood stone), and then incorporated into the churchyard of the church of All Saints (Fig. 6). Similarly, a menhir can be found at the outer wall of the cathedral of Le Mans in France (Michell 1982: 90f.). At Avebury the local church was perhaps raised from some of the stones of the

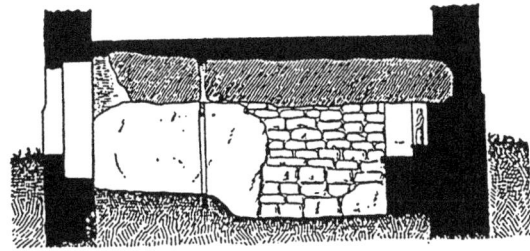

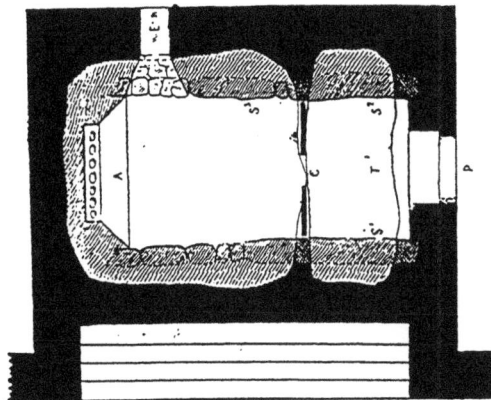

Figure 4. Chapelle des Sept–Saints in Plouaret, North Brittany: the church built around a megalithic tomb (after Mortillet 1897).

prehistoric henge monument. But the majority of the stones of Avebury, when they were buried, may deliberately not have been demolished in order to avoid *upsetting* the Devil (Burl 1979: 37; cf. Ucko *et al.* 1991: 179f.). In Knowlton, Dorset, the Norman church has been erected in the centre of a henge monument. Similarly, at Stanton Drew, Avon, the church stands in close vicinity to a larger megalithic complex including three stone circles and two stone avenues (Grinsell 1977). In Langenstein, Germany, a huge menhir of approx. 10 tons weight has formed part of the churchyard's wall for almost a millennium now (Fig. 7; Dobiat 1987). It is revealing that the whole village's name is *Langenstein*–long stone. Of more recent origin but perhaps drawing on a similar perception of both megaliths and the prehistoric past is a gravestone in the form of a menhir that can today be found on the cemetery of Locmariaquer (Fig. 8; Willing 1995: 28). Sometimes churches were deliberately built next to prehistoric (and therefore pagan) remains in the landscape. At Midmar, Aberdeenshire, a stone circle is situated in a

Figure 5. Alcobertas: dolmen as a side chapel.

Figure 6. All Saints Church, Rudston, Humberside.

Figure 7. Menhir as part of churchyard's wall in Langenstein, Germany (from Dobiat 1987).

Figure 8. Gravestone in the form of a menhir on the cemetery of Locmariaquer (photograph by Matthias Willing, reproduced by permission).

churchyard. It may also be no coincidence that the cathedral of Santiago de Compostela in Galicia was sited in an area rich in megalithic monuments; perhaps it absorbed an old megalithic cult (Fleure 1931: 17; Howes 1925).

But things were perhaps not as simple as they may appear from what I have written so far. Nico Roymans recently questioned a too simplifying dichotomy of the available choice for action of the Christian Church against prehistoric monuments: a negative choice leading to neglect and complete destruction, and a positive choice leading to continuity of place and assimilation, of which only one could be chosen. Roymans emphasised instead a spatial distinction made by the Christian Church in early modern village territories. In an 'outer zone' with negative, non–Christian connotations prehistoric funerary monuments were left intact but *at the same time* 'diabolised'. In an 'inner zone', on the other side, which was 'perceived as Christian, civilised and cultural', pagan monuments have been either destroyed or 'christianised' by connecting them with the cult of a saint (Roymans 1995: 18f., 33).

It is still today a hotly debated question whether there is a direct continuity of the practices and customs that are reported for the Medieval Age from prehistoric times. This is not the place to discuss the matter of continuity fully.[3] What matters here is that magical practices of various kinds took place at prehistoric monuments in Medieval times, whether in continuity from prehistoric customs or not (Flint 1991). Partly, they may have been connected with old pagan beliefs, and hence were combatted by the Christian church and Medieval law (Uslar 1972; Bender 1993: 258f.). Generally speaking, magic and religion are two quite different spheres, although at times they may overlap. While religions involve the worshipping of gods, magic is restricted to attempts to enforce control over nature by spiritual forces (see Hutton 1991: 289–292). The Christian Church tried to blur this distinction and declared all magic as 'pagan', but magic and religion may well have been practised on different occasions by the same Christian people (Barb 1963). The range of magical practices at megaliths was extensive, but many related to fertility or health (Wood–Martin 1902: chapter VI; Kirchner 1955: 653–661). Others were connected to prophecy.

The Christian Churches of the present have no strong feelings about prehistoric monuments, nor (to the best of my knowledge) any policies of how to deal with them. Paganism is encountered elsewhere. But this is not to say that the megaliths and barrows have lost all of their spiritual aura. Some elderly inhabitants of Blieskastel, Saarland, Germany, remember well that the menhir 'Gollenstein' used to be the target point of Easter processions by people from the surrounding villages (Holtorf forthcoming (b)). Perhaps in an effort to 'christianise' the site, at the beginning of the last century, a little niche was cut into the monument and may

originally have been filled with a Saint's figurine; nowadays a candle is put in there occasionally. Quite a few pilgrims who come to Blieskastel as a place of Roman Catholic pilgrimage afterwards visit the Gollenstein. A lot of people nowadays, and by far not only New Age supporters and modern druids (see Carr–Gomm 1991), are attracted by a somehow magical mystery which surrounds prehistoric monuments. Some consider menhirs in general as places of magical practices which were part of ancient fertility cults; in their shape they resemble phalli clearly enough. Even some of the Medieval magical practices at megaliths are still known, and occasionally carried out (Eliade 1958: 221–225). Other 'old' practices are in fact not–so–old and turn out to be fairly recent creations (Hutton 1991: 294f.; Johnson 1992: 14). In the Saarland I met someone who had an idea to celebrate pagan weddings at the Gollenstein and considers such rituals as a possible alternative to what the Christian church offers.

Conclusions about Constructions

In this paper I hope to have shown, at the example of Christian receptions of megaliths, how 'constructions' of monuments in the mind of people can be approached. I have demonstrated what roles megaliths can play as part of larger understandings of landscapes and of the world: in a 'Christianity' landscape, prehistoric stone monuments were seen as convenient building material. Others were known to the Church and many Christians as symbols of a foreign 'pagan' world, associated by theologians with the Devil, and therefore perhaps sometimes demolished. Many more ancient ritual monuments were 'Christianity' and in some cases turned into places of Christian worship. In addition, megaliths were considered by some local believers to be appropriate places to conduct (or continue) magical practices in order to influence the course of nature. By developing a Radical Constructivist research interest and methodology[4], archaeology can complement geographical studies on the meanings of monuments as elements of the landscape, contributing also to an 'archaeology of mind'.

Secondly, I have mentioned a number of specific monuments and fragments of their individual histories. The later history of megaliths in the landscape is, however, a field that has been much overlooked in the past.[5] It is as if archaeology only deals with birth and death of the stones: the Neolithic, when most megaliths were first erected, and the Present, when megaliths become frozen on tourist–sites or demolished by ploughing on the fields. But strangely enough, all the millenia of adolescence, maturity, and senility(?) of megaliths seem not to have attracted much interest by

---

[3] While earlier scholars such as Walter Johnson (1992), Herbert Fleure (1931), and Glyn Daniel (1972: 19–21, 38, 59) have been astonishingly optimistic about such a continuity, today much more caution is generally uttered (e.g. Morris 1989: chapter 2; Hutton 1991: chapter 8; Dark 1993: 134f.). There is, of course, also the possibility of 'created' continuities (see Bradley 1987).

[4] One commentator wrote in response to this paper that 'the practice of Radical Constructivism looks very much like Conservative Empiricism; and all the more persuasive for that'. Unfortunately much current academic research seems all the more persuasive for some, when it appears to imitate 'Conservative Empiricism'. Unlike such research, a Radical Constructivist approach only looks like Conservative Empiricism in as much as that helps in persuading, while in essence the two have little in common. Radical Constructivists neither attempt to represent (a specified part of) the world nor explain its phenomena using scientific methodology alone; see the introductory section above.

[5] This remains true even though there are a few important exceptions, e.g. Daniel 1972; Michell 1982; Bradley 1987; Mohen 1990: chapter 1; Chippindale 1994; Roymans 1995. See also Holtorf forthcoming (a).

archaeologists. The relations of Christians to prehistoric monuments is a particularly complex and interesting field of study which deserves to be dealt with more intensively, as part of a larger interest in the later history of archaeological monuments.

Finally, in a reflexive manner, I turn the focus of attention on my own role as the author of this paper. It may have gone largely unnoticed, but I have also demonstrated in this paper how I myself, and other (mostly) academics to which I have referred, construct megaliths, landscapes, and the past: very different from how Christians have done it. To me, megaliths were first and foremost an object of study. I have presented megaliths and details of their history as evidence for my argument about Christian landscapes of pagan monuments. I did so within the limitations of my personal preferences and interests, the scope of my reading and creativity; in any case my argument could not be larger than what would fit into a 20 minute lecture slot first and a book chapter later. The past which I wrote about in this paper was a deliberate construct of mine that was employed in order to fulfil various purposes, including to write and read a paper at TAG, with slides; to re-write and finally publish an illustrated article; by doing this, to participate in the academic discourse; and as more than a side-effect, hopefully also to create some intelligibility and to make sense about a chosen topic. If this last point is what I have achieved, I suppose my attempt to construct constructions of megaliths was worth the effort: mine, the editors', the publisher's, and your's–the reader's.

Acknowledgements

Thanks to George Nash for first inviting me to give a paper at the session 'The Social Construction of Landscape' at TAG 1994, on which this chapter is based, and then editing the present volume. Ronald Hutton, Ross Samson, David Selwyn, and Alex Woolf have all read earlier drafts of this paper and I have benefited considerably from their suggestions and critical comments, although they are not to be held responsible for anything I wrote. I am also grateful to Philine Kalb for her hospitality and for introducing me to the Portuguese megaliths that have been transformed into chapels. Miguel A.de Blas Cortina and Mark Patton have both very kindly replied to my letters and supplied me with more valuable information than I could use in this article alone. Finally, thanks to Gretel and Tony in whose bookshelf I first came across Richard Morris' seminal book, during a house–sitting weekend in 1994.

References

Barb, A.A. 1963. 'The Survival of Magic Arts,' in *The Conflict between Paganism and Christianity in the Fourth Century*. Edited by A.Monigliano, pp. 100–125. Oxford: Clarendon.

Barber, C, and Williams, J G. 1989. *The Ancient Stones of Wales*. Abergavenny: Blorenge.

Bede. 1968. *A History of the English Church and People*. Harmondsworth: Penguin.

Bender, B. 1993. 'Stonehenge – Contested Landscapes (Medieval to Present–Day),' in B.Bender (ed.): 245–279.

Bender, B, Editor. 1993. *Landscape: Politics and Perspectives*. Providence and Oxford: Berg.

Blas–Cortina, M. A. de. 1979. La decoracion parietal del dolmen de la Santa Cruz (Cangas de Onis, Asturias). *Boletin del Instituto de Estudios Asturianos* 98, 718–757.

Bradley, R. 1987. Time regained: the creation of continuity. *Journal of the British Archaeological Association* 140, 1–17.

Burl, A. 1979. *Prehistoric Avebury*. New Haven: Yale University Press.

Carr–Gomm. 1991. *The elements of The Druid Tradition*. Shaftesbury: Element.

Chippindale, C. 1994. *Stonehenge Complete*. Second edition. London: Thames and Hudson.

Coleman–Norton, P. R. 1966. *Roman State & Christian Church. A Collection of Legal Documents to A.D. 535*. 3 Vols. London: S.P.C.K.

Cosgrove, D. 1989. 'Geography is Everywhere: Culture and Symbolism in Human Landscapes,' in *Horizons in Human Geography*: Edited by D.Gregory & R.Walford, 118–135. Basingstoke: Macmillan.

Daniel, G. 1972. *Megaliths in History*. London: Thames and Hudson.

Dark, K. R. 1993. 'Roman–Period Activity at Prehistoric Ritual Monuments in Britain and in the Armorican Peninsula,' in *Theoretical Roman Archaeology: First Conference Proceedings*. Edited by E.Scott, 133–146. Worldwide Archaeology Series Vol. 4. Aldershot: Avebury.

Dobiat, C. 1987. *Der Menhir in Langenstein, Stadt Kirchhain, Kreis Marburg–Biedenkopf*. Archäologische Denkmäler in Hessen 65 (brochure).

Eliade, M. 1958. *Patterns in Comparative Religion*. London and New York: Sheed and Ward.

Eriksen, P. 1990. *Samsos store stengrave*. Skippershoved.

Fleure, H. J. 1931. *Archaeology and folk tradition*. Sir John Rhys Memorial Lecture, 1931. London: British Academy.

Flint, V. 1991. *The Rise of Magic in Early Medieval Europe*. Princeton: Princeton University Press.

Ginzburg, C. 1992. *The cheese and the worms: the cosmos of a sixteenth–century miller* [1976]. London: Penguin.

Glasersfeld, E. von. 1987. *The Construction of Knowledge*. Seaside: Intersystems Publications.

1991. 'Knowing without Metaphysics: Aspects of the Radical Constructivist Position,' in: *Research and Reflexivity*. Edited by F.Steier, 12–29. London: Sage.

Grinsell, L. V. 1973. 'Witchcraft at some Prehistoric Sites,' in *The Witch Figure*. Edited by V.Newall, 72–79. London: Routledge and Kegan Paul.

1976. *Folklore of Prehistoric Sites in Britain*. London: David & Charles.

1977. *Stanton Drew Stone Circles, Somerset*. Department of the Environment: Ancient Monuments and Historic Buildings. (brochure)

1981. The Later History of Ty Illtud. *Archaeologia*

Cambrensis CXXX, 131–139.

1986. The Christianisation of prehistoric and other pagan sites. *Landscape History* 8, 27–37.

Haas, A. 1913. Mönchguter Altertümer aus vorgeschichtlicher Zeit. *Mannus* 5, 235–248.

Holtorf, C. J. 1995. 'Problem–orientated' and 'object–orientated' approaches of archaeological research–reconsidered. *Hephaistos* 13, 7–18. URL: http://news.acs.lamp.ac.uk/Hephaistos.html.

forthcoming (a). 'Constructed Meanings: the Receptions of Megaliths after the Neolithic,' in *Megalithic Tombs–Their Context and Construction.* Copenhagen: The National Museum. URL: http://news.acs.lamp.ac.uk/Kalundborg.html.

forthcoming (b). 'Landscapes of Monuments as Landscapes of the Mind. The Contemporary Meanings of Megaliths,' in *Megaliths and Landscapes.* Edited by J.Nordbladh. URL: http://news.acs.lamp.ac.uk/Falköping.html.

Howes, H. W. 1925. The Cult of Sant–Iago at Compostela. *Folklore* 36, 132–150.

Hutton, R. 1991. *The Pagan Religions of the Ancient British Isles.* Oxford: Blackwell.

Johnson, W. 1992. *The Later History of the Megaliths.* [First published 1908.] Loughborough: Heart of Albion Press.

Kaul, F. forthcoming. 'Redeeming the Soul of Neolithic Man. The Megaliths of Britanny in Contemporary Christian Iconography,' in *Megalithic Tombs – Their Context and Construction.* Copenhagen: The National Museum.

Kirchner, H. 1955. *Die Menhire in Mitteleuropa und der Menhirgedanke.* Akademie der Wissenschaften und der Literatur, Mainz. Abhandlungen der Geistes– und Sozialwissenschaftlichen Klasse. Nr.9, 609–817.

Leisner, G. & Leisner, V. 1956. *Die Megalithgräber der Iberischen Halbinsel.* Vol. 1.1. Berlin: Walter de Gruyter & Co.

Marcus, R. A. 1970. 'Gregory the Great and a Papal missionary strategy,' in *The Mission of the Church and the Propagation of the Faith.* Edted by G.J.Cuming, 29–38. Cambridge: Cambridge University Press.

1990. *The End of Ancient Christianity.* Cambridge: Cambridge University Press.

Meinig, D. W. 1979. The Beholding Eye. Ten Versions of the Same Scene, in Meinig (ed.): 33–48.

Editor. 1979. *The Interpretation of Ordinary Landscapes: Geographical Essays.* Oxford: Oxford University Press.

Michell, J. 1982. *Megalithomania.* London: Thames and Hudson.

Mohen, J–P. 1990. *The World of Megaliths.* New York: Facts on File.

Morris, R. 1989. *Churches in the Landscape.* London: Dent & Sons.

Mortillet, A. de. 1897. Les Monuments Mégalithiques Christianisés. *Revue Mensuelle de l' école d'Anthropologie de Paris* 7, 321–338.

Reynolds, S. 1991. Social mentalities and the case of

medieval scepticism. *Transactions of the Royal Historical Society* (Sixth Series) 1, 21–41.

Roymans, N. 1995. The cultural biography of urnfields and the long–term history of a mythical landscape (with comments and reply). *Archaeological Dialogues* 1995.1, 2–38.

Rusch, G. 1987. *Erkenntnis, Wissenschaft, Geschichte: von einem konstruktivistischen Standpunkt.* Frankfurt/M.: Suhrkamp.

Shook, L. K. 1960. The Burial Mound in Guthlac A. *Modern Philology* 58.1, 1–10.

Spindler, K. 1994. *The Man in the Ice* [1993]. London: Phoenix.

Ucko, P. J., Michael Hunter, Alan J.Clark & Andrew David. 1991. *Avebury Reconsidered. From the 1660s to the 1990s.* London: Unwin Hyman.

Uslar, R. von. 1972. 'Zu den tumuli paganorum und corpora flamma consumpta,' in *Studien zu Volkskultur, Sprache und Landesgeschichte. Festschrift Matthias Zender.* Edited by E.Ennen & G.Wiegelmann, 481–489. Bonn: Röhrscheid.

Willing, M. 1995. Im Zentrum von Armorika: Die bretonische Megalithkultur der Region Morbihan (NW–Frankreich). *Das Altertum* 41, 23–54.

Wood–Martin, W. G. 1902. *Traces of the Elder Faiths of Ireland. A Folklore Sketch. A Handbook of Irish Pre–Christian Traditions.* Vol. II. London: Longmans, Green, and Co.

The Materially–Structured Social Environment of the Maltese Islands During the Temple Building Phase

by Andrew Townsend

Acknowledgements

I would like to thank The Directors of the Gozo Archaeological Project (Professor A. Bonanno, Dr T. Gouder, Dr C. Malone, Dr S. Stoddart and Dr D. Trump) for allowing me to discuss the Brochtorff Circle excavations and use the illustrations of their finds from the site, in particular, Drs Caroline Malone and Simon Stoddart. I would also like to thank Mr Nicholas Vella for reading and commenting on earlier drafts of this paper. The writer is responsible for any ambiguity or errors. Drawings of the finds and the site reconstruction are by Steven Ashley, and are reproduced by courtesy of the Project Directors.

Excavations undertaken at the Brochtorff Circle (Gozo) between 1987 and 1994 have produced a rich source of data pertaining to mortuary practices during the Temple Period on the Maltese Islands (c.4100–2500 BC). It is advanced here, that when evaluated in conjunction with data from other known monuments on Malta and Gozo,[1] the recent discoveries enable us to formulate new hypotheses concerning the social order on the islands during this phase. Furthermore, hypotheses that can be advanced from a theoretical standpoint that radically departs from the traditional culture–historical or diffusionist approaches to this particular issue. In the following pages, I will advance a theory which proposes that the significance of natural features of the islands' landscape were subsumed within a social environment that was reliant on the interplay between material forms that were either mobile or static.

Introduction

As recently as the 1980s, our most detailed knowledge of Maltese Prehistory was based primarily on the work of John Evans (Evans 1953; 1956; 1971) and David Trump (Trump 1961; 1966).[2] Apart from the pioneering work of Themistocles Zammit (Zammit 1915–16; 1916–17; 1918–20; 1930a; 1930b) at Tarxien (Malta), it is probably fair to say that virtually all the potentially useful contextual information from sites excavated in the nineteenth and early twentieth centuries had been lost or destroyed. Now, the Brochtorff Circle excavations have furnished us with fresh contextual data, and as such, have created the opportunity for new avenues of research. They are a giant step forward and effect a counterbalance to the archaeological vacuum on Malta that spans between the 1950s and 60s, through to the 1980s, as well as to the debacles of the nineteenth and early twentieth centuries. Having said this, they do form part of only a small handful of excavations that have taken place on the islands since the opening decades of the present century. The Hal Saflieni Hypogeum (Evans 1971: 44–67), and the Tarxien Complex (Evans 1971: 116–149, Zammit 1915–16; 1916–17; 1918–20; 1930a; 1930b) on Malta, qualify as the last truly massive (spatially) monuments of the early prehistoric phase to be excavated.[3] This colossal void of knowledge created mainly by the early, non–scientifically–controlled, excavation work must be seen as a key limiting factor in terms of our understanding of prehistoric lifeways on the Maltese Islands. In view of the paucity of contextual evidence from the majority of monuments on the islands, it comes as no great surprise that today, the study of Maltese Prehistory remains thwart with difficulties. A number of important issues warrant discussion in brief here:

– The majority of monuments on Malta and Gozo were excavated during the nineteenth and early twentieth centuries. Whilst a number of temples still survive as magnificent standing structures presiding over the landscape, a great deal of contextual information was lost or destroyed at the time of excavation in that they were hastily emptied–out by their excavators. Unfortunately, only objects considered worthy of museum display were retained. In essence, we lack detailed contextual information from these sites.

– Smaller intermediate shrines, or the like, are either archaeologically invisible or await discovery. Assuming that this component of the built environment did once exist, then it too would have been highly significant in terms of the *materially–structured social environment* of the islands that I am proposing in this paper.

– Erosional processes have claimed portions of, or perhaps even whole sites situated on cliff tops or at other coastal locales.[4] It is plausible to suggest that these sites in particular may have served to demark the interface between the islands themselves, and what may have been perceived (conceptually and physically) as the outside world. Needless to say, their complete or even partial loss, effects a significant imbalance when attempting to make any inference about the distribution of temple structures on the islands.

– There is a dearth of prehistoric settlement evidence which must place any inference concerning social developments and change on shaky foundations. At present, evidence for 'domestic' structures of the Temple Period is extremely scarce. Trump (1966) located a number of structures at Skorba (Zebbug, Mgarr, Ggantija phases), while Malone *et al.* (1988) discovered the remains of what have been interpreted as 'domestic' structures of the Temple Period at Ghajnsielem Road on Gozo. Recent soundings at Tac–Cawla (Gozo) have also revealed what appear to be the remains of a large Tarxien phase ('domestic'?) structure there (Calvert 1995).

---

[1] Namely temples and hypogea.
[2] The chronology proposed by Renfrew (1972) has also provided the temporal framework for the discussion of Maltese Prehistory.

[3] A highly important temple site, although not as extensive as Tarxien, is that excavated by David Trump at Skorba on Malta (Trump 1961; 1966).
[4] Ghajn Zejtuna (Malta) for instance (Evans 1971: 29).

If we can assume that settlements of varying sizes were established, and continued to develop on the islands, then it is quite possible that a number these lie under modern conurbations. It is also possible that a number of settlement sites have simply disappeared due to the processes of erosion, or destruction arising from the construction of later buildings and other land usage such as agricultural terracing. The potential for obtaining settlement evidence exists, but awaits to be fully addressed.

– During the present century, the study of Maltese Prehistory has generally taken place under a theoretical regime consisting of two main components:
a) The culture–historical approach and,
b) Archaeomythology.

a) *The culture–historical approach.* The work of Evans and Trump cited above have proved to be recognised landmarks for the study of Maltese Prehistory, and indeed, provide the temporal and cultural underpinning for the present discussion. However, during the considerable time lapse between their work and the Brochtorff Circle project, few advances were made. It is probably for this reason that up until now, Maltese Prehistory has generally been studied within a culture–historical context.[5] The new evidence from Gozo provides us with an opportunity to build–on the advances of the 1950s and 60s with the effect that the study of Maltese Prehistory can enter the sphere of current archaeological reasoning and debate.

b) *Archaeomythology.* At the other extreme, the study of Maltese Prehistory has been plagued with the antics of the so–called 'fringe–archaeology', not least in relation to the temples and cult paraphernalia derived from them. The figurines and statuary that functioned in the *materially-structured social environment* of prehistoric Malta have all too frequently fallen victim to ill–founded, intuitive theories as to what they represent, or to what purpose they might have served. A key issue here, and indeed a highly controversial one, concerns a mythical entity, commonly referred to as the *Mother–Goddess* or *Great Earth–Mother* (see Meskell 1995). It is not altogether denied here that *Goddesses* could have been an integral component of belief systems in prehistory, but at this stage, any theory or discussion concerning this 'concept' must surely be relegated to the level of pure speculation. Nevertheless the *Mother–Goddess* of Malta hypothesis has entrenched itself particularly at the level of lay discussion, and has been further popularised by a number of highly speculative, if not theoretically–alarming, publications (i.e., Ferguson 1989, Gadon 1989, Gimbutas 1991, Veen 1992; 1994, Veen and Van der Blom 1992). The argument has also been carried further to include gender issues: is the anthropomorphic statue from the Tarxien Temples (Evans 1959: Plate 60; 1971: Plate 49.11–13, Zammit 1916–17: Plate XXXIX.a, Zammit and Singer 1924: Plate XII.38) a priest or a priestess? (Biaggi 1989). It is held in this paper that such arguments have little import in

terms of our understanding of social developments and change on prehistoric Malta. In their recent discussion of figurines and statuary from the Brochtorff Circle, Malone *et al.* (1995) have rightly dismissed the *Mother–Goddess* hypothesis and issues of gender as frequently applied to the numerous examples from the Maltese Islands.

We shall leave the *Mother–Goddess* debate for others to contest, and instead, turn our attention to issues of greater archaeological concern. What was the social landscape of the Maltese Islands in prehistory? Why did the Temple Culture apparently come to an abrupt end at c.2500 B.C.?

Island Societies: Some Island–Specific Variables

It is widely acknowledged that an island or small group of islands, can provide the archaeologist with a very convenient 'laboratory' (Evans 1973: 520) or 'theatre' (Kirch 1980: 39), within which to study cultural developments through time and across space. Unlike the majority of mainland situations, on offshore marine islands there is a far more tangible 'whole' created by their bounded or circumscribed nature. But islands cultures are also heavily dependant on what are quite often extremely limited (biogeographically) environments. Any study involving island societies must therefore consider a whole constellation of island–specific variables that encompass both socio–economic and biogeographical factors (Evans 1973: 520). Island biogeographies vary considerably throughout the world, and each specific case will offer different opportunities and challenges to founding populations, that in turn, relate to other variables such as contrasts in geology, soils and availability of water resources (Cherry 1990: 198, Spriggs 1986: 6). In the Mediterranean for example, it is clear that the first human colonists of Cyprus (Knapp [with Held and Manning] 1994) and Crete (Broodbank and Strasser 1991) would have been faced with challenges and opportunities that were markedly different from those encountered by the first colonists of Malta. The divergent types of 'beachhead bottleneck' and 'niche shifts' experienced by colonists, as well as varying responses to human–induced degradation of the natural environment (Keegan and Diamond 1987), are all factors that come into play when we consider the highly divergent cultural trajectories of different island civilisations. In each case, different but related island–specific processes (physical and social) would have been at play. In the case of the Maltese Islands, it is clear that early farming groups successfully subdued the numerous island–factored obstacles of the alien habitat which confronted them.

When considering the above criteria, an obvious question arises: Why were the Mediterranean islands colonised by human groups in the first instance? Suggestions have included concepts of 'missionary zeal', 'sense of adventure', 'spirit of discovery' and 'wanderlust' in addition to more obvious reasons such as pressure on local resources on mainlands stimulating the need for more land.[6] Here, it might only be stressed that we are probably looking at

---

[5] Incorporating diffusionist theories.

[6] The fortification of a number of Stentinello Culture sites on Sicily may be indicative of social stress related to the increased pressure on available local resources.

'purposive behaviour' (Cherry 1981: 42; 1990: 146) on the part of human groups. If we can assume that the Maltese Islands were at one stage tree–covered, and by implication, offered a potentially rich resource for human settlement, then this may well have been noted by visitors (perhaps casual voyagers or fishing parties) from Sicily, prior to full colonisation taking place by early farming groups.

One highly important aspect of many island societies is their penchant for exaggerated and often bizarre cultural traits such as the construction of large ceremonial and religious complexes (Evans 1973: 519), as well as the creation of extraordinary cult imagery in a number of cases. It is a phenomenon which can be observed in islands of the Pacific for instance (see Kirch 1990, Kolb 1994, Sahlins 1955), as well as the Mediterranean. In most cases, such cultural traits are a radical departure from those on adjacent mainlands and as such, are frequently cited as a product of insular cultural developments on the island(s) in question.

When compared to developments on adjacent mainlands, some island cultures have even been referred to as 'cultural backwaters' or 'out of step' (see discussion by Held 1993: 25). Conversely, the Temple Culture of the Maltese Islands developed, possibly in isolation (Stoddart *et al.* 1993) to what may be envisaged as a ranked, if not centralised, society, and without the use or exchange of metals. The monuments, cult imagery, and by implication, social landscape of the Tarxien phase, all attest to a level of social development well above that of the egalitarian farming community. Far from being considered as 'backward' or 'out

of step', it would perhaps seem more plausible to suggest that we are looking at a series of *highly–specific* socio-economic responses on the part of human groups, that themselves, were determined by the particular island environment in question.

Here, our island 'laboratory' or 'theatre' is in fact the Maltese Islands between c.5000 and 2500 BC, where human intervention radically changed the natural landscape and in the process, created a social environment which I shall argue, was eventually centred on buildings and objects of various scales. Before proceeding to discuss this aspect of my paper however, it needs to be recognised that the different resources available to prehistoric populations on the Maltese Islands, in addition to geographical variables, are prime factors that need to be taken into account when attempting to evaluate social processes taking place. Hence, an overview of important geographical factors of the Maltese Islands will now follow.

The Geography of the Maltese Islands: An Overview

The Maltese Islands form a closely–knit group located approximately 90 km to the South of Sicily, and some 300 km from the coast of North Africa. The largest of the islands is Malta (28 x 13 km) followed by Gozo itself (14 x 7 km) and then Comino (2 x 2 km) (see Fig.1). Two smaller islands also forming part of the group are Cominotto and Filfla. Until the Early Holocene, it appears that the Maltese Islands were joined to Sicily, and they must therefore be considered as 'land–bridge' islands (Keegan and Diamond

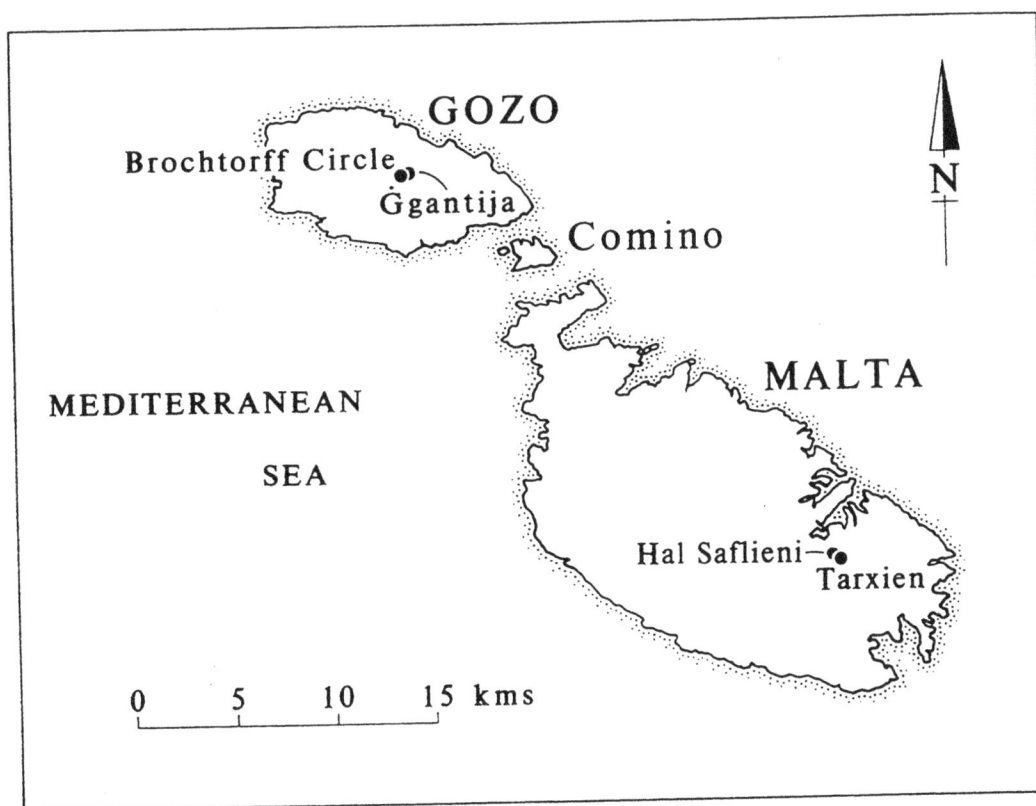

Figure 1. The Maltese Islands showing the location of the Brochtorff Circle, Ġgantija, Hal Saflieni and Tarxien (Stoddart *et al.* 1993).

1987: 64). Late Quaternary rises in sea level are responsible for the small, relatively isolated, group of islands we see today (Shackleton *et al.* 1984). The 90 km strait between Sicily and the Maltese Islands that now exists, perhaps a formidable crossing in the context of early marine transport, was successfully navigated by the first human colonists of the islands.[7] Exactly how they did this is not certain, but a combination of skilful seamanship, the availability appropriate sea–craft, and use of ocular navigational phenomena, would have facilitated perhaps a relatively easy sea crossing from Sicily to the Maltese Islands, especially when compared to developments in the Pacific (for instance, see Finney 1977).

The intervisibility of Malta and Sicily,[8] whilst serving as an on–going visual link for the communities of each island, was a facility entirely lost to seaborne voyagers (Stoddart *et al.* 1993: 5). When visible however, the summit of Mount Etna on Sicily may itself have been of special significance for human populations on the Maltese Islands, to the extent that it may have featured as a component of their own symbolic universe — more so no doubt when occasional volcanic activity was in progress. It may also have served as a constant visual reminder of the ancestral homeland lying over the distant horizon.

In contrast to the distance of the Maltese Islands from Sicily and North Africa, a relatively short sea crossing (5 km) separates Malta and Gozo,[9] and as such, would have presented a minimal physical barrier to prehistoric populations living on the islands. Nevertheless, it is plausible to suggest that the two islands may have been separated conceptually as well as physically. Cases are actually known where island populations ascribe special symbolic meaning to the geographical morphology of their lands (Glass 1988). Whether it was Malta or Gozo that was colonised first is still an open debate. What is fairly certain, is that the islands taken as a group, were first colonised at c.5000 BC, probably by farming groups from Sicily[10] (Evans 1984).

The morphology of island landscapes throughout the world is highly varied. The Maltese Islands boast a highly distinctive form of Mediterranean landscape which is governed primarily by the nature of their principal geological components (limestones, clay, sand), combined with the processes of tectonic movement and erosion. The typical tree–stripped environment of the Mediterranean as a whole, is also a noticeable feature of the Maltese Islands. Such environmental degradation is also thought to have commenced, and proceeded fairly rapidly, after the initial human settlement of the islands took place (Stoddart *et al.* 1993: 5), and it has certainly left its mark. Any visitor to the islands today will be instantly struck by the barren, although highly evocative, landscape that millennia of erosional processes have created. The potentially disastrous

consequences of land erosion need not be repeated here, but do warrant acknowledgement in respect of the resulting morphological characteristics they impart on the landscape. Perhaps, one of the most dramatic aspects of the Maltese landscape however, as we see it today, are the towering cliffs which dominate the coastline to the south–west of both Malta and Gozo. Resulting from tectonic uplift, these cliffs have created a formidable coastline. Nevertheless, both Malta and Gozo incorporate broken coastlines which include stretches of shoreline that could have been easily breached by human colonists in the late sixth millennium BC.

Natural–Physical Environments and Materially–Structured Social Environments of Islands: The Concept

It is the island environment (pre–colonisation on the part of humans) that is unaffected by human activities that I will be referring–to as the *natural–physical environment*. This is in contrast to the island environment (post–colonisation) that has undergone human–induced (culturally–factored) physical alterations. With the latter, a built–up social environment (settlements, ritual centres, etc.) becomes an integral and highly visible part of the landscape through time. Material culture objects are also 'used' and 'function' (Talalay 1993) within the built–up environment as determined by the prevailing social order. It is this particular island environment that is mainly dominated by human activities and resultant cultural traits, that I will term the *materially–structured social environment*.

The Natural–Physical Environment of the Maltese Islands

Precisely what form the *natural–physical* environment of the Maltese Islands took at the time of their colonisation by humans is virtually impossible to ascertain at present. Limited environmental information, and the faunal assemblage noted below, are the sole evidence we have.

A number of species of wild animals are known to have inhabited the islands prior to human colonisation and their remains have been found at a number of locales. The cave site of Ghar Dalam (Malta) produced remains of Dwarf Elephant, Pygmy Hippopotamus and Red Deer (Evans 1971, Morana 1987). It should be noted that a number of these animals are either 'gigantisms' or 'dwarfisms'. The morphological changes seen in some of these animals result from being confined to the island habitat situation, and can also be observed on other Mediterranean Islands (Davis 1985; 1987, Reese 1975, Schüle 1993, Sondaar 1977; 1986). Whether or not it was human agency that brought about their extinction in cases is still an area of much debate.[11]

Although it is recognised that the basic geology and configuration (shape and size) of the Maltese Islands have changed little since prehistoric times (Trump 1990: 15), at present, there is not a great deal more we can realistically say about the *natural–physical environment* that once existed – save perhaps that we know that human–induced

---

[7] And perhaps even earlier casual visitors to the islands.

[8] From elevated locales and during fairly clear weather conditions only.

[9] The islands of Comino and Cominotto are located in the channel which separates Malta from Gozo.

[10] Generally acknowledged to be the Stentinello Culture of Sicily.

[11] In the case of Cyprus for instance, see Simmons (1988; 1991a; 1991b), and Simmons and Reese (1993).

degradation of the natural environment has taken place over the course of time. Human–induced alterations to the natural environment, and ultimately the social landscape (environment) of the islands, is a key issue in terms of the present argument, and to which we now turn.

The Materially–Structured Social Environments of the Maltese Islands (Diagram 1)

As far as cultural developments are concerned, one of the most prominent characteristics of the islands between c.3600–2500 BC (the Temple Period) is the construction of limestone monuments (traditionally referred to as 'temples') and subterranean rock–cut mortuary hypogea.[12] This cultural trait is accompanied by the production of cult imagery in the form of figurines and statuary (primarily anthropomorphic), relief carving in stone (abstract and zoomorphic forms), as well as numerous cultic objects.[13] It is also clear that two–dimensional rupestral art played an important role as paintings found at the Hal Saflieni Hypogeum on Malta indicate (see Evans 1971: Plans 14.C,D).

material correlates. The final result was an island landscape in which material forms created the necessary impact for the maintenance of the prevailing social order. It is proposed here that the natural topographical features, such as hilltops and plateaus, although possibly still active components of the social landscape, were insufficient in their own capacity to maintain the social order of the Temple Period. Hence, an additional component was required that transcended the symbolism associated with the purely natural aspect of the islands. In essence, this was attained via a gradual shift from a natural symbolism (the natural landscape) to a form of symbolism that was manifested in temples, hypogea, and, above all, art forms. The latter were either static or portable, and readily served as vehicles for the transmission of (social) information (Pace 1994: 42). We now turn to the archaeological record itself for the material evidence of what I am proposing.

Prehistoric Developments on the Maltese Islands c.5000–2500 BC

To briefly recap, this paper focuses on social developments

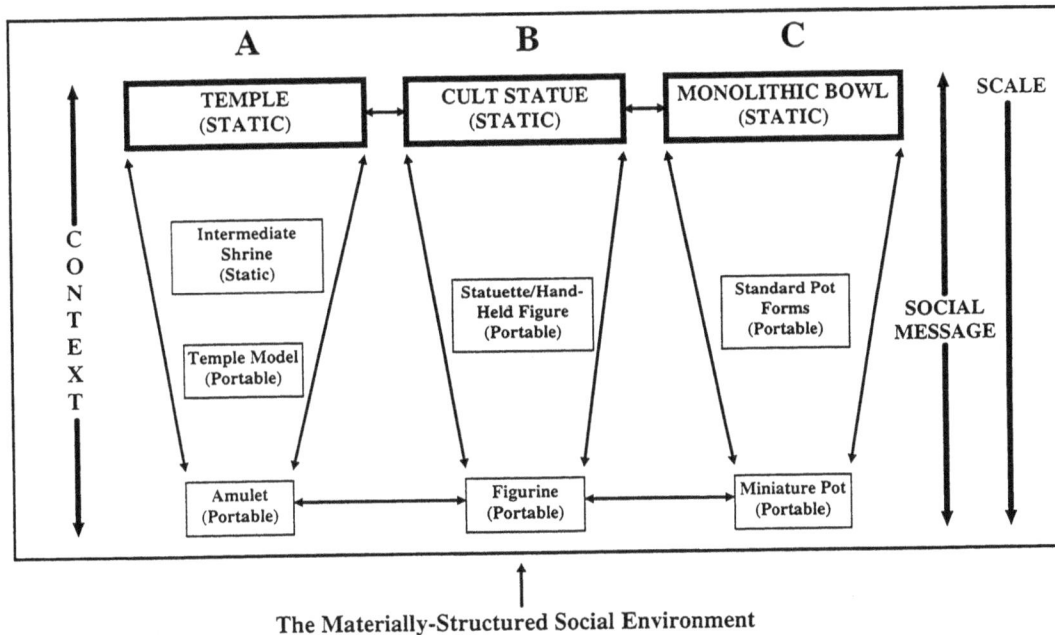

Diagram 1. The materially–structured environment of the Maltese Islands during the Tarxien phase: The scalar relationship between static (context–specific) and portable (trans–contextual) objects.

The Maltese temples and hypogea of the Temple Period provide us with clear evidence of a social order that was radically different to those of earlier phases of the islands' occupation. Changes in the natural environment of the islands brought about by human intervention were an integral part of developments leading up to the Temple Period. Farming practice and the extraction of natural resources for construction purposes, through time, created irreversible effects on the landscape and in doing so, triggered various social responses that manifest themselves to us in the form of

that were taking place on the Maltese Islands between c.5000 BC and c.2500 BC: developments that ultimately resulted in the construction of limestone monuments[14] across the landscape, and the production of cult imagery of various forms, materials, scale, and importantly, *portability*. I have suggested that the *natural–physical environment* of the islands that had been colonised by early farming groups was gradually transformed by human agency through time to one over which a far more complex social order prevailed. With the latter, only large monuments, located at specifically-chosen locales across the landscape, combined with the functional properties of cult imagery could possibly operate

---

[12] At present, the only two hypogea known are the Hal Saflieni Hypogeum on Malta, and the Brochtorff Circle on Gozo.

[13] For example, 'phallic niches' from the Tarxien Temples (Evans 1971: Plate 50.10,11), and a 'Floral Altar' from Hagar Qim (Evans 1959: Plate 79; 1971: Plate 41.8).

[14] And perhaps other structures that no longer survive.

and maintain such a social order on the islands. In essence, the *natural–physical environment* of c.5000 BC was transformed through time to one which is *materially–structured* at the social level during the Temple Period.

The Colonisation of the Maltese Islands by Humans: The Ghar Dalam Phase

Although there is still some debate amongst workers concerning the approximate calendar date, and precise nature of the arrival of the first human colonists on the Maltese Islands, the archaeological evidence available to hand indicates that this took place at c.5000 BC (the Ghar Dalam phase). Furthermore, the biogeographical constraints of the Maltese Islands are recognised to have made farming practice a pre–requisite of their colonisation (Stoddart *et al.* 1993: 5), there being no archaeological evidence on the islands to suggest otherwise at this stage. The same also applies to other islands in the Mediterranean of course (Cherry 1981: 41, Evans 1977: 14). It is plausible to suggest that the earliest farmers on Malta brought with them practices and technologies at a level that was sufficient to induce rapid physical changes in the island environment they initially encountered. It is probable that the that the removal of tree cover for the creation of fields and construction of buildings would have taken place from the outset, although the environmental evidence presently available prevents us from making a full assessment of each and every process.

The only known Ghar Dalam structure reported to date, is that found by David Trump at Skorba (Malta), and this consists of an oval hut at least 4.2 m x 6.00 m in plan (Trump 1966: 10). But, in addition, there are also surface finds from various locales around the islands that possibly indicate the presence of occupation horizons in their immediate vicinity. When compared to the material culture of later phases on the islands, the Ghar Dalam phase would seem to be somewhat impoverished. For instance, there is very little evidence for what might be termed Ghar Dalam 'cult objects' during this phase. Save perhaps for two zoomorphic handle fragments (Evans 1959: Plate 72; 1971: Plates 32.7,8), the finds from this particular phase have little artistic import, and perhaps correlate with what one might expect from farming groups establishing themselves within a totally new (alien) environment. However, in view of the limited excavation work carried out, the dearth in evidence for cult practices during the Ghar Dalam phase may be apparent rather than real. According to Evans (1984: 491), the Ghar Dalam community of the Maltese Islands can be envisaged as mixed farmers living in villages (also frequenting caves) with domestic animals (sheep/goat, cattle, pigs) and crops (wheat, barley, lentils).

On–Going Developments:

The Ghar Dalam phase (c.5000–4500 BC) is followed by the Grey Skorba (c.4500–4400 BC) and Red Skorba (c.4400–4100 BC) phases. It is in the latter phase that we have the first real evidence for what is traditionally defined as 'ritual activity' on the islands. This evidence takes the form of two rooms, 8.4 x 5.4 m max. (oval–shaped) and 5.6 x 3.2 m max.

(D–shaped) found by Trump (1966: 11) at Skorba.

The 'North Room' produced fragments of anthropomorphic figurines (see Evans 1971: Plate 34.2, Trump 1966: Plate XXVI, XXVII and Fig.30) and these represent the first known examples of cult imagery produced on the islands. All would have been highly portable objects (Malone *et al.* 1995: Category 3) in their complete state (four of terracotta and one of stone) and could, if required, have been used in a multiplicity of contexts. Further evidence from the 'North Room' also suggests that this building served some special purpose. In addition to some worked tarsal bones of cattle,[15] six goat skulls were found with their horns intact, but with facial bones removed. Based on the figurine evidence, and taking other variables into account, the 'North Room' has been interpreted as a form of 'shrine' for votive offerings (Trump 1966: 14).

So far then, we have seen continuous cultural developments on the islands from the time of their initial colonisation by humans around 5000 BC, through the Grey and Red Skorba Phases (Evans 1984: 493). Up until this point, we have only minimal evidence for ritual activity and the use of special purpose buildings. Nevertheless, even if more structures such as the 'North Room' at Skorba come to light in the future, this would only serve to enhance our knowledge of ritual practices taking place at a comparatively basic (perhaps 'domestic') level, especially when compared to those inferred for the limestone temples and hypogea of the Temple Period. The Temple Period is the main focus of this paper, and to which we now turn.

The Temple Period

Although the majority of Maltese temples are known to have been constructed during the Ggantija phase (c.3600–3300/3000 BC) the long–term processes by which they eventually came about commenced few centuries earlier in the Zebbug phase (c.4100–3800) and, in essence, it is from the latter that an uninterrupted cultural sequence can be observed that takes us through to the end of the Tarxien Temple phase (c.2500 BC), when profound cultural changes take place at the pan–archipelago level.

A major characteristic of the Zebbug phase is the appearance of rock–cut tombs (used for collective burial), and the appearance of a new form of pottery on the islands (Baldacchino and Evans 1954, Evans 1971: 166–169). As with earlier phases, there are also similarities with contemporary cultural traits on Sicily (i.e., San Cono/Piano Notaro/Conzo pottery), but as yet, it is far from certain whether or not the Zebbug phase denotes the arrival of new human groups on the Maltese Islands (Evans 1984: 493). There is also very little evidence for any settlements, the key evidence again coming from Skorba (Trump 1966: 14), in the form of hut remains.

Anthropomorphic imagery is also produced during the Zebbug phase and, going by the evidence to date, takes–on

---

[15] Trump (1966: 14) suggests that these may be phallic symbols.

94

two distinct forms. The first type is the so–called 'statue–menhirs', one coming from the Zebbug Tombs on Malta (Baldacchino and Evans 1954: Plate III, Evans 1959: Plate 48; 1971: Plate 61.7,8, Fig.57), and a further example from the Zebbug phase tomb at the Brochtorff Circle on Gozo (Stoddart *et al.* 1993: 7). A second type is represented by anthropomorphic bone pendants which at present are exclusive to the Brochtorff Circle (Stoddart *et al.* 1993: Fig.5). As with the Red Skorba figurative work noted above, both the 'statue–menhirs' and the bone pendants of the Zebbug phase are portable objects, but in this case are associated with a mortuary context in the first instance. Other important finds from the Zebbug phase tomb at the Brochtorff Circle include exotica (obsidian, greenstone, ochre) which themselves indicate that the Maltese Islands, at least until the Ggantija/Tarxien phases, were involved in some form of exchange network along with other Central Mediterranean communities (Stoddart et al. 1993: 7). It is plausible to suggest that the possession of exotic goods was part of an on–going strategy by emerging elites on the islands to maintain their authority by dominating access to such resources (see Knapp [with Held and Manning] 1994: 428), but that is the subject of another paper.

The Temple Period[16] of the Maltese Islands is primarily characterised by the construction of limestone monuments during the Ggantija phase (c.3600–3300/3000 BC) with a continuum through to the end of the Tarxien Temple phase (c.3300/3000–2500 BC), and it is evident that a number of these structures were added–to, and elaborated through time. Whereas in earlier phases, special purpose buildings, and perhaps prominent natural features constituted the ritual landscape of the islands, there were now large ritual centres that formed an integral part–of, and indeed, dominated that landscape. The middle ground between these centres may have been occupied by intermediate shrines,[17] or the like, and of course, it would seem that there are also the settlements to be considered.

The actual distribution of the temples across the islands has been the subject of much debate concerning social development and change taking place there between c.3600 and 2500 BC. A number of temple–specific arguments have been advanced which attempt to define the nature of social order (for example, a 'chiefdom' type society) on the islands during the Temple Period.

The temple–specific model suggested by Colin Renfrew (1973) proposes that during the Temple Period, the islands were divided into six territories,[18] each comprising a chiefdom. Using criteria derived from semi–arid South Iran, Renfrew suggested that the human population of the islands would have been in the order of 11000 (minimum). The basis of his hypothesis was that, after colonisation of the islands took place, population growth created a demand for intensive agriculture, which in turn, eventually led to the emergence of a chiefdom–type society. It is held in

Renfrew's argument that the chief in each territory was able to mobilise tribesman in order to construct monuments. Furthermore, 'priests' would have officiated in the temples.

Whilst it can be observed that the temples do in fact fall into recognisable clusters that are, perhaps, indicative of territories or social groups, it is surely misleading to use such data in isolation to formulate models about the prevailing social order as a whole. Far more work on the islands is required in order to establish the relationship between settlement location and monuments. Within the limits of present knowledge, 'ritual centre' is probably the most realistic term to use when speaking about the so–called 'temples'.

Taking an entirely different approach to Renfrew, Stoddart *et al.* (1993) have proposed a model for social development and change which is non temple–specific, and instead, takes into account funerary remains and associated objects[19] found at the Brochtorff Circle. In essence, their model proposes that there was intra–community rivalry during the Zebbug phase, and this was centred on the exchange of exotica. Later, and as the islands appear to have become physically and culturally isolated, such intra–community rivalry was then focused on the construction of temples (commencing in the Ggantija phase). With the apparent collapse of the Temple Building society (c.2500 BC), the islands once more became integrated within the exchange network of the Central Mediterranean (during the Tarxien Cemetery phase), and it is at this time that a whole new package of cultural traits[20] appear on the islands.

It is advanced in the present paper, that the production of cult imagery during the Temple Period served the purpose of providing stationary foci within the ritual centres themselves, as well as portable devices that could function in various contexts (temple, shrine, hypogeum, house) across the islands. It is also contended here that, during the Temple Period, social order was maintained on the islands by the continuous reference to monuments and objects, and there is some good evidence available to maintain such a hypothesis. The lack of settlement evidence for the Temple Period has been noted. Going on what we do know, it would seem that a dichotomy exists between the enormous amount of labour invested in the construction of monuments and that for the rather slight 'domestic' structures such as that discovered at Ghajnsielem Road on Gozo (Malone *et al.* 1988). If this reading of the data is correct, then it would reinforce the visual, and by implication, rhetorical, importance of the Temple Period monuments and cult objects.

Perhaps the most elaborate of all the temples, and one that has certainly produced a plethora of evidence for ritual activity,[21] is the Tarxien complex on Malta (Evans 1971: 116–149, Trump 1990: 67–77, Zammit 1915–16; 1916–17; 1918–20; 1930a; 1930b) (Fig.2). A cursory glance at the

---

[16] A transitional Mgarr phase (c.3800–3600 BC) links the Zebbug and Ggantija phases (Trump 1990: 21).

[17] For example, see Stevenson (1986: 72).

[18] Based on the distribution of the temples.

[19] Lithic objects formed from exotic materials (greenstone, obsidian).

[20] Cremation (urn) cemeteries, the use of metals (copper axes and daggers), insubstantial architecture, dolmens, new pottery types and figurines (Evans 1956; 1959: 168–188; 1971: 149–166, Pace 1995, Trump 1976).

[21] Dagger and bones in the Spiral Altar (Evans 1971: Plate 20.5, Trump 1990: Plate 6).

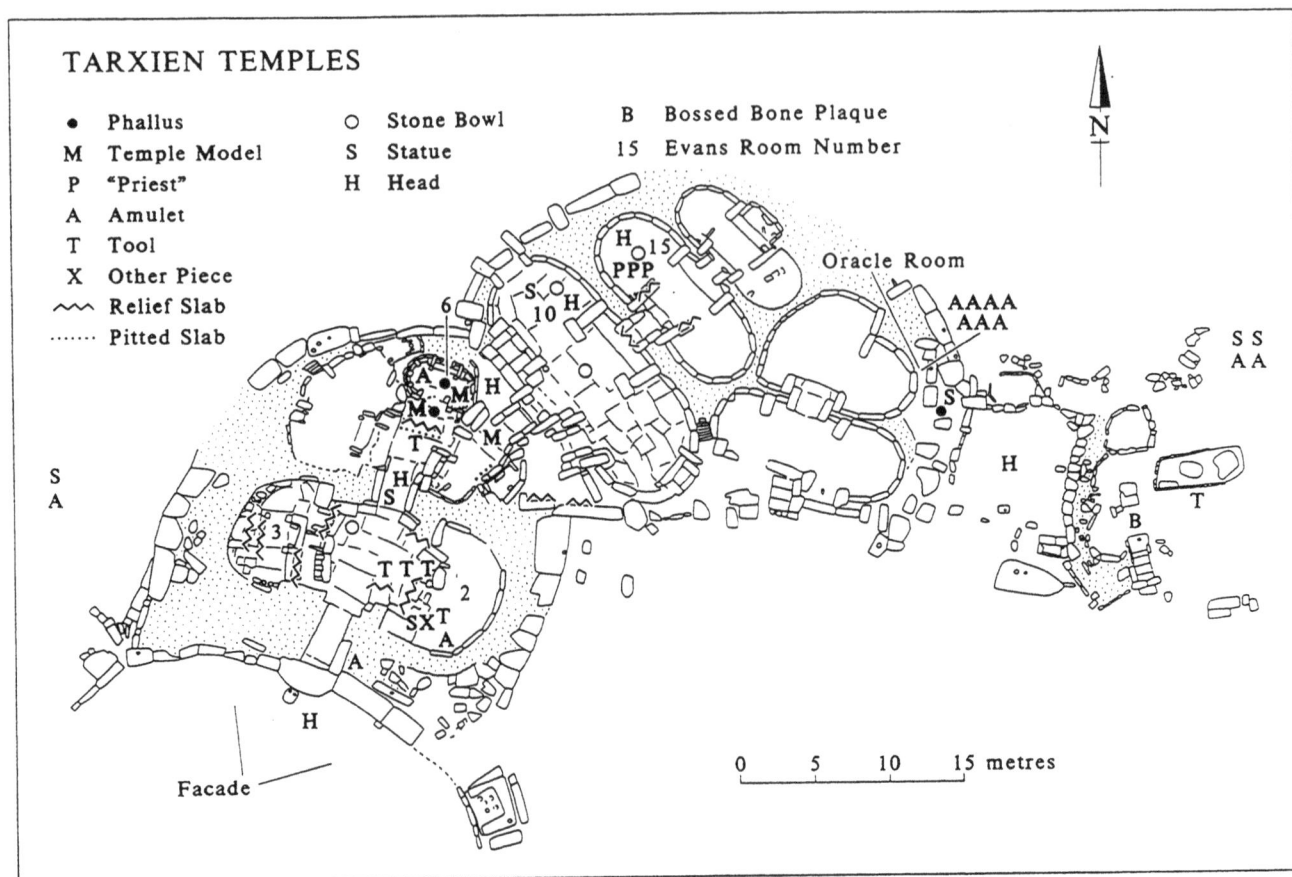

TARXIEN TEMPLES

- • Phallus
- M Temple Model
- P "Priest"
- A Amulet
- T Tool
- X Other Piece
- ⌒⌒ Relief Slab
- ······ Pitted Slab
- ○ Stone Bowl
- S Statue
- H Head
- B Bossed Bone Plaque
- 15 Evans Room Number

Figure 2. Plan of the Tarxien Temples (Malta) showing the distribution of figurative and rupestral art (Stoddart *et al.* 1993)

plan of this monument instantly communicates to the observer, a structured use of space throughout. Closer examination reveals the strategic placing of anthropomorphic, zoomorphic and abstract imagery throughout a large portion of the complex.[22] There is not the space here to discuss the nature and placing of representational work within the temple in detail,[23] but the location of one particular object warrants particular reference. Standing in apse 2 (see Fig.2) of the South Temple, the remains of an enormous limestone statue (Evans 1971: Plate 15.2,19.5, Trump 1990: Plate 5, Zammit 1915–16: Plate XV–Fig.2; 1980: Plate 2, Zammit and Singer 1924: Plate XIV.43), were found, estimated by Trump (1990: 70) to have originally stood some 2.75 m high,[24] but now truncated.[25] Having entered the South Temple and passed through a short passage, Apses 2 and 3 are in fact the first two internal compartments that one encounters. Apse 3 is directly opposite Apse 2 and houses relief panels depicting abstract and zoomorphic imagery (i.e., Evans 1971: Plate 16.1, 18.3).[26] It is argued here that the large anthropomorphic cult statue standing in Apse 2 noted above, was strategically placed close to the entrance of the temple with the intention of creating a long–lasting visual impact for anyone entering, or leaving the building. A statue of such proportions would have been an awesome spectacle to the entrant(s), and would have created a visual impact far in

excess of that which could have been achieved by smaller objects such as figurines or statuettes (more below). Furthermore, such an object was static (Malone *et al.* 1995: Category 1), and as such, was single context (monument) specific in nature. Who would have had internal access to the temple is open to question, but as Stoddart *et al.* (1993: 13) have noted, it is plausible to suggest that towards the end of the Tarxien phase, the majority of monuments on the islands may, ever increasingly, have become exclusive domains in favour of a privileged or select few. It will be argued later that a concept of scale was at play which was dependant on the interrelationship between large, intermediate and small material manifestations across space and context; in other words, the interplay between static (context–specific) and portable (trans–contextual) material forms.

The Brochtorff Circle

The Brochtorff Circle is a multi–phase subterranean mortuary complex[27] located on the Xaghra Plateau on the island of Gozo (see Fig.1), and has been partially excavated by an Anglo–Maltese team since its 'rediscovery' in 1987.[28] 'Rediscovery' is the correct word to use here, for the site was partially excavated by the Lieutenant Governor of Gozo, Otto Bayer, in the 1820s and then subsequently lost. Thanks to the artistic work of the painter Charles de Brochtorff, we

---

[22] Generally confined to the South and Middle Temple.

[23] A most useful account is given in Stoddart et al. (1993: 11–13).

[24] The original is now on display in the Museum of Archaeology, Valletta.

[25] A large cult statue (Malone et al. 1995: Category 1) is built into the temple wall at Hagar Qim (Malta).

[26] Originals now on display in the Museum of Archaeology, Valletta.

---

[27] The only other known subterranean burial complex is the Hal Saflieni Hypogeum on Malta (Evans 1971: 44–67).

[28] The final season of excavation work took place in 1994, although the Gozo Survey continues.

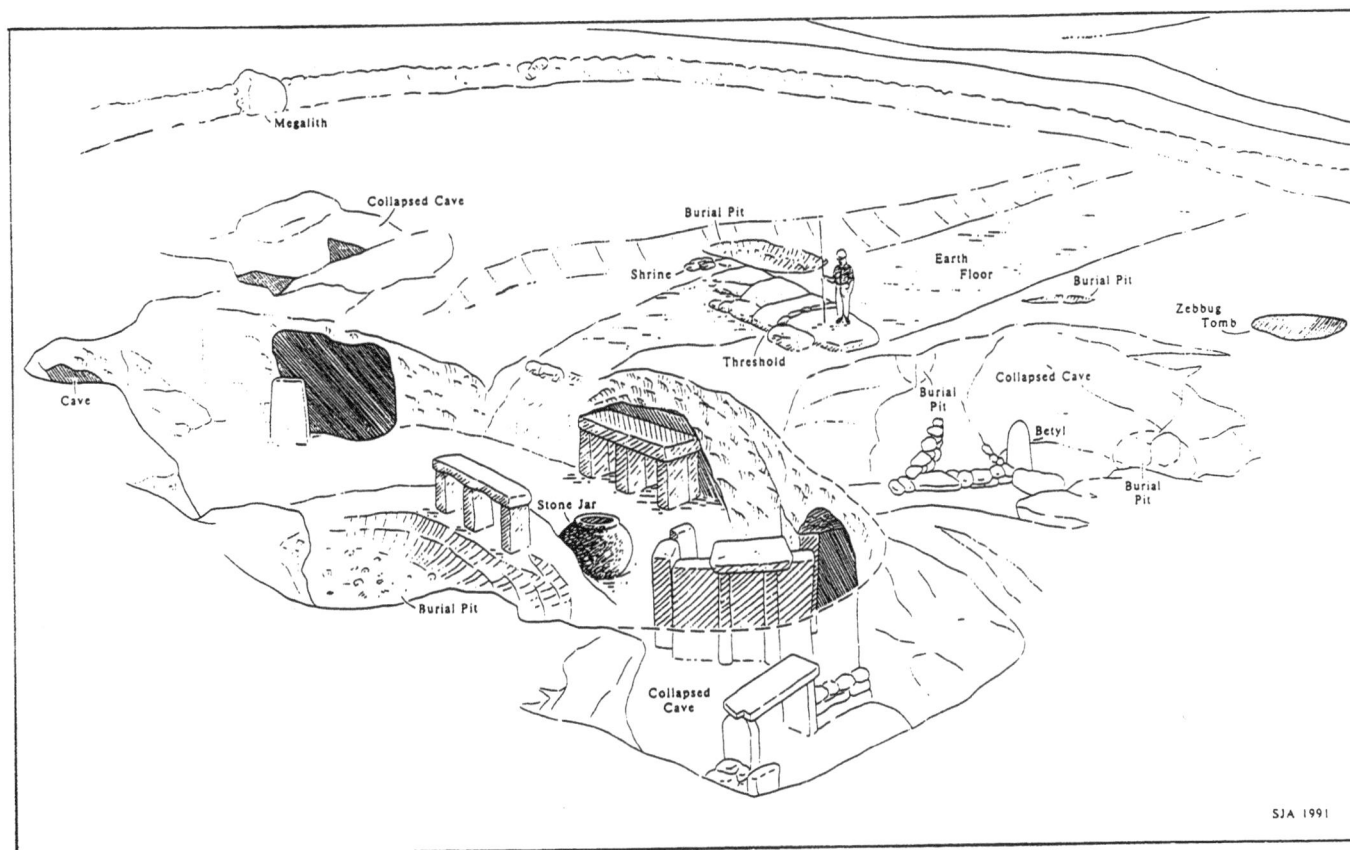

Figure 3. Reconstruction of the Brochtorff Circle.

have a contemporary record of Bayer's work (see Bonanno 1990: Plate 21 top, Evans 1971: Plates 29.3,4). From what we can tell, the Brochtorff Circle would originally have been delimited by a linear arrangement of standing stones forming a circle, with a large megalithic entrance facing the Ggantija Temple a few hundred meters to the north–east[29] – features actually shown on Brochtorff's painting.[30] In terms of its island context, the Brochtorff Circle would seem to form part of a small cluster of monuments located on the Xaghra Plateau, with the small Santa Verna temple to the west, and large Ggantija Temple to the north–west (Bonanno et al. 1990). An artist's reconstruction of the site[31] is shown in Fig.3. In view of the sheer complexity of this monument, only key aspects that pertain to the present theme will now be discussed.[32]

Zebbug Tomb. A twin–chambered tomb dating to the Zebbug phase (c.4100–3800 BC) presents the earliest evidence for use of the site (see Fig.4: 'Rock–cut Tomb'). Analysis of the human bones, in addition to other evidence, indicates that the tombs contained the remains of large family groups buried together (Stoddart *et al.* 1993: 7). Notable amongst the finds, are carved bone anthropomorphic pendants (Stoddart *et al.* 1993: Figure 5), which to date, would seem to be exclusive to the Brochtorff Circle, and a so–called 'statue menhir' similar to the example found at the Zebbug Tombs on Malta (Baldacchino and Evans 1954: Plate III, Evans

1959: Plate 48; 1971: Plate 61.7,8). Whilst such simplistic imagery hardly compares with the highly sophisticated art forms of the Tarxien phase later on, they can nevertheless be judged as formative elements in the on–going social processes that would culminate in the object– and monument–saturated *materially–structured social environment* of the islands. As noted above, the finds from this tomb include objects manufactured from materials that are exotic to the Maltese Islands (Liparian and Pantellerian obsidian, Sicilian ochre, Calabrian greenstone) and their presence suggests some form of on–going contact (perhaps exchange process) with Sicily and mainland Italy, at least during this particular phase (Stoddart *et al.* 1993: 7).

Tarxien Phase. Due to the long–term use and reworking of the site in prehistory, only residual evidence remains (mainly diagnostic pottery) from the intermediate phases (Ggantija, Saflieni) of its use. Consequently, we have to leap over some 800 years to find intact contextual evidence pertaining to the further use of the site – that is, to the Tarxien Temple phase (c.3300/3000–2500 BC). By this time, the site had been developed to incorporate a number of use–factored 'modules' (Stoddart *et al.* 1993: 10), which in some cases, were partially delimited by standing stone architecture (see Fig.4).

Two of these modules stand out in particular insofar as the finds from them indicate their possible use or function. One module is a burial pit that contained the remains and partial remains of many individuals (Malone *et al.* 1993, Stoddart *et al.* 1993). Here, our main interest lies in the small anthropomorphic figurines (Fig.5) that were deposited in the

---

[29] See Bonanno et al. (1990: Fig. 3).

[30] A small number of these stones still remain in–situ.

[31] Drawing by Steven Ashley.

[32] For interim reports, see Bonanno et al. (1990), Malone et al. (1993), Malone and Stoddart (1995), Stoddart et al. (1993).

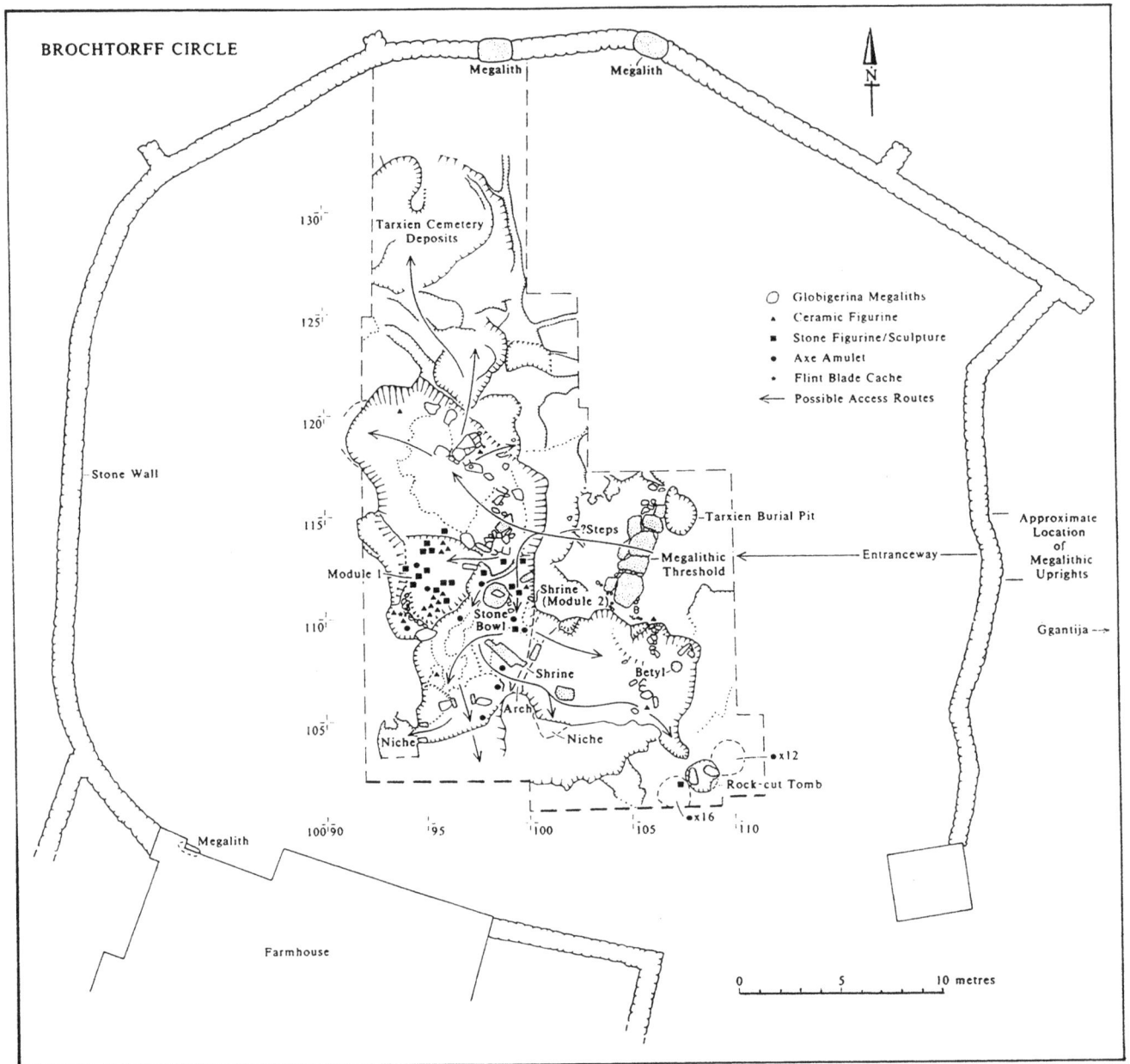

Figure 4. Plan of the Brochtorff Circle as excavated (Stoddart *et al.* 1993).

pit, ostensibly with the interred individuals (for other examples, see Malone *et al.* 1995: Figure 6). Adjacent to the bone pit lies a second module, in this case, referred to as a 'shrine' (Stoddart et al. 1993: 10). It was in this area during the 1991 season that a number of highly important discoveries were made. One is a twin–figure statuette carved from globigerina limestone (Fig.6), the other, a bundle of stone (globigerina limestone) idols (Fig.7), tentatively described as the tool kit[33] of a ritual specialist or shaman (Stoddart *et al.* 1993: 11)[34]. The shrine also contained a huge stone bowl, the function of which is far from clear.[35]

Yet another highly significant find from the site, are the fragments of what once would have been a large static object (Malone *et al.* 1995: Fig.3) (Fig.8). These fragments were found scattered over the site and initially give the impression of forming part of a large anthropomorphic cult statue[36] that, at some point, has been deliberately broken or effaced. For a comparable object, one instantly thinks of the large cult statue from Hagar Qim (Evans 1971: Plate 40.8).[37]

Tarxien Cemetery Phase. No actual structures from this phase were located on the site, although the presence of Tarxien Cemetery phase pottery and other deposits, indicate

---

[33] The bundle also included a miniature Tarxien pot (Malone et al. 1993: 82).
[34] The staff figures vary in terms of their stage of manufacture and range from 'roughout' to completed object (Stoddart et al. 1993).
[35] For a similar example, this time from the Tarxien Temples on Malta, see

Zammit (1916–17: Plate XXXIII–Figs.2,3; 1980: Plate 9).
[36] The statue is estimated to have been some 1.00 m in height (Malone et al. 1995: 7).
[37] As seen (i.e., with head missing) 486 mm in height (Evans 1971: 92).

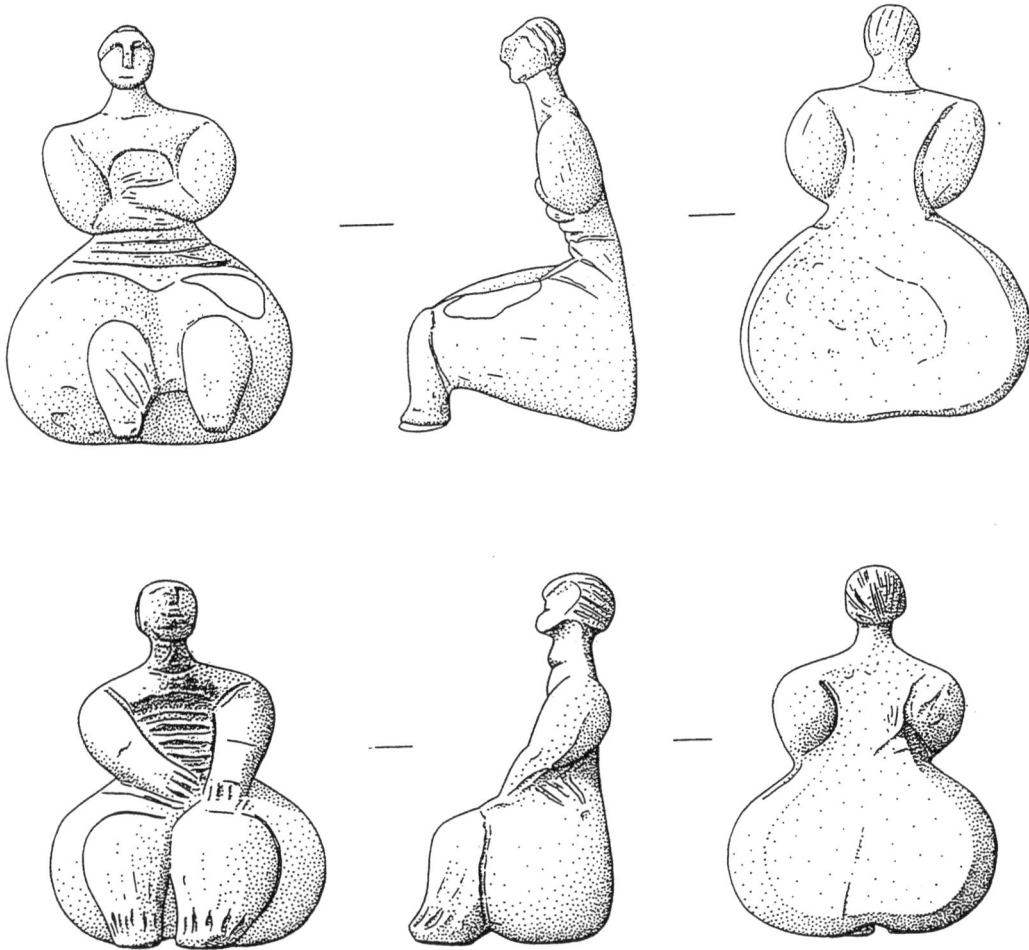

Figure 5. Ceramic anthropomorphic portable figurines from the Brochtorff Circle.

Figure 6. Globigerina limestone twin–anthropomorphic statuette from the Brochtorff Circle (height 12.5 cm).

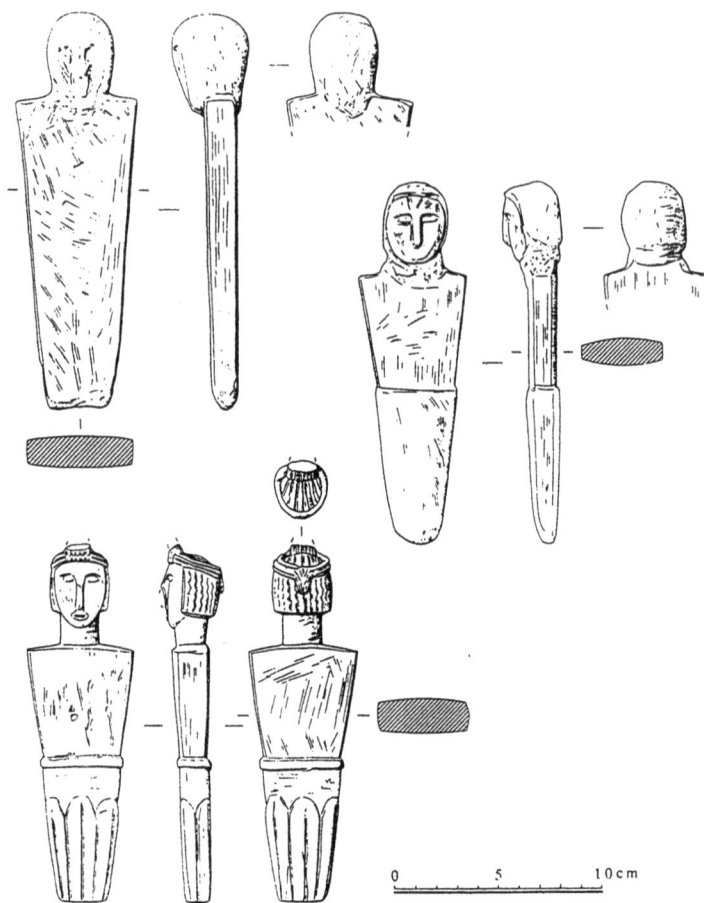

Figure 7. Globigerina staff figures from the 'shamans bundle' found at the Brochtorff Circle.

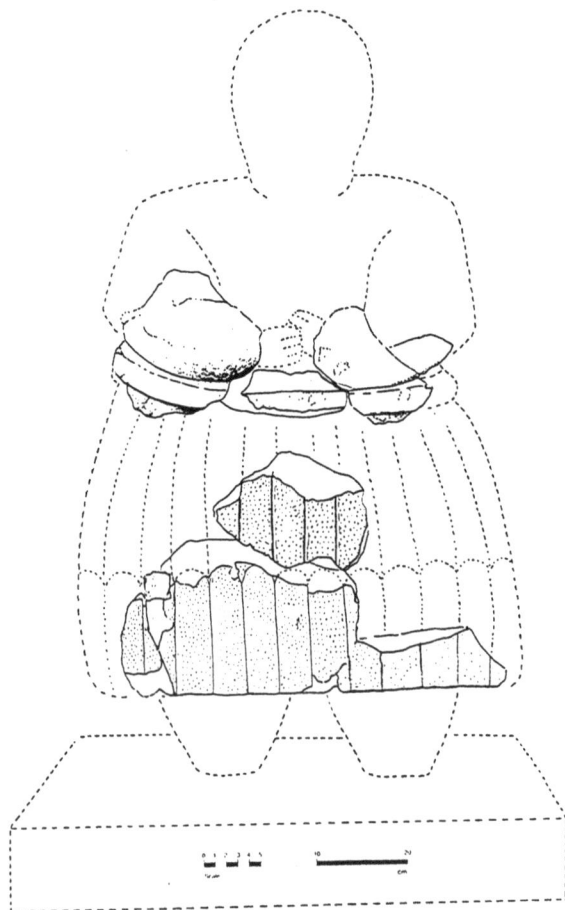

Figure 8. Reconstruction of cult statue found at the Brochtorff Circle. (Malone *et al*. 1995).

that light structures once stood in at least two locales within the site boundary. Furthermore, it would seem that the Tarxien Cemetery people held some kind of respect for the site as indicated by the presence of intact pottery vessels deliberately placed in chosen locales around the site. No Tarxien Cemetery burials were located at the Brochtorff Circle.

Discussion

Based on criteria set out in Malone *et al.* (1995), it is possible to categorise the figurative work from the Brochtorff Circle during the Tarxien phase as follows:

- Large Cult Statues (Category 1).
- Statuettes and Hand–Held Objects (Categories 2a and 2b).
- Figurines (Category 3).

By analysing the formal properties[38] of these objects, we can start to make inferences regarding factors such as their transportability, curatability, and hence the active role they might have played in the maintenance and functioning of the *materially–structured social environment* advanced in this paper. In brief:

- Large cult statues (Category 1) such as the example at Tarxien, and that from the Brochtorff Circle (Fig.8), would have been manufactured with the intention of the object remaining in–situ and would have served as an 'attention-focusing device' (Renfrew 1985: 18) within a said context.

- Smaller statuettes (Category 2a), such as those from Hagar Qim (Evans 1971: Plates 39.17–20,40.1–9) or the Brochtorff Circle (Malone *et al.* 1995: Fig. 4) (Fig.6), although probably monument-specific in terms of their context, are portable enough to have functioned in a multiplicity of contexts – perhaps also in a small shrine or even within the 'domestic' context elsewhere on the islands. They too, may have served as 'attention–focusing devices' as noted above.

- Small figurines (Category 3) are highly portable objects that could have functioned in a multiplicity of contexts and as such, would have been readily interchangeable between such contexts. A number of these small figurines are derived from monuments on Malta, such as the alabaster examples found at the Hal Saflieni Hypogeum (Evans 1959: Plates 51,52; 1971: Plates 36.4,5), as well as ceramic and stone examples from the Brochtorff Circle (Malone *et al.* 1995: Fig.6) (Fig.5). It would seem unlikely that this class of object would have been 'attention–focusing' in the same sense as the statuettes and large cult statues noted above. Even smaller than the figurines, are animal phalanges carved in the form of anthropomorphic busts (Malone *et al.* 1995: Fig.6, top right). It would also seem that small, highly portable objects, such as figurines (or carved phalanges), although having functioned in other contexts during their life span, were perhaps produced with the intention of being deposited with

the deceased. Conversely, statues (Category 1) and statuettes (Category 2a) may have been produced with the intention of curation over long (trans–human generation) periods of time.

The above dictum is clearly based on a concept of scale, and by implication, on the transportability of a given object. Furthermore, it is based solely on figurative objects found at the Brochtorff Circle and other monuments on the islands. I now wish to argue that the concept of scale just noted, can be further elaborated to take into account both buildings and objects, and hence, will apply to the *materially–structured social environment* of the islands as a whole.

Diagram 1 shows the scalar interrelationship between buildings and objects functioning within the *materially-structured social environment* of the islands. The largest phenomenon (A) is the temple itself, diminishing to the smaller temple or shrine, to the temple model (i.e., Evans 1971: Fig.51, Plate 47.7–9),[39] and even down to a small amulet carved with the representation of a temple (Evans 1971: Plate 51.6).[40]

The next phenomenon is the figurative work (B) discussed above, starting with the large cult statues diminishing in scale to the statuettes,[41] then to the figurines, and even down to the small carved animal phalanges.

The same concept can also be applied to containers (C), the largest being massive (static) monolithic bowls, such as the example found at the Tarxien Temples on Malta (Zammit 1916–17: Plate XXXIII–Figs.2,3; 1980: Plate 9) and one from the Brochtorff circle on Gozo (see Fig.3). The next (intermediate) category down the scale would be portable vessels – in essence, the standard form of Tarxien pot. The lower end of the scale is represented by miniature pots, such as the example found with the 'shaman's bundle' at the Brochtorff Circle (Malone *et al.* 1993: 82) and other known examples, such as that from Hal Saflieni (Evans 1971: Plate 35.14).[42] One sherd from a miniature pot of Saflieni type was also found by Malone et al. (1988: Figure 3.B) at Ghajnsielem Road on Gozo.

Towards the end of the Tarxien phase, it can perhaps be envisaged that the *materially–structured social environment* of the Maltese Islands, through time, had reached saturation levels in terms of the sheer quantities of buildings and objects functioning within. More information is needed in order to understand the processes that brought about the apparent end of the Temple Culture at c.2500 BC. However, if the various material forms discussed above had served as a form of 'safety valve' for society or individuals, then pressures unknown to us at present had become too great, and were sufficient to trigger radical social change on the islands, or even perhaps, their temporary abandonment (see also Trump 1976).

---

[38] Amongst other variables: scale, type of material, etc.

[39] Found at Tarxien (Malta).
[40] Found at Tarxien (Malta).
[41] Which would include hand–held objects from the Shaman's Bundle found at the Brochtorff Circle (Malone et al. 1995: Category 2b, Plate III, Fig.5).
[42] Height: 3 cm (Evans 1971: 62).

Conclusion

The two and a half millennia that span c.5000 to c.2500 BC is a chapter of the Maltese Islands' past that has left us with the material evidence for a rather abstruse series of social developments (island–factored) through time and space. It can be reckoned that such changes went hand–in–hand with irreversible (human–induced) changes to the natural (physical) environment of the islands.

Although the model advanced in this paper will undoubtedly warrant revision in the light of future archaeological discoveries, as well as further investigation of the data available to hand at present, at this stage, it is important to acknowledge a number of fundamental issues, notably though, the relationship of building/object–scale across context. The *materially–structured social environment* of the Maltese Islands that I have proposed could not be maintained solely by a combination of large temples, large cult statues and large stone vessels. Conversely, a whole scalar–spectrum of forms was required, starting with the gargantuous (i.e., the temple itself) down to the miniature object (i.e., the amulet carved with the representation of a temple). It was important that objects were capable of being transported, and were thus interchangeable between different contexts. It was also important to have stationary foci such as large temples or cult statues, as these disseminated rhetorical forces throughout the islands – or if such a thing existed, their respective territories. Material forms had taken over from where natural symbolism, functioning in its own right, had left off. Perhaps it is only within an 'arena' or 'laboratory' as unique as the Maltese Islands that such a magnificent experiment could have taken place.

Bibliography & References

Baldacchino, J.G. and Evans, J.D., 1954. Prehistoric Tombs Near Zebbug, Malta. *Papers of the British School at Rome* XXII (N.S.IX), pp.1–21.

Biaggi, C., 1989. The Priestess Figure of Malta. In, Hodder, I., (ed.), 1989: *The Meanings of Things: Material Culture and Symbolic Expression.* Pp.103–121. London: Unwin Hyman Ltd.

Bonanno, A., 1990. The Archaeology of Gozo: From Prehistoric to Arab Times. In, Cini, C. (ed.), 1990: Gozo: *The Roots of an Island.* Pp.11–45. Valletta: Said International Ltd.

Bonanno, A., Gouder, T., Malone, C. and Stoddart, S., 1990. Monuments in an Island Society: The Maltese Context. *World Archaeology* 22 (2), pp.190–205.

Broodbank, C. and Strasser, T.F., 1991. Migrant Farmers and the Neolithic Colonization of Crete. *Antiquity* 65, pp.233–245.

Calvert, J., 1995. British Team Discovers Remains of Prehistoric Dwelling in Gozo. *The Times of Malta*, Thursday April 13, pp.6–7.

Cherry, J.F., 1981. Pattern and Process in the Earliest Colonization of the Mediterranean Islands. *Proceedings of the Prehistoric Society* 47, pp.41–68.

Cherry, J.F., 1990. The First Colonization of the Mediterranean Islands: A Review of Recent Research. *Journal of Mediterranean Archaeology* 3 (2), pp.145–221.

Davis, S., 1985. Tiny Elephants and Giant Mice. *New Scientist* 105 (1437), pp.25–27.

Davis, S.J.M., 1987. *The Archaeology of Animals.* London: B.T. Batsford Ltd.

Evans, J.D., 1953. The Prehistoric Culture–Sequence in the Maltese Archipelago. *Proceedings of the Prehistoric Society* (N.S.) XIX, pp.41–94.

Evans, J.D., 1956. The 'Dolmens' of Malta and the Origins of the Tarxien Cemetery Culture. *Proceedings of the Prehistoric Society* 22, pp.85–101.

Evans, J.D., 1959. *Ancient Peoples and Places: Malta.* London: Thames and Hudson.

Evans, J.D., 1971. *The Prehistoric Antiquities of the Maltese Islands: A Survey.* London: The Athlone Press.

Evans, J.D., 1973. Islands as Laboratories for the Study of Culture Process. In, Renfrew, C. (ed.), 1973: *The Explanation of Culture Change: Models in Prehistory.* Pp.517–520. London: Gerald Duckworth and Co. Ltd.

Evans, J.D., 1976–77. Archaeological Evidences for Religious Practices in the Maltese Islands During the Neolithic and Copper Ages. *Kokalos* 22–23 (1), pp.130–146.

Evans, J.D., 1977. Island Archaeology in the Mediterranean: Problems and Opportunities. *World Archaeology* 9 (1), pp.12–26.

Evans, J.D., 1984. Maltese Prehistory – A Reappraisal. In, Waldren, W.H., Chapman, R., Lewthwaite, J. and Kennard, R–C. (eds.), 1984: *The Deya Conference of Prehistory. Early Settlement in the Western Mediterranean Islands and Their Peripheral Areas. Part ii.* Pp.489–497. Oxford: BAR IS 229 (ii).

Ferguson, I., 1989. Malta: Builders of Temples, Builders of Dolmens. *Journal of Indo–European Studies* 17 (3–4), pp.215–237.

Finney, B.R., 1977. Voyaging Canoes and the Settlement of Polynesia. *Science* 196 (4296), pp.1277–1285.

Gadon, E.W., 1989. Malta: The Temple as the Body of the Goddess. In, Gadon, E.W., 1989: *The Once and Future Goddess.* Pp.57–68. New York: HarperCollins Publishers.

Gimbutas, M., 1991. *The Civilization of the Goddess: The World of Old Europe.* San Francisco: HarperSanFrancisco.

Glass, P., 1988. Trobriand Symbolic Geography. *Man* (N.S.), 23, pp.56–76.

Held, S.O., 1993. Insularity as a Modifier of Culture Change: The Case of Prehistoric Cyprus. *Bulletin of the American Schools of Oriental Research* 292, pp.25–33.

Keegan, W.F. and Diamond J.M., 1987. Colonization of Islands by Humans: A Biogeographical Perspective. *Advances in Archaeological Method and Theory* 10, pp.49–92.

Kirch, P.V., 1980. Polynesian Prehistory: Cultural Adaptation in Island Ecosystems. *American*

Scientist 68, pp.39–48.

Kirch, P.V., 1990. Monumental Architecture and Power in Polynesian Chiefdoms: A Comparison of Tonga and Hawaii. *World Archaeology* 22 (2), pp.206–222.

Kolb, M.J., 1994. Ritual Activity and Chiefly Economy at an Upland Religious Site on Maui, Hawai'i. *Journal of Field Archaeology* 21 (4), pp.417–436.

Knapp, A.B. (with S.O. Held and S.W. Manning), 1994. The Prehistory of Cyprus: Problems and Prospects. *Journal of World Prehistory* 8 (4), pp.377–453.

Malone, C., Bonanno, A., Gouder, T., Stoddart, S. and Trump, D., 1993. The Death Cults of Prehistoric Malta. *Scientific American* 269 (6), pp.76–83.

Malone, C., Stoddart, S. and Trump, D., 1988. A House for the Temple Builders: Recent Investigations on Gozo, Malta. *Antiquity* 62, pp.297–301.

Malone, C. and Stoddart, S., 1995. Discoveries at the Brochtorff Circle. *Treasures of Malta* 1 (2), pp.15–19.

Malone, C.A.T., Stoddart, S.K.F. and Townsend, A.P.J., 1995. The Landscape of the Island Goddess? A Maltese Perspective of the Central Mediterranean. *CAECVLVS* II, pp.1–15. (Papers on Mediterranean Archaeology, Archaeological Institute, Groningen University).

Meskell, L., 1995. Goddesses, Gimbutas and 'New Age' Archaeology. *Antiquity* 69, pp.74–86.

Morana, M., 1987. *The Prehistoric Cave of Ghar Dalam.* Malta: M.J. Publications.

Pace, A., 1994. Prehistoric Art Forms from Megalithic Malta. *Treasures of Malta* 1 (1), pp.39–43.

Pace, A., 1995. Malta and the Dawn of the Metal Ages. *Treasures of Malta* 2 (1), pp.55–59.

Reese, D.S., 1975. Men, Saints, or Dragons? *Expedition* 17 (4), pp.26–30.

Renfrew, C., 1972. Malta and the Calibrated Radiocarbon Chronology. *Antiquity* XLVI, pp.141–144.

Renfrew, C., 1973. *Before Civilization. The Radiocarbon Revolution and Prehistoric Europe.* London: Jonathan Cape Ltd.

Renfrew, C., 1985. *The Archaeology of Cult: The Sanctuary at Phylakopi.* (The British School of Archaeology at Athens: Supplementary Volume No. 18). London: Thames and Hudson.

Sahlins, M.D., 1955. Esoteric Efflorescence in Easter Island. *American Anthropologist* 57, pp.1045–1052.

Schüle, W., 1993. Mammals, Vegetation and the Initial Human Settlement of the Mediterranean Islands: A Palaeoecological Approach. *Journal of Biogeography* 20, pp.399–411.

Shackleton, J.C., Van Andel, T.H. and Runnels, C.N., 1984. Coastal Paleogeography of the Central and Western Mediterranean During the Last 125,000 Years and its Archaeological Implications. *Journal of Field Archaeology* 11, pp.307–314.

Simmons, A.H., 1988. Extinct Pygmy Hippopotamus and Early Man in Cyprus. *Nature* 333, pp.554–557.

Simmons, A.H., 1991a. Humans, Island Colonization and Pleistocene Extinctions in the Mediterranean: The View from Akrotiri Aetokremnos, Cyprus.

Antiquity 65, pp.857–869.

Simmons, A.H., 1991b. One Flew Over the Hippo's Nest: Extinct Pleistocene Fauna, Early Man, and Conservative Archaeology in Cyprus. In, Clark, G.A. (ed.), 1991: *Perspectives on the Past: Theoretical Biases in Mediterranean Hunter–Gatherer Research.* Pp.282–304. Philadelphia: University of Pennsylvania Press.

Simmons, A.H. and Reese, D.S., 1993. Hippo Hunters of Akrotiri. *Archaeology* 46 (5), pp.40–43.

Sondaar, P.Y., 1977. Insularity and Its Effect on Mammal Evolution. In, Hecht, M.K., Goody, P.C. and Hecht, B.M. (eds.), 1977: *Major Patterns in Vertebrate Evolution.* Pp.671–707. London: Plenum Press.

Sondaar, P.Y., 1986. The Island Sweepstakes. *Natural History* 9, pp.50–57.

Spriggs, M., 1986. Landscape, Land Use, and Political Transformation in Southern Melanesia.In, Kirch, P.V. (ed.), 1986: *Island Societies: Archaeological Approaches to Evolution and Transformation.* Pp.6–19. Cambridge: Cambridge University Press.

Stevenson, C.M., 1986. The Socio–Political Structure of the Southern Coastal Area of Easter Island: AD 1300–1864. In, Kirch, P.V. (ed.), 1986: *Island Societies: Archaeological Approaches to Evolution and Transformation.* Pp.69–77. Cambridge: Cambridge University Press.

Stoddart, S., Bonanno, A., Gouder, T., Malone, C. and Trump, D., 1993. Cult in an Island Society: Prehistoric Malta in the Tarxien Period. *Cambridge Archaeological Journal* 3 (1), pp.3–19.

Talalay, L.E., 1993. *Deities, Dolls, and Devices. Neolithic Figurines from Franchthi Cave, Greece.* Bloomington and Indianapolis: Indiana University Press.

Trump, D.H., 1961. Skorba, Malta and the Mediterranean. *Antiquity* XXXV, pp.300–303.

Trump, D.H., 1963. A Prehistoric Art Cycle in Malta. *The British Journal of Aesthetics* 3 (3), pp.237–244.

Trump, D.H., 1966. *Skorba.* (Reports of the Research Committee of the Society of Antiquaries of London, No.22). London: The Society of Antiquaries.

Trump, D.H., 1976. The Collapse of the Maltese Temples. In, Sieveking, G. de G., Longworth, I.H. and Wilson, K.E. (eds.), 1976: *Problems in Economic and Social Archaeology.* Pp. 605–610. London: Gerald Duckworth and Co. Ltd.

Trump, D.H., 1990. *Malta: An Archaeological Guide.* Valletta: Progress Press Co. Ltd.

Veen, V., 1992. *The Goddess of Malta: The Lady of the Waters and the Earth.* Malta: Inanna–Fia.

Veen, V., 1994. *Female Images of Malta: Goddess, Giantess, Farmeress.* Malta: Inanna–Fia.

Veen, V. and Van der Blom, A., 1992. *The First Maltese: Origins, Character and Symbolism of the Ghar Dalam Culture.* Malta: Fia.

Zammit, T., 1915–16. The Hal–Tarxien Neolithic Temple, Malta. *Archaeologia* 67, pp.127–144.

Zammit, T., 1916–17. Second Report on the Hal–Tarxien Excavations, Malta. *Archaeologia* 68, pp.263–284.

Zammit, T., 1918–20. Third Report on the Hal–Tarxien Excavations, Malta. *Archaeologia* 70, pp.179–200.

Zammit, T., 1930a. *Prehistoric Malta: The Tarxien Temples*. Oxford: Clarendon Press.

Zammit, T., 1930b. The Prehistoric Remains of the Maltese Islands. *Antiquity* IV, pp.55–79.

Zammit, T., 1980. *The Copper Age Temples of Hal–Tarxien, Malta.* (Seventh Edition), Malta: Union Press.

Zammit T. and Singer, C., 1924. Neolithic Representations of the Human Form from the Islands of Malta and Gozo. *Journal of the Royal Anthropological Institute* LIV, pp.67–100.

Experiencing Space and Symmetry: The Use, Destruction and Abandonment of La Hougue Bie Neolithic Passage Grave, Jersey

George Nash

Introduction

The Neolithic passage grave of La Hougue Bie (No.6), located on the south–east of the island of Jersey, is regarded as one of the most important Neolithic monuments in Europe (map 1). Discovered in 1924, the passage and chamber area – cruciform in shape – is one of the largest, and now best–preserved, of its kind. La Hougue Bie is one of eight passage graves on Jersey and has a number of direct architectural associations with Chalcolithic monuments of Brittany. Unlike the passage grave traditions of the Boyne Valley (Eire) and Anglesey, the monuments of Jersey appear to be constructed earlier; the first phase of La Hougue Bie, dating from the Middle Neolithic – c.3500 BC (Patton 1995:35). The size and shape of La Hougue Bie suggests that its builders were concerned with visuality and display; and arguably constituted a high degree of social stratification and organisation. The monument is sited on a small rise (86 O.D.), one of the highest points on the island. Both La Hougue Bie and the nearby smaller Faldouet passage grave (No.7) would have 'controlled' the landscape around the south–eastern part of the island. In order to enhance the visuality of the La Hougue Bie monument, its builders made additions to the facade over probably a number of centuries. These included modifications to the primary cairn, the construction of two support buttresses and two horns (secondary cairn). The two horns appear to be 'fashion accessories', as this type of 'addition' is present on many communal graves throughout western (Atlantic) Europe. Indeed, it might succeed or copy the horn facades of the British trapezoidal monuments such as those of the Severn–Cotswold type. Radio–carbon dates for both appear to be roughly contemporary. Only recently has any attention been paid to the mound and facade area which includes both the primary and secondary cairn.

The Architecture of the Facade Area

It has now been established that both the primary and

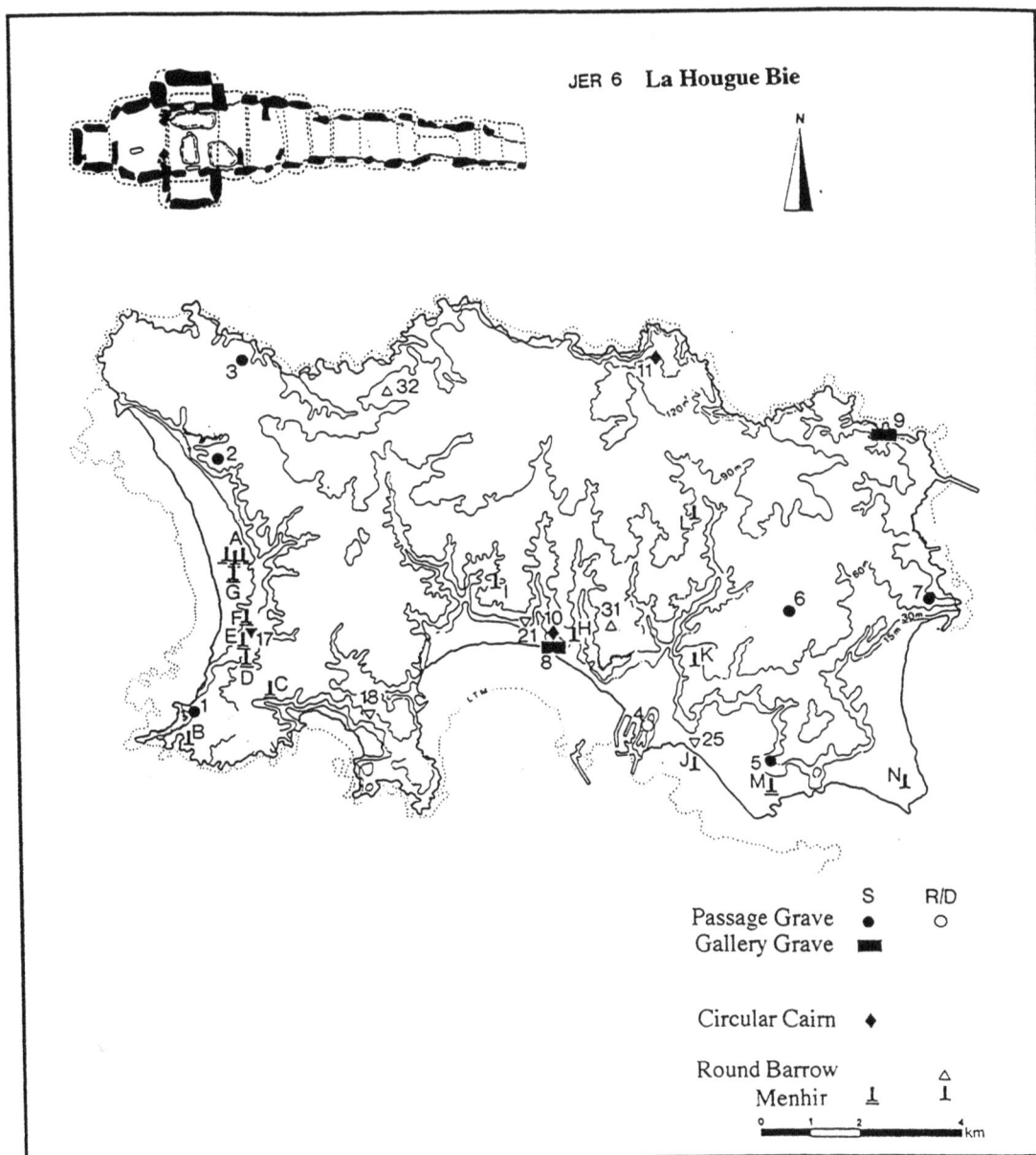

Map 1. Passage graves of Jersey and associated monuments (adapted from Kinnes & Hibbs 1988).

Plate 1. Three phases of history: Primary Cairn, Buttress and Secondary Cairn (southern part of the facade, close to the entrance).

Plate 2. Neolithic land surface and secondary cairn (southern horn). Bottom right of the photograph is lower stratigraphy of the Bronze Age blocking material.

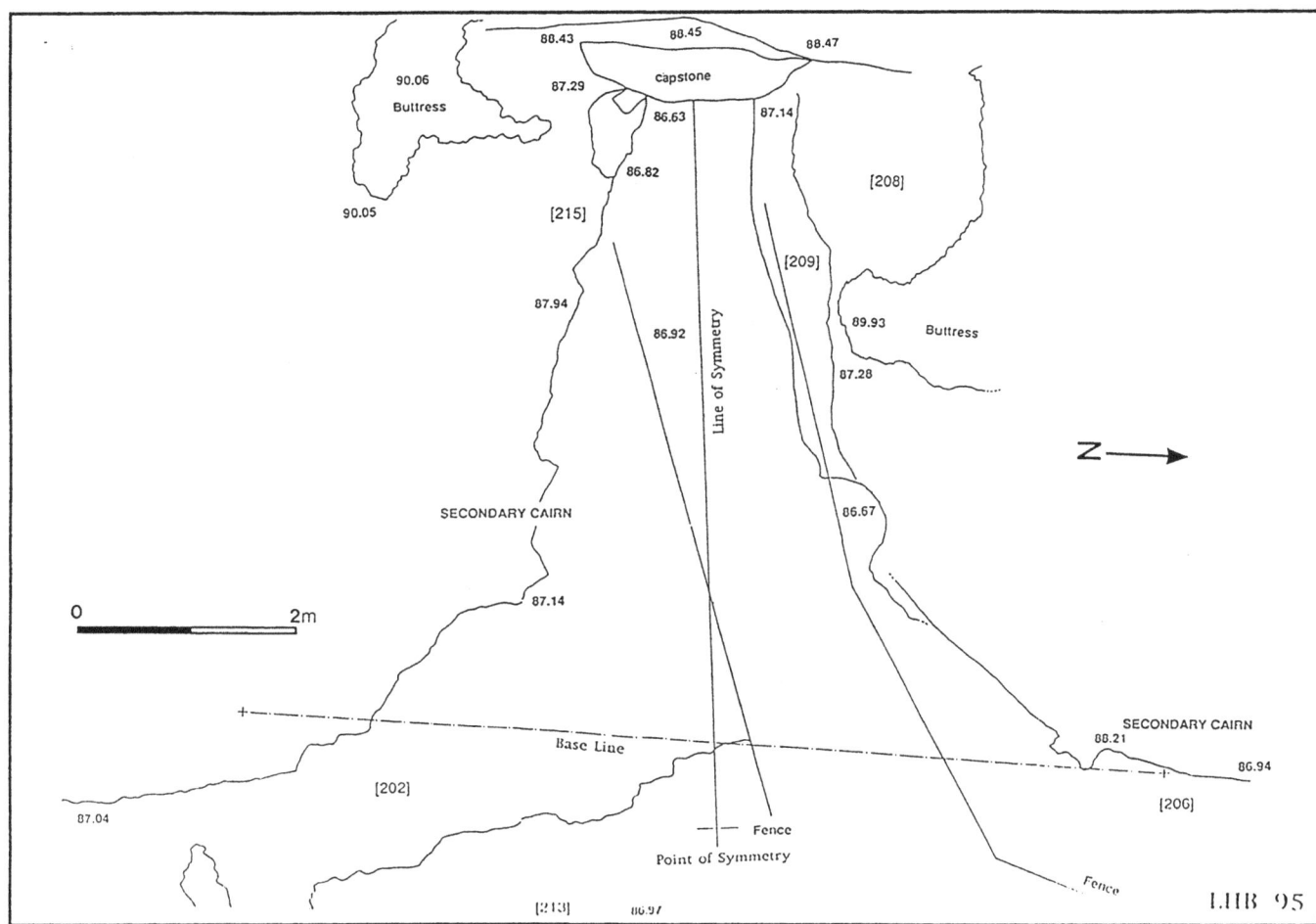

Figure 1. La Hougue Bie Passage Grave, Jersey – Facade Area

secondary cairns are completely independent of each other (Nash 1996:17). Primary cairn on both the southern and northern ends of the facade run behind the two horns (secondary cairn) (fig.1). It was only at the southern end, near the entrance, that both structures bond into each other (Plate 1). One can only assume that the same merging occurred on the northern side. The blocking, when removed, revealed both primary and secondary drystone cairn walling. Radiocarbon dates from both phases range from 4760±70 Bp to 4110±60 Bp (Patton 1995:594).

On either side of the primary cairn, are two buttresses. The southern buttress appears to be supporting unstable primary cairn. The buttress on the northern side, however, is constructed similarly, but does not support unstable cairn. Both buttresses achieve near perfect bi-lateral symmetry when viewed from the central point within the facade area.

Both blocking phases around the entrance area overlie both buttresses, which suggests they were constructed before the Late Neolithic (*c.*2250 BC) and prior to the final blocking phase. The buttress facing, although irregular in places, is, nevertheless, laid in a similar fashion to the primary cairn. Recent tree-root damage, plus Victorian building and demolition, has disturbed the upper sections of both buttresses and surrounding cairn.

The final excavation programme in 1995 was concerned with

the excavation and subsequent restoration work of the facade area (Nash 1997). The primary objectives were to establish the extent of the Neolithic land surface, as well as the original outline of the northern and southern facade walls for both the primary and secondary cairns. This required further removal of extensive Bronze Age blocking material.

Above the Neolithic land surface was a Bronze Age blocking deposit which, I would suggest, was the final ritual and/or political act before the tomb became abandoned (Plate 2). The extent of the blocking material was, in places, at least 4.5m thick and covered an area roughly 7m x 9m – and appears to be a universally diagnostic act that is repeated in many tombs throughout western Europe. The process of blocking possibly represents political instability and a change from corporate burial practice to single, prestige, status burials (Thomas 1991, Whittle 1985).

Prior to the 1991 excavation programme, the facade area and primary cairn were completely covered by natural wind-blown deposits (aeolian) and later by Medieval and Post-Medieval debris. Either side of the facade area, the mound has a 42° sloped contour, similar to other areas of the mound. During the Regency period, a large folly, the Prince's Tower, was built over the facade area and incorporated two 15th century chapels. The 1995 excavation uncovered a latrine cutting into the northern secondary facade wall and is probably contemporary with the tower.

Between 1994 and 1995, an extensive deposit identified as blocking material was removed from within the facade area. This deposit, consisting mainly of large angular and sub–angular ignimbrite blocks and intermixed within a fine dark brown organic soil, extended about 6m beyond the facade proper, up to the B46 (and beyond). Desaintpaul *et. al.* (1996:3) refers to the rockfill material as granite and rhyolite fragments. Prior to the 1995 excavation, the facade area was cut by a concrete passage which lead from the tomb entrance and extended approximately 6m into the central facade area. Built after the 1924 excavation, the concrete passage had damaged part of the primary cairn around the entrance on both the northern and southern extent.

Establishing a mound diameter and height

After the final phase excavation in late 1995, attention was turned to the origin of the extensive blocking rubble deposit. There are two probabilities as to where it might have originated, just prior, and during the initial blocking phase. Firstly, the rubble may have been brought up from Queen's Valley, approximately 1.2km to the south. This seems unlikely, as stone was readily available close to, and on the site. Alternatively, the rubble, which is similar in geology to the infil of the primary cairn, may have come from the top of the mound. Dispersed within the rubble blocking was a small quantity of faced stone, mainly pink granite (<10%) and

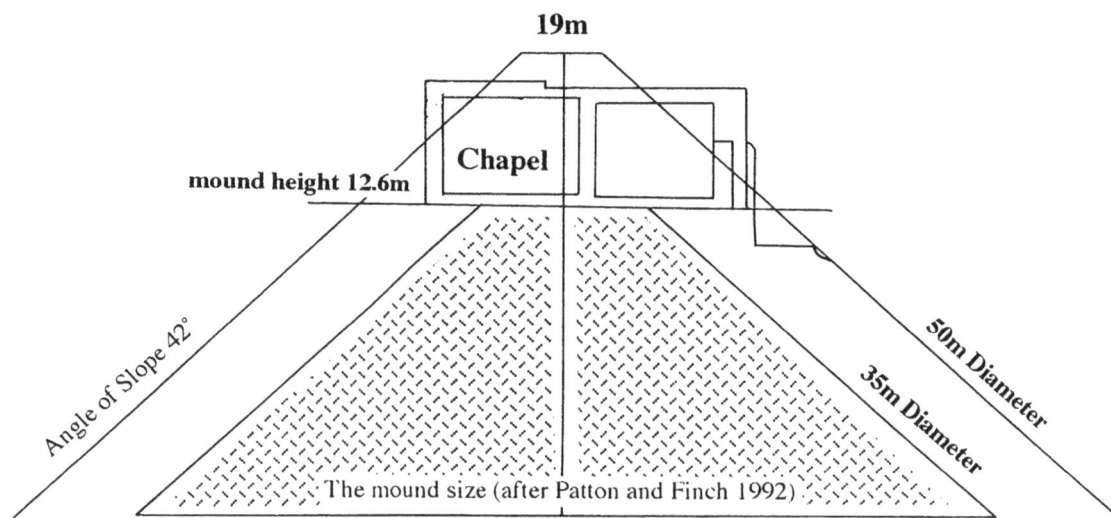

Figure 2. Diagramatic cross–section of La Hougue Bie.

Plate 3. The Faldouet Passage Grave looking west.

occasional dolerite blocks (>2%), similar to facing–stone on the lower primary cairn.

Previously, Kinnes and Hibbs (1988:75) have estimated the original height of the mound to be around 15m. Furthermore, it has been estimated that the transportation of construction material from the Queen's Valley would have taken 200 people, 200 days. Johnson (1982:65) and Joussaume (1985:82) have suggested similar dimensions. Kinnes and Hibbs (1988:39) suggest that the cubic capacity of the present mound is approximately 50,000m³ with a diameter of (>)50m (ibid. 25). However, this estimate appears to be rather conservative. Desaintpaul (*et. al.* 1996:3) suggests that volume is 18,000 tons. The author has estimated that the cubic volume is 11,033m³.

However, was the mound higher? A possible answer may lie with the intervisibility of nearby monuments. The cubic metre of the blocking (>290m³) is enough to raise the mound by approximately 6.4m, higher than the present height of 12.6m (19m). The missing upper section of the mound is estimated at 273m³ (fig.2). From the top of the mound, there appears to be a visual relationship with the Faldouet passage grave (Plate 3), approximately 2km to the east. Consequently, both monuments are similar in ground plan and shape. However, no mound is present at Faldouet. From the top of La Hougue Bie, the sea is visible, and, during the Neolithic, so was the Faldouet monument. I would argue that, in order to enhance the visibility of La Hougue Bie, the mound would have been considerably higher than at present. Furthermore, and contrary to previous ideas of shape of the mound is conical, rather than a circular stepped pyramid. The excavation of the facade area, plus the removal of the covering earths above the entrance, suggest a conical shape.

The Maths

Total Mound Volume (cone)

$$V = \pi r^{2x} h \div 1/3$$

$$V = 1/3 \, \pi \, 25.0m^2 \times 19.0m = 11,306$$

Missing upper cone

$$1/3 \, \pi \times 6.7m^2 \, (r) \times 6.4 \, (h) = 273m^3$$

$$= 11,306m^3 - 273m^3$$

$$= 11,033m^3$$

The Present Mound Volume (A Frustum) = 11,033m³

A number of hypothetical calculations concerning the diameter of the primary cairn and mound have been put forward by Patton and Finch 1992, Desaintpaul (1996 *et. al.*) and more recently by Patton (1995:53). Here, there appears to be much contradiction and confusion. Patton and Finch (1992:117) have claimed that the diameter of the primary cairn is approximately 35m. However, the diameter of the mound including the deposition of later deposits exceeds 55m. A plan from the same paper, though, shows the mound to be 60m (east to west) x 66m (north to south). The problem arises here as to which set of figures to use. The mound seems to have been (correctly) surveyed once during the 1924 excavation (Baal *et. al.* 1925). The plan and section may be considered reasonably accurate, although Baal had little or no idea of the actual shape and diameter of the primary and secondary cairns (figs. 3 and 4).

During the 1994 season, the primary cairn, along with

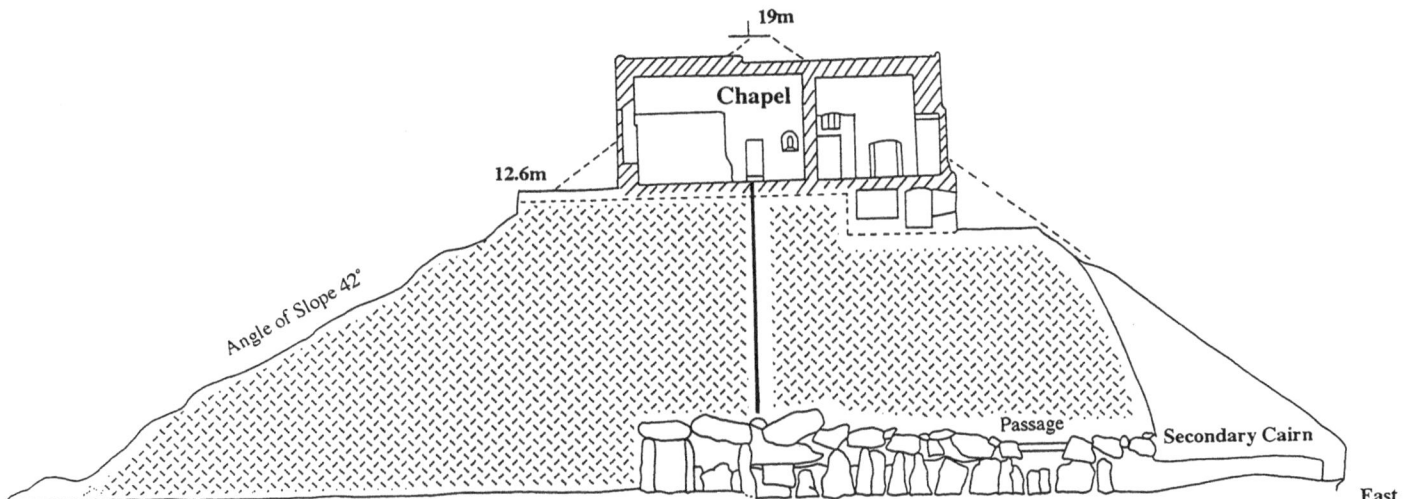

Figure 3. Cross–section of La Hougue Bie (redrawn and adapted from Baal *et. al.* 1925).

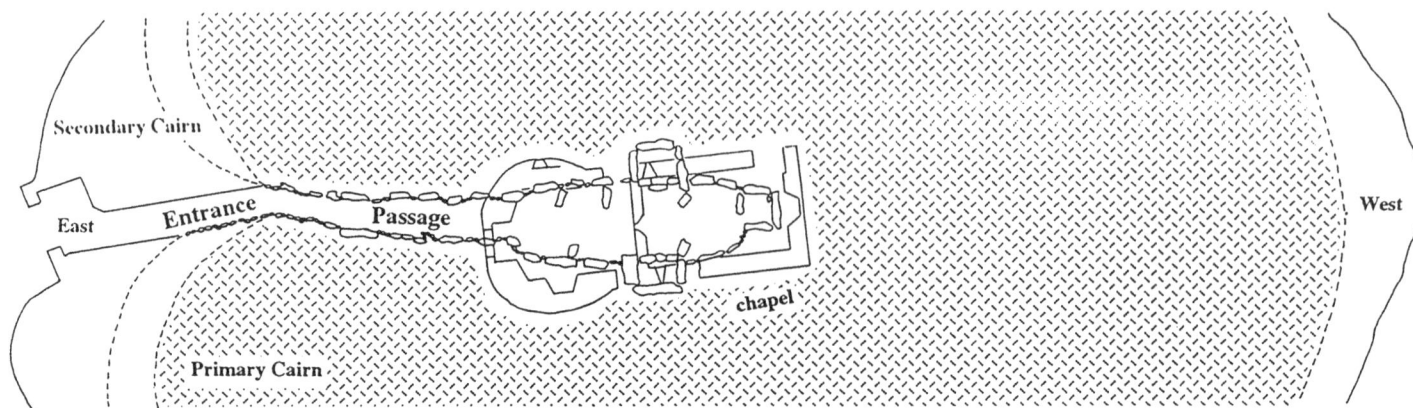

Figure 4. Plan of the central section of La Hougue Bie (redrawn and adapted from Baal *et. al.* 1925).

associated wind–blown deposits, was exposed in section on the northern side of the facade. The primary cairn, here, extended approximately 2.5m from the edge of the secondary cairn. In section, sediments were 0.75m thick and consisted of two soils – wind–blown deposits and recent brown–earths (outer turf layer) (Plate 4). On the western side, deposits were confined to recently formed brown–earths. Indeed, in places, the primary cairn was partially exposed. The monument itself overlies an extensive loess deposit (>5m) which was probably formed by easterly winds blowing across exposed beach levels during the early post–glacial period – *c.*11000 BP (Bishop & Bisson 1989:90). However, it should be noted that the same deposit is also present within the upper Neolithic stratigraphy of La Hougue Bie. Therefore, I would suggest either that the wind–blown soils are reworked or sediments are being constantly blown across the eastern part of the island throughout the Holocene. Indeed, the sediment fraction of the surrounding fields would suggest this.

Wind blown deposits from the mound originate from a regionalised deterioration in climate around the Neolithic–Early Bronze Age, most probably after the final blocking phase and the subsequent abandonment of the tomb. Simmons & Tooley (1981:133) suggest that prevailing winds around the English Channel lifted fine silty sediments from coastal dune areas and deposited these inland.

Patton and Finch (1992:118) have suggested that these deposits are in fact earthen terraces which were laid over the cairn. However, this particular hypothesis is problematic, as no sedimentological tests to argue soil change were undertaken, nor were there any artifacts present within the deposit. Furthermore, in places, the wind–blown deposits over lie the Early Bronze Age blocking, suggesting the deposit was much later. During the latter part of the 1994 excavation, a series of six sediment samples were taken (at 20cm intervals) from a vertical section within the northern area of the facade, where the primary and secondary cairn converged, and where wind–blown deposits are thickest (>1.5m). Samples were later individually analysed for soil change (sediment fraction and colour) within the section. Each sample comprised roughly 85% silt, 10% fine–grained sand and 5% clay – a typical wind–blown deposit. It appeared conclusive that the soil deposit was uniform throughout, suggesting a gradual

deposition over time, rather than a human–induced terrace. It should also be noted that the (original) height and size of La Hougue Bie displays monumentality, and in order to enhance this one would not cover or hide a mound of this size and proportion; it is there to be seen.

Plate 4. The facade area of La Hougue Bie prior to the removal of the 1920s tunnel.

George Nash

Making a Molehill out of a Mountain

If one accepts (in part) that the rough diameter of the mound lies between 55m and 60m (Patton and Finch 1992:118), and subtract approximately 3m from the eastern (facade) end and between 0.5m and 1.5m from the western end, the diameter of the primary cairn will be between 50m and 53m. Desaintpaul (1996 *et. al.*), although using (now) problematic data from Patton and Finch, has calculated the mean angle of slope either side of the facade at between 36° and 42°. Within the facade area itself, the angle is more acute, and above the capstone on the southern side, the primary cairn stands almost vertical. Approximately 2.7m above the capstone, and beyond the vertical facing, the primary cairn resumes an approximate angle of between 47° and 50°, although this area has been subjected to much damage over the last 150 years. Indeed, reconstruction of primary cairn above the capstone can be only considered a matter of conjecture.

In assessing the mean angle of slope (42°), as well as the lower diameter of the primary cairn, one can calculate the diameter of the upper part of the mound. Indeed, if one accepts the hypothesis put forward by Patton and Finch that the mound is 35m in diameter, then the two Medieval chapels would simply not fit onto the present mound summit. It is already known that the deposit (in section) overlying the primary cairn on the northern side of the facade is only, on average, 0.75m thick. It is therefore obvious that the diameter of the mound must be considerably greater. Auto CAD (13) graphics (figs. 5 and 6) have calculated the tolerances using the data from Patton & Finch (1992), as well as calculations used in this paper.

Symmetry and Instability around the faced during the Neolithic

On either side of the primary cairn, are two buttresses. The southern buttress discovered in 1994, appears to be supporting

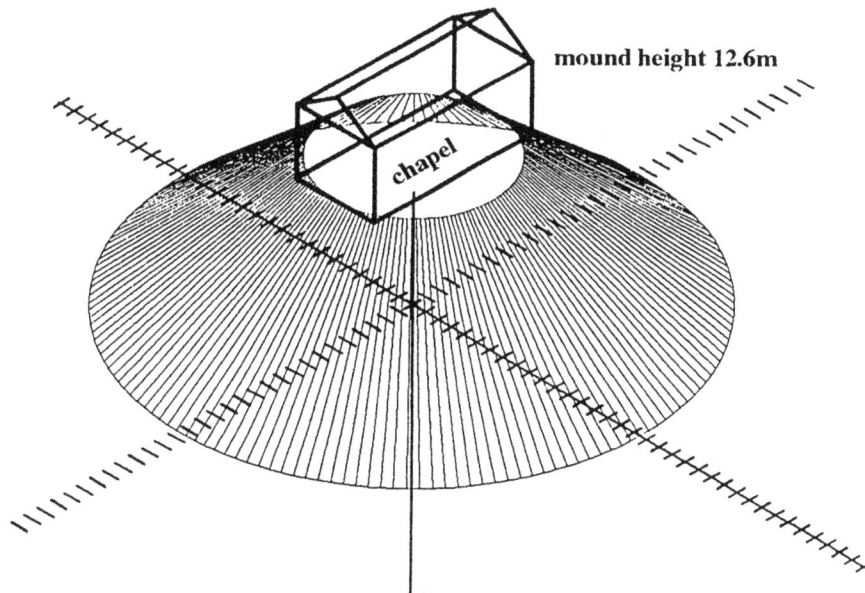

Figure 5. CAD (computer aided design) of the La Hougue Bie mound (35m diameter).

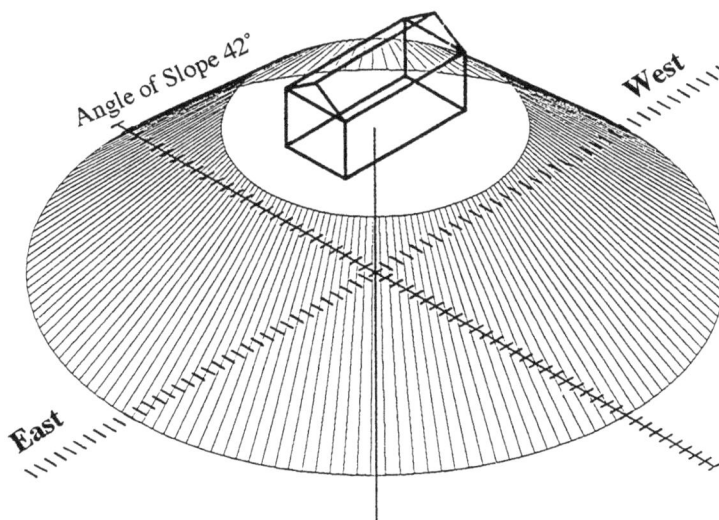

Figure 6. CAD (computer aided design) of the La Hougue Bie mound (50m diameter).

111

unstable primary cairn above. The angle of cairn slope above the buttress is 90°. The buttress on the northern side is similarly constructed, but does not support any unstable cairn, therefore it appears to be more of a cosmetic feature, adding a visual, rather than a structural benefit to the primary cairn. Indeed, both buttresses achieve near–perfect symmetry when viewed from the central point within the facade area. I would suggest these two structures should be regarded as a separate construction phase of the primary cairn itself. It was assumed both were built on to the upper slope of the secondary cairn and therefore could well be regarded as the final phase of the facade cairn (phase III). However, when excavating behind the secondary cairn on the northern side, the buttress foundations were firmly set approximately 1.20m below the upper ridge of the secondary cairn. One could argue they were either built whilst the secondary cairn was being constructed, or that both buttresses were constructed against the primary cairn, well before the secondary cairn was built. A third, but unlikely option is that they were added after the secondary cairn was built. However, in order to construct a suitable foundation base, deep foundations would have been necessary to support the loading of the upper buttress cairn material. This method would have de–stabilised the secondary cairn.

The buttress 'facing' although irregular in places is nevertheless laid in a similar fashion to the primary cairn. Indeed, excavation on the southern side of the facade area has revealed a small area of faced cairn which is, in fact, lower buttress material. The upper sections of both buttresses are rough and irregular.

As well as attempting to expose further cairn material, the excavation programme concentrated on the removal of the remaining Late Neolithic and Early Bronze Age blocking area(s) around the facade entrance. From the previous excavation in 1994, Patton (1995) was able to place this blocking into two phases – 1c and 1d. Both phases indicate the tomb fell into disuse at least twice. Radiocarbon dates from both phases range from 4760±70 (1c) to 4110±60. (1d) BP (Patton 1995).

Excavated as a Narrative

The exposure of the facade area has answered many questions regarding its the final use. Indeed, one could not have envisaged the final visual display of the inner facade until the 1920's tunnel had been fully demolished. It was only then that the full impact of the facade proper could be understood. Outlined below are ideas from this, and the latter part of the 1995 excavation and discusses briefly, the chronology of the monument.

The Primary (wall) cairn (phase I) – construction commenced around the Middle Neolithic and is contemporary with the passage grave tradition elsewhere on Jersey. The construction consists of drystone wall facing which is back–filled by mainly ignimbrite debris. Cairn stones are flushed in order to create a (smooth) faced wall. Key stones are intermediately placed within the cairn matrix. The cairn forms a large mound that was covered initially by wind–blown (prehistoric) deposits, Victorian debris (originating from a tower) as well as rubble

(from subsequent damage) of the 1924 excavation. Phase 1 marks a period whereby corporate monumentality is in practice. Although stratified, the whole community would have used the monument for social/ritual purposes, including burial.

The buttresses (phase II), in my opinion, were constructed soon after the first phase, and were built as a result of instability (caused by settlement loading) to the upper cairn. The southern buttress appears to support upper cairn material, whilst the northern buttress acts purely as a cosmetic feature. Both buttresses are in near perfect symmetry. The base of the southern buttress was fully excavated and revealed a semi-dressed structure which was flushed against the existing primary cairn. In places, a small quantity of (brown-yellowish) wind–blown soil lay between the two structures possibly indicating a 'bonding layer'. Amongst the cracks, and on top of horizontally jutting cairn stones on the buttresses (and cairn), a small quantity of pottery and flint was recovered as well as many charcoal flecks. I would suggest the charcoal is a result of extinguishing (ritual) fires constructed, possibly on a small platform, on top of the mound – the debris was disposed of, by pushing the embers and associated debris over the edge of the mound.

The secondary (horn) facade cairn (phase III) was constructed towards the late Middle Neolithic, at around the same time that other structures throughout Western Europe were either being built with protruding horns (trapezoidal in form) or 'additions' were being made to existing (circular) monuments. The secondary cairns appear to restrict the visual access to both the facade area and the passage (and chamber area) from either side of the mound. Both horns are in near perfect symmetry and are constructed of flushed drystone walling. Next to the entrance capstone on the southern side is a line of vertical (up right) kerbing extending out towards the outer facade area. The kerbing, different in construction to the cairn proper, appears to add to the monumentality of the entrance area (along with the orthostat and capstone). The restricted visual access within the facade area, is an important concept to consider. In many contemporary religions, sacred special space is reserved for special people. This idea would suggest the facade area, the passage and the chamber were used by a social hierarchy. One is able to experience the visual access from various points around the facade area as well as from inside the tomb itself.

There are three main building phases for La Hougue Bie. Each was completed within a short period of time. However, the question arises as to the damage caused to the top of the mound prior to, and during, the construction of the two Medieval chapels and the later Prince's Tower.

Meagre Finds

Finds around the facade area are meagre. However, within the Early Bronze Age blocking material, a few metres east of the facade, a number of artifacts regarded as prestige were recovered (fig.7). Among these was a single fragment of polished stone ring (rare in the Channel Islands) and three pieces of polished stone axe – two of which originate from the Le Pinnacle axe factory in the north–west of the island. The other derives from the west coast of Brittany. Two transverse arrowheads, a selection of flint waste, Middle Neolithic coarse red pottery sherds and a large collection of red rhyolite pebbles were also recovered. This artifact assemblage within the blocking material signifies a period of possible social and political change. I would suggest that the 'old order' (i.e. the prestige artifacts) is being replaced by new ideas, especially with burial practice (single burial) and the accumulation of new prestige items. Prestige items may have come from the top of the mound, either prior to, or during, the destruction phase. All were recovered within the lower blocking phase, a few centimetres above the Neolithic land surface (Plate 2). At around the same time, La Hougue Bie, during the Late Neolithic/Early Bronze Age, changed from a corporate monument to a single–status tomb. The 1924 excavation revealed a single male cist burial within the main chamber area (Baal *et. al.* 1925). It is most probably the final blocking phase, which indeed is extensive, that ends La Hougue Bie's function

as a mortuary building. However, the monument and surrounding area may have continued to play an important role as a socio–political meeting place, hence its continuous use up until the Medieval period (15th century).

Acknowledgements

I wish to thank the following people for their comments on this paper. Firstly, sincere thanks to Trevor Kirk and Mark Patton (Trinity College, Carmarthen), Olga Finch (Jersey Museum Service), Robert Bourne, John Mullis (Babtie Consultants & Berkshire County Council) and George Children (Cambridge) for comments and support on the first draft. Also, a big thank you to Jayne Pilkington for help with the mathematics. Finally, thanks to Bradley Tyley for the production of Auto–CAD drawings of the chapels and mound, and Jane Crossely for the reconstruction drawing and finds.

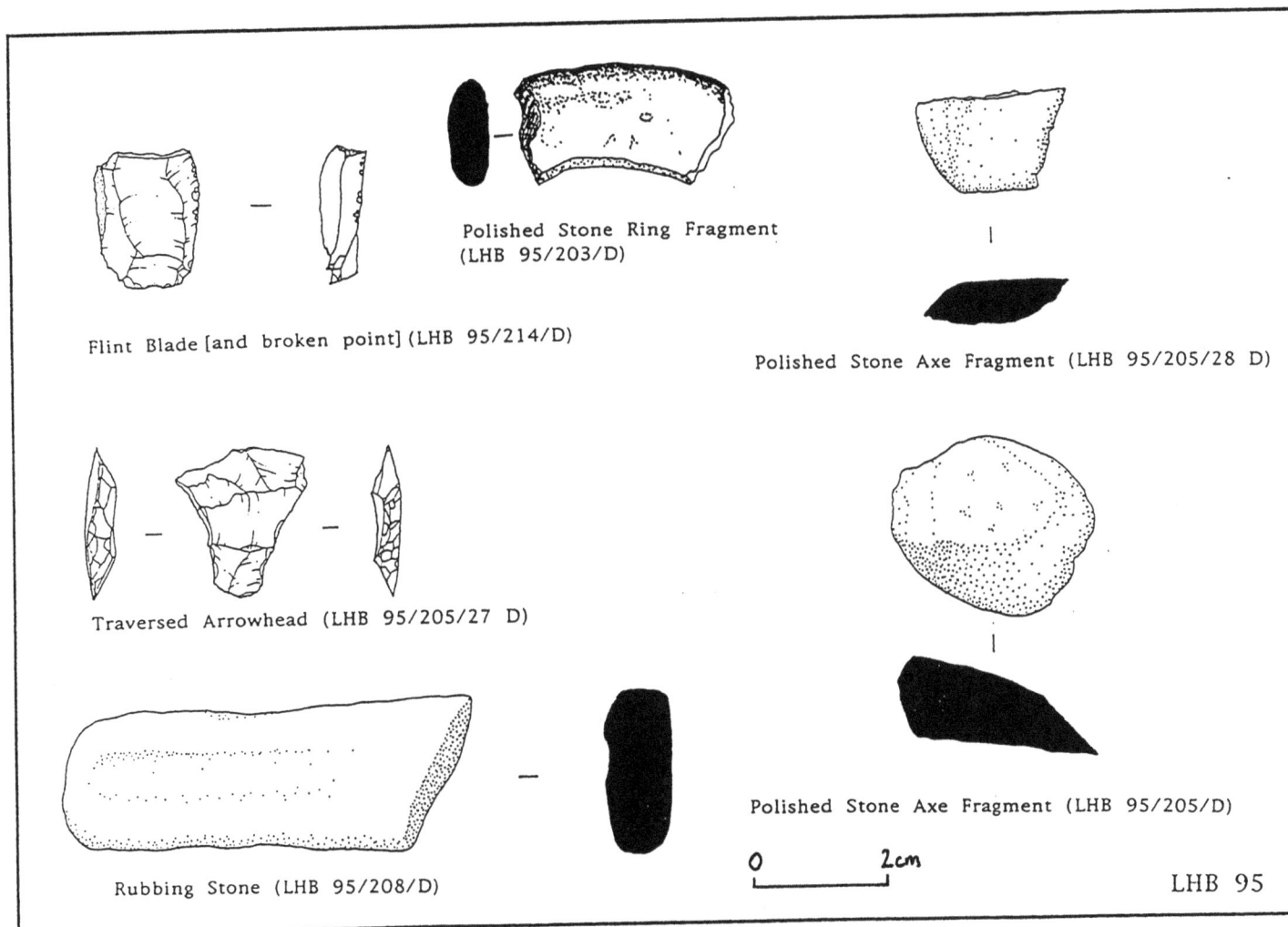

Figure 7. Artifacts from the Bronze Age blocking material and Upper Neolithic land surfaces.

Addressing the outline

One tends to think of landscape as a wide open expanse. Indeed, I have previously referred to this as the 'macroscape'. But what of the 'microscape'? The experience of, say, an individual in a small room is different to being within a cathedral (referred to as 'the sense of occasion'). In this paper, I explore particular components that involve the built environment. In particular, I discuss the relevance of monumentality within the corporate phases of the Middle and Late Neolithic. In particular, I am interested in discussing the architecture and building logistics of a large Neolithic passage grave. Between 1994 and 1995, I was director for the final excavation programme at the Neolithic passage grave of La Hougue Bie, Jersey. This series of excavations were similar to many others. However, the microscape of the facade area posed a number of questions and went beyond the now too familiar 'dig and record' strategy. The shape, size and form of the monument can be considered important when determining the mechanisms that control and manipulate Neolithic society. Further, it asks a number of fundamental questions concerning the visuality and monumentality of building such a large monument as well as the mechanics and construction methodology used.

Bibliography

Baal, A.D.B., Godfray, A.D.B., Nicolle, E.T. & Rybot, N.V.L. (1925) 'La Hougue Bie', *Societe Jersiaise Annual Bulletin* 10:178–236.

Bishop, A.C. & Bisson, G. (1989) *Jersey; British Geological Survey and Channel Islands sheet No.2.*

Desaintpaul, F., Pine, R.J. & Sharp, J.C. (1996) '*An Assessment of the Static and Dynamic Stability of a Neolithic (6,000 year old) Rockfill Burial Mound*'. Paper to be submitted at Eurock '96, Turin, Italy, Sept 2–5 1996.

Joussaume, R. (1985) *Dolmens for the Dead: Megalith Building throughout the World.* Batsford, 82–3.

Johnston, D.E. (1981) *The Channel Islands: an archaeological guide*, Philmore, London.

Kinnes, I.A. & Hibbs, J.L. (1988). *The Dolmens of Jersey*, Jersey: La Haule Books/Channel Television.

Mourant, A. (1933) 'Dolmen de le Hougue Bie. Nature and provenance of materials'. *Ann. Bull. Soc. Jersiaise*, No.12: 217–20.

Mourant, A. (1974) 'Reminiscences of the excavation of La Hougue Bie', *Societe Jersiaise Annual Bulletin* 21:246–53.

Nash, G.H. (1995a) Phase IV Excavation of the La Hougue Bie Passage Grave, Jersey. Interim Strategy Report No.1

Nash, G.H. (1995b) Phase V Excavation of the La Hougue Bie Passage Grave, Jersey. Interim Strategy Report No.2

Nash, G.H. (1995c) Phase V A Feasibility Study for Replacing the Missing Orthostat at La Hougue Bie, Jersey. Interim Strategy Report No.3

Nash, G.H. (1997) Report on Early Bronze Age Blocking Material within the Facade Area, La Hougue Bie Passage Grave, Jersey. Interim Report No.4 *Societe Jersiaise* (forthcoming).

Patton, M.A. (1990) 'Neolithic Stone Rings from the Channel Islands', *Societe Jersiaise* Vol.25, pt 2. 347–352.

Patton, M.A. & Finch, O. (1992). 'Excavations at La Hougue Bie, Jersey: First interim report', *Societe Jersiaise Annual Bulletin* 25: 632–40.

Patton, M.A. & Finch, O. (1993). 'Excavations at La Hougue Bie, Jersey: Second Interim Report', *Societe Jersiaise Annual Bulletin* 26: 116–32.

Patton, M.A. (1995a) *Neolithic Communities of the Channel Islands.* Oxford: British Archaeological Reports. British Series 240.

Patton, M.A. (1995b) 'New light on Atlantic seaboard passage–grave chronology: radiocarbon dates from La Hougue Bie (Jersey)', *Antiquity* Vol.69, No.264. 582–86.

Simmons, I. & Tooley, M. J. (1981) *The Environment in British Prehistory.* Duckworth. 133–134.

Thomas, J. (1991) *Rethinking the Neolithic.* Cambridge. Cambridge University Press.

Whittle, A. (1985) *Neolithic Europe: A Survey*, Cambridge World Archaeology, Cambridge University Press.

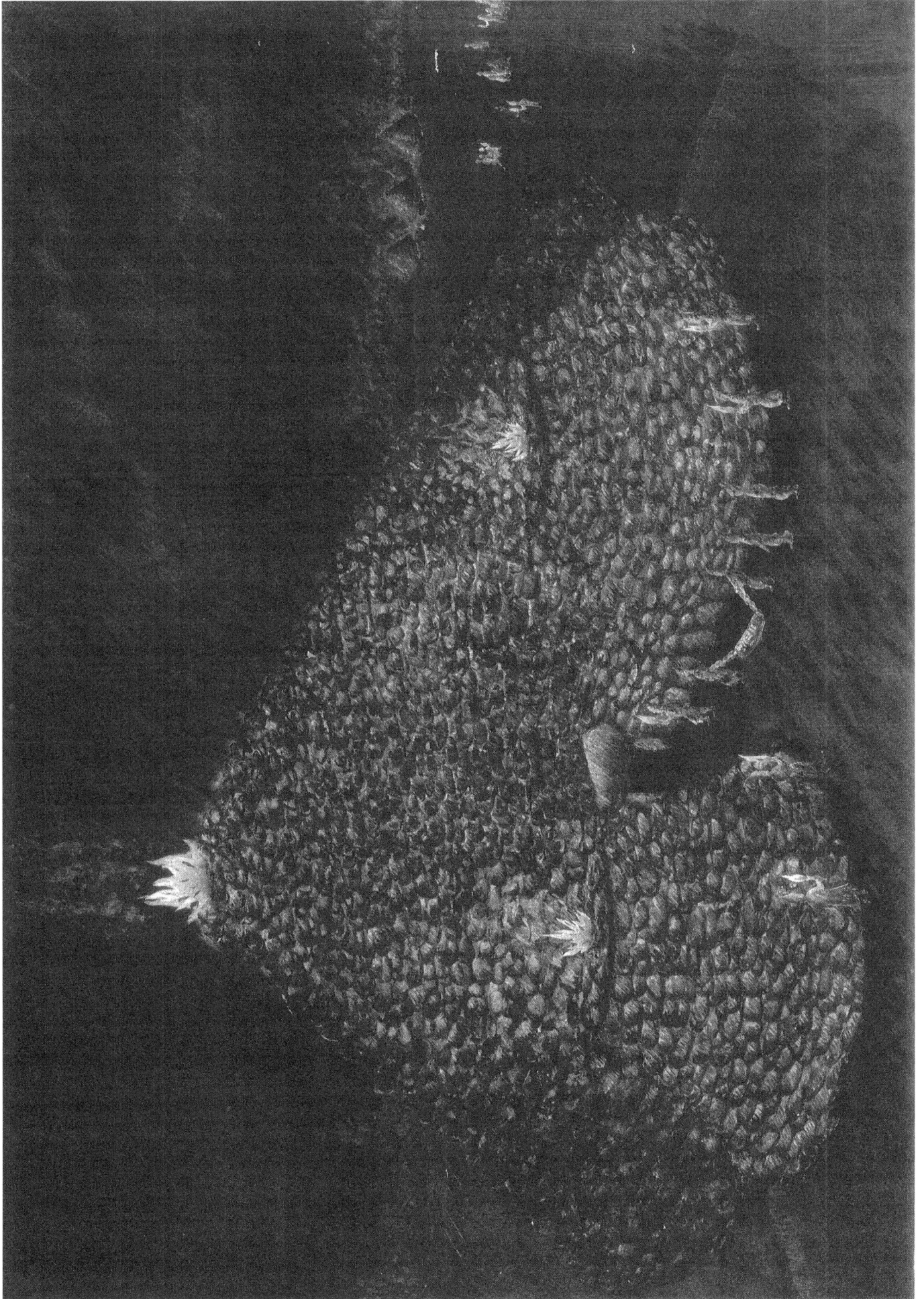

Figure 8. Reconstruction of the conical mound of La Hougue Bie. Drawing by Jane Crossley.

Appendix 1

CONTEXT DESCRIPTION

AREA i (Lower southern facade)

CONTEXT [200]	A fine, grey sandy silt (60%) loess (wind-blown) soil with few inclusions.
INTERPRETATION:	Natural deposit underlying Neolithic land surface. No artefacts were recorded in this layer.
CONTEXT [201]:	A tightly compacted gritty deposit, running horizontally 4 cm. below the cairn. Inclusions include small broken pieces of ignimbrite. A few waste fragments of flint recorded.
INTERPRETATION:	Neolithic land surface.
CONTEXT [202]:	Same as [207]. A fine moist sandy silt (90%) underlying the blocking area and running up and underneath the lower cairn.
INTERPRETATION:	Upper Neolithic land surface possibly linked to the Late Neolithic abandonment phase. Inclusions include waste flint, pebbles and pottery sherds.
CONTEXT [205]:	Same as [213] and [72]. Large stone boulders, tightly compacted within a dark silty soil. Leaching through this deposit has caused localised iron-panning and maganese coagulants. Artefacts recovered include two fragments of polished stone axe, two transverse arrowheads, one stone ring fragment and numerous waste flint and pottery sherds - all Neolithic in date.
INTERPRETATION:	Early Bronze Age blocking material.

AREA ii (lower northern facade)

CONTEXT [206]:	Same as [202] and [207]. A fine moist sandy silt (90%) underlying Early Bronze Age blocking material. This deposit runs against and underneath the secondary cairn. Artefacts recovered include waste flint, pebbles and pottery sherds.
INTERPRETATION:	Late Neolithic land surface.
CONTEXT [207]:	Fine sandy silt, approximately 0.45m in depth. Inclusions include 1920's wall fragments, flint and pavement gravel. Deposit is the same as [209].
INTERPRETATION:	A disturbed deposit, linked to the construction of the 1920s' tunnel.

George Nash

AREA iii Upper facade (southern area).

CONTEXT [214]: A moderately fine moist silty loess located between the primary and secondary cairn. Possibly same as [208]?

INTERPRETATION: 'Dumped' soil, part of the construction of the secondary cairn (phase iii).

CONTEXT [215]: Same as [214]. Soil deposit consisting of a tightly compacted sandy silt (90%). Deposit is well exposed due to earlier tree root damage.

INTERPRETATION: 'Dumped' soil, part of the construction of the secondary cairn (phase iii).

CONTEXT [203]: Same as [74], [208] and [57]. Rubble and tightly compacted sandy silt (90%) overlying [214] and [215]. May be contemporary with [72]. Artefacts assemblage include flint debetage, pebbles and small pottery sherds.

INTERPRETATION: Late Neolithic or Early Bronze Age blocking material.

CONTEXT [204]: Loose rubble and tightly compacted sandy silt (90%) running against the 1920s' tunnel construction.

INTERPRETATION: Modern re-deposited rubble and soils compacted against tunnel wall.

AREA iv Upper facade (northern area)

CONTEXT [208]: Same as [57] and [74]. Rubble and tightly compacted sandy silt (90%) running against the 1920s' tunnel construction.

INTERPRETATION: Late Neolithic/Early Bronze Age blocking material.

CONTEXT [209]: Loose rubble and sandy silt against tunnel wall. Also included is modern house brick rubble and concrete fragments.

INTERPRETATION: Modern re-deposited rubble packing between the tunnel wall and the inner secondary cairn soils [216].

CONTEXT [216]: Finely compacted loess silty deposit in front of the buttress foundation but behind the secondary cairn. Same as [215]. Artefact assemblage includes waste flint, small pebbles and pottery sherds.

INTERPRETATION: 'Dumped' soil, forming part of the secondary cairn.

AREA (v) Blocking phase on southern side of outer facade

117

CONTEXT [213]   Same as [205] and [72]. Blocking rubble with moderately compacted dark brown earth. Artefact assemblage include polished stone ring fragment, two quern fragments, grinding stone, pottery sherds and flint. All artefacts date to the Neolithic. This deposit extends at least 8.0m from the inner facade area to beyond the present hedge boundary and road.

INTERPRETATION: Extension of the Early Bronze Age blocking phase.

© George Nash

www.ingramcontent.com/pod-product-compliance
Lightning Source LLC
Chambersburg PA
CBHW061300270326
41932CB00029B/3415